D0821943

Pattern, Price & Time

Wiley Trading Advantage Series

Pattern, Price & Time

Using Gann Theory in Trading Systems

James A. Hyerczyk

John Wiley & Sons, Inc.

New York · Chichester · Weinheim · Brisbane · Singapore · Toronto

The Gann charts were produced using Ganntrader 2.1; copyright © 1996 by Peter A. Pich. Release: 2.113, SN: 35182. Gannsoft Publishing Company, 509-548-5990.

Microsoft Excel is a registered trademark of Microsoft Corporation.

Navigator Software is a registered trademark of Genesis Financial Data Services.

TradeStation, SuperCharts, and System Writer Plus are registered trademarks of Omega Research Inc.

This text is printed on acid-free paper.

Copyright © 1998 by James A. Hyerczyk.

Published by John Wiley & Sons, Inc.

All rights reserved. Published simultaneously in Canada.

Reproduction or translation of any part of this work beyond that permitted by Section 107 or 108 of the 1976 United States Copyright Act without the permission of the copyright owner is unlawful. Requests for permission or further information should be addressed to the Permissions Department, John Wiley & Sons, Inc., 605 Third Avenue, New York, NY 10158-0012.

This publication is designed to provide accurate and authoritative information in regard to the subject matter covered. It is sold with the understanding that the publisher is not engaged in rendering legal, accounting, or other professional services. If legal advice or other expert assistance is required, the services of a competent professional should be sought.

Library of Congress Cataloging in Publication Data:

Hyerczyk, James A.
    Pattern, price & time: using Gann theory in trading systems / James A. Hyerczyk.
      p.   cm.—(Wiley trading advantage series)
    Includes index.
    ISBN 0-471-25333-2 (alk. paper)
    1. Speculation.   2. Gann, William D., b. 1878.   I. Title.
II. Series.
HG6015.H94   1998
332.64′5—dc21   97-37322

Printed in the United States of America

10 9 8 7 6 5 4 3 2 1

Preface

When I was first approached by Pamela van Giessen, of John Wiley & Sons, to consider writing a book about trading using the methodology of W. D. Gann, I had to think about it for a while. After all, Gann analysis is a complicated subject. My first thought was that I couldn't do it; there was no way I could write about all the material Gann had covered in his books. Furthermore, I didn't know how to go about doing it. Should I update his course? Should I update *How to Make Profits in Commodities?* Where should I start? These were some of the questions going through my mind. After much more thought and internal debate, I finally decided that a book about Gann's methodology wasn't necessary because many books and courses were already published on the subject. Then it occurred to me to write a book about what I consider to be the major themes of Gann's work: pattern, price, and time. As I outlined the book, I decided the simplest approach would be to show how each method worked individually and how each method worked when combined.

My experience in the futures business showed me that too often traders become hooked on either pattern, price, or time in their analyses. The most common mistakes are systems built around the time to enter and price to exit, or price to enter and time to exit. In addition, traders who use pattern often enter or exit at poor prices or with poor timing. These observations provided further evidence that a combination of all three methods is necessary for success in the marketplace. It is on this premise that I have based my book.

After a brief introduction to W. D. Gann and his background, the book begins with a simple explanation of the trend indicator. Upon mastering this technique, the reader is introduced to various patterns created by the trend indicator charts, then the concepts of price and time are introduced. Throughout the chapters various ways to link together price and time are discussed. Finally, in the last chapter trading strategies using all three concepts are presented.

This book is intended to be educational. It is by no means intended to replace the books and courses written by W. D. Gann. If anything, it should be used by the novice as an introduction to the subjects of pattern, price, and time, and by the expert for enhancing his or her trading abilities. While Gann analysis concepts are discussed in this book, it is not intended to be a book *on* Gann analysis as many original ideas and techniques are introduced throughout the text. Although at times limited by page size in this book, I believe pattern, price, and time analysis is presented in a detailed but clear manner. I hope that you find the ideas in this book as useful as I have.

JAMES A. HYERCZYK

Palos Park, Illinois
January 1998

Acknowledgments

I would like to thank Nick Flambouras for introducing me to the analysis methodology of W. D. Gann. Although I was just an Associated Person with little or no money in my book of business, Nick allowed me to study the various tools he used to analyze the futures markets. My fascination with technical analysis began at the time when I was exposed to the many Gann charts he had in his office. I will always be grateful to Nick for the opportunity to view a real Gann expert at work.

I would also like to thank Nikki Jones for perservering during tough times to make the Gann courses and books available to the public, for helping me research Gann material, and for answering questions about W. D. Gann whenever I needed help.

My thanks also go out to Peter Pich who developed Ganntrader 2. Without this software my life would be a nightmare. Before the program, I spent weeknights and weekends copying data and making charts by hand. Since the development of this program, I have had more time to analyze markets and develop trading strategies.

I would also like to acknowledge Les Rosenthal and Jack Sandner who helped me during some tough times. Thanks also to Lewis Borsellino. Although we didn't see eye-to-eye very often, I did learn a lot about trading and mental toughness from him.

Dave Hightower and Terry Roggensack also deserve thanks for allowing me to develop my skills as a market analyst. Finally, many thanks to Bob Boshnack who believed in my methodology and gave my career a much needed boost.

J. A. H.

Contents

Pattern, Price & Time

1   Who Was
W. D. Gann?

If not the first technical market analyst, W. D. Gann was certainly among the more successful. Creating and publicizing a new approach to analyzing markets, Gann claimed to have made a world's record in leverage and accuracy more than once, that he had developed trading strategies for speculators, and that he could predict market moves to exact price levels.

William Delbert Gann was born on a cotton ranch on June 6, 1878, in Lufkin, Texas. He displayed a strong aptitude in mathematics during his early years, completed a high-school education, and started trading in 1902 at the age of 24. By his own admission, Gann's early trading was based on "hope, fear and greed," all of which he later realized were not compatible with a successful trading strategy.

After losing significant sums of money, Gann began to observe that markets followed mathematical laws and certain time cycles. He was particularly interested in the connection between price and time, a relationship he referred to as the "square" of price and time. He began studying this interaction diligently, even traveling to England, India, and Egypt to research mathematical theory and historical prices.

In developing his theories, Gann was undoubtedly one of the most industrious technical analysts. He made thousands of charts displaying daily, weekly, monthly, and yearly prices for a wide variety of stocks and commodities. He was an avid researcher, occasionally charting a price back hundreds of years. At a time when most market analysis was strictly fundamental, Gann's revolutionary theories relied on natural laws of mathematics, time cycles, and his unshakable conviction that past market activity predicted future activity.

Gann moved to New York City in 1908. He opened brokerage offices at 18 Broadway and began testing his theories and techniques in the market. Within a year it was clear to others that Gann's success was based on more than just luck. A 1909 article in *The Ticker Digest* explained that ". . . Mr. Gann has developed an entirely new idea as to the principles governing stock market movements."[1]

---

[1]From an article in the December 1909 issue of *The Ticker and Investment Digest* reprinted in the W. D. Gann Commodities Course, Lambert-Gann Publishing Co., Inc., Pomeroy, Washington, p. 178.

In this article, Gann asserted that most traders enter the market without any knowledge or study, and that most eventually lose money. He explained that he noticed a cyclic recurrence in the rise and fall of stocks and commodities, and decided to study and apply natural laws to trading strategy. Gann indicated that months of studying at the British Museum in London revealed what he called *the Law of Vibration*.

This law determines the exact points to which a stock would rise or fall, and predicts the effect well before the Street is aware of either the cause or the effect. Beyond this vague explanation, Gann was reticent about his strategies and unwilling to explain his theories in any detail.

Although past success is not an indication of future results, Gann's trading was extremely successful, at least to a point. An analysis of his trading record over 25 market days revealed that Gann made 286 trades, 264 of which were profitable. His success rate of 92.31% turned an initial investment of $450 into $37,000.

A colleague of Gann's said, "I once saw him take $130.00 and in less than one month run it up to over $12,000.00. He can compound money faster than any man I ever met." It is not surprising that the press concluded ". . . such performances as these . . . are unparalleled in the history of the street."[2] Although Gann's theories were apparently profitable at times, he was equally subject to the potentially substantial risk of loss that is inherent in commodities futures trading.

Gann issued annual market predictions of major moves and exact support and resistance levels. Newspapers around the country kept track of his predictions for 1921, 1922, and 1923, substantiating his accuracy. In January 1929, he issued an annual forecast that read:

> September—One of the sharpest declines of the year is indicated. There will be a loss of confidence by investors and the public will try to get out after it is too late. . . . A "Black Friday" is indicated and a panicky decline in stocks with only small rallies.[3]

His facility in analysis and prediction extended to areas other than the market. He predicted the exact date of the Kaiser's abdication, the end of World War I, and the elections of Presidents Wilson and Harding. Gann also predicted the occurrence of World War II thirteen years in advance and described the stealth bomber sixty-one years before its invention.

Gann's original reticence about his success later turned into an almost religious fervor to share his knowledge. He had begun writing during his trading

---

[2]Ibid., p. 180.

[3]From "1929 Annual Stock Market Forecast" in *Truth of the Stock Tape* (originally published in 1923 by Financial Guardian Publishing Co.; reprinted by Lambert-Gann Publishing Co.), p. 36.

career, starting with the *Truth of the Stock Tape*, written in 1923 (originally published by Financial Guardian Publishing Co.; reprinted by Lambert-Gann Publishing Co.) This book was intended to help traders analyze market activity using a standard stock tape. In 1927, he wrote *The Tunnel Thru the Air: Or, Looking Back from 1940* (originally published by Financial Guardian Publishing Co.; reprinted by Lambert-Gann Publishing Co.). This seemingly autobiographical novel provides insight into Gann's trading theories and his morals. (It also includes his predictions of World War II and the stealth bomber.) He went on to write books and courses explaining his new discoveries, including *New Stock Trend Indicator, How to Make Profits in Commodities*, and *45 Years in Wall Street* (originally published in 1936, 1942, and 1949, respectively; all three books were later reprinted by Lambert-Gann Publishing Co.). He also created home study courses for stocks and commodities and taught weekend seminars to explain the use of special price and time calculator tools he had invented. These materials were considered valuable enough that in 1932 people were paying $1,500 for his home study commodity course, and $5,000 for his master price and time calculator seminar.

Gann continued to refine his techniques and teach them to others until his death on June 14, 1955. From notes and papers, some of which were dated just two weeks before he died, it is evident that Gann was continuing his pursuit of a perfect trading system. For example, there is written evidence that he was developing a three-dimensional chart that incorporated price, time, and volume and how they applied to the market.

Since his death, rumors of a $50,000,000 fortune have circulated throughout the futures and stock industries. However, this figure is unsubstantiated by the material that was left after his death. For one thing, market movement and volatility did not offer such an opportunity. Also, brokerage statements indicate that he traded an account with a balance in excess of $2,000,000, and his will, filed in Miami, indicates a figure considerably below $50,000,000.

Most of the evidence of Gann's trading success is found in the numerous articles by newspaper writers who witnessed and verified his short-term trading activity. These articles, which have been reprinted in many of his books, highlight his trading successes in terms of both accuracy and trading results. Since Gann was a great promoter of his trading books and courses, only his successes are highlighted. Although his losing streaks and major losses are never cited, Gann always warned about the danger of trading without stop-loss orders.

Following Gann's work in chronological order shows that he experienced losses when he first started to trade. In addition to trading losses, Gann also lost money in bank and brokerage firm failures. These events probably played a major part in his desire to succeed in the market. Like many traders today, Gann initially derived income from selling his advisory service and his books while simultaneously trading. His obituary lists him as an author and a stock broker; as his popularity and success grew, however, it is probably safe to assume that he turned more of his attention to trading.

As he got older, his health began to fail, which made writing and lecturing very difficult. During this time he sold his publishing rights to Ed Lambert and formed Lambert-Gann Publishing. Based on this business deal, he was able to maintain some income by reprinting his books and courses, but, in my opinion, he focused more attention on deriving an income from the market. In May 1954, he stated "I am nearing my 76th birthday and am writing this new course of instructions, not to make money (for I have more income than I can spend). . . ."[4]

Based on the physical evidence left behind and the substantiated articles highlighting his trading activity, Gann did trade the markets successfully but did not amass the huge fortune alleged by rumor.

---

[4]From the W. D. Gann Commodities Course, Lambert-Gann Publishing Co., Inc., Pomeroy, Washington, p. 1.

2   Gann Theory in a Nutshell

Gann Theory can be described as the study of pattern, price, and time relationships and how these relationships affect the market. Gann Theory looks at pattern, price, and time as the key important elements in forecasting the future movement of the market. While each element has its own characteristics, each also has a unique, overlapping quality.

The focus of Gann Theory is to find the interlocking relationship between these three primary indicators of changes in trend and market direction. In other words, in certain instances a pattern has a large influence on the market, while at other times price and time exert their dominance. It is the balance of these three elements, especially price and time, that creates the best trading opportunities that can lead to more success in the market. Gann Theory helps the trader to determine the best combinations of pattern, price, and time to initiate successful trades. While trades can be triggered by each element individually, a trader who weights his signal too much toward one of these elements may experience a large number of losses, whereas a trader who is patient enough to wait for a proper balancing of pattern, price, and time may experience more success.

Pattern study consists of the proper construction of minor, intermediate, and main trend-indicator swing charts and closing-price reversal patterns. Price study consists of Gann angle analysis and percentage retracements. Time study looks at swing timing, cycle timing, and historical dates. The combination of these three time factors helps the trader decide when and where to buy or sell. In this book, I describe techniques that help the trader determine how to discover these elements through proper chart construction and how they are related in trading activity.

While there is much material available *about* Gann Theory, very little of it explains *how* to put the Gann tools to practical use in a trading system. I used to think that this sort of material was valuable until I placed a stop according to some huge astrophysical law. In other words, information about the origins of cycles and price and time relationships is very interesting, but if it cannot be converted to practical use in a trading system then I consider it essentially useless. Research that reveals that a sixty-year cycle bottom is due in 1998 plus or minus two years does not help you trade soybeans profitably today. This is why you have to focus your attention on the market and what pattern, price, and time are telling you at the present.

It is my intention to focus you on the portions of Gann Theory that can be used to create a profitable trading system. My studies of Gann's original work show that he primarily used swing charts, Gann angle clusters, and cycle counts from former tops and bottoms. There also is evidence that he used astrology to initiate some trades. This latter topic is not discussed in great detail, however, as it involves a great deal of background research before it can be utilized. Since it does fall under the concept of time, which is a key element of Gann analysis, I do discuss some simple examples of how Gann applied financial astrology to the markets. In addition, Gann created and used a series of master price and time charts, which he used to determine current and future support and resistance points.

Many of his writings contain rules for trading hypothetical examples. The only evidence I found of an actual trade recommendation was in his *Master Egg Course*. This information, however, became the basis for my research, as it made clear to me what was important and what was not in developing a Gann-based trading system. Each paragraph highlighted how Gann combined pattern, price, and time into a trading strategy. In the following paragraph,[1] he speaks of his use of the Master Chart:

> Example: May 3, 1949, October Eggs high 5025. This was on the timing of 168, which is 14 years, and 169 is the square of 13. Note that the price of 5010 hits 7/16 point of the circle at 5010, which would make this a resistance and selling level based on the Master Square Chart. See notes and time periods on the right hand of this Master Chart.

This example concerns his use of support and resistance angles:

> I wired Chicago last night that October Eggs was a sure sale today. The reasons were as follows: Based on the angles on the daily high and low chart, the angle of 4 × 1, which moves 2 1/2 points per day from the first top at 4760 made December 6, 1948, crossed at 5020. The 45 degree angle moving up from the low of 4685 on March 16, 1949, crossed at 5020. The angle of 67½ degrees, which moves up 20 points per day from the low of 4785 on April 18, crossed at 5020 and the angle moving up from 4735 on

---

[1]All quotations in this chapter about the *Master Egg Course* are from the W. D. Gann Commodities Course, and are reprinted with permission per Nikki Jones of Lambert-Gann Publishing Co., Inc., Box O, Pomeroy, Washington 99347.

February 14 crossed at 5005, making 4 important angles coming out at this high point. A sure point for great resistance because the time from the starting of the option was over 6 months. The time from the first important top on December 6, 1948, was close to 5 months and the angle from this top called the top exactly.

In the next example, Gann speaks of the importance of a price scale:

Since receiving 1 letter stating that the contracts for Eggs were changed on February 1 and that 1 point now equals $1.44, I did some experimenting to adjust angles to the money value because that is very important. I wanted to get something that would work to an angle of $11\frac{1}{4}$ angle and by multiplying 144×8 it gave 1152 or $11.52 profit on 8 points. This would give an angle 5×4 or about 39 degrees, moving up at the rate of 8 points per day, instead of the 45 degree angle which moves 10 points per day.

A discussion of the swing chart and angles appears in the following paragraph:

Years of this research and experience have proved that the first advance from which a reaction runs more than 3 days will set an angle for an important top later. This rule works on weekly and monthly charts also. After there is a second or third top and when there is a greater decline from the third top, an angle from that bottom must call bottoms and tops of the next advance. You will note that on the greatest decline from January 24 to February 8, the price declined to the angle from the extreme low of 4485, and the angle of 2×1 from the third top called the second and also the last bottom at 4560. From this low of 4560 we start the angle moving up at the rate of 8 points per day. It calls the low for March 2, next it called the top at 4850 on March 30 from which a 2-day reaction followed, and finally on May 3 this angle in green crossed the first top angle at 5020, on May 3, 1949.

In the next paragraph, Gann combines a percentage retracement point, the swing chart, and angles:

The market closed at the halfway [of] the range of the day on May 3. May 4 was signal day. The opening was at 50 cents; the high was 5005; the low for the day was 4980; the market closed at 4985. This was the first day since April 18 that the market had broken the low of the previous day and closed under. The total time from 4560 to 5025 was 58 market days in view of the fact that the option is over 6 months old a greater reaction can be expected. The 45 degree angle from the last low of 4795 is the most important one to watch for support and a secondary rally. The decline should run at least 5 days with not more than 1 day rally.

He then interprets the data obtained from the swing chart:

Other reasons for the top on May 3 were as follows:

First move up from 4485 to 4760—total gain 275 points.
First move down 215 points.
Second move up from 4560 to 4850—total gain 290 points.
Second move down 4850 to 4775—loss 75 points.
Third move up 4775 to 5025—total gain 250 points. This was 25 points less than the first gain and 40 points less than the second gain up.

In this paragraph, Gann discusses the importance of timing using the swing chart:

The greatest time period from January 24 to February 8 was 11 market days. And the last advance from April 18 was 11 market days; therefore, when the market declines more than 11 days, it will overbalance the greatest time period. When it declines more than 75 points it will overbalance the last price declines or space reversal, and indicate lower prices.

The next four paragraphs use the Master Chart to interpret the market. Also, time and price are discussed in geometric terms.

Study the Master Chart against previous tops and bottoms and you will see how it confirms the geometrical angles on other charts.
   Example: 5010 is opposite 180 degrees from 60 cents, 4890 is on a 45 degree angle from 1050, the extreme low price. 4950 is 180 degrees from 45 cents. From 30 cents, which is half of 60, the 45 degree angle crosses at 48 cents. This is why the market made 3 bottoms around 48 cents on April 13 to 18. The Master Chart shows the same resistance levels and by using the time period with it you will learn the basic mathematical and geometrical law for market movement.
   By going over back records and carefully studying all the important tops and bottoms you will see the working of the law.
   Since the fluctuation of Eggs on the minimum of 5 points now equals $7.20 which is 2 circles of 360 degrees, ½ of this is 360 and makes an angle moving at the rate of 2 1/2 points per day very important. The fluctuations will now work better to the circle of 360 degrees. In a few days I will send you another Master Chart showing each 15 degree angle and the resistance levels which will help you to determine resistance and turning points.

Finally, after analyzing swing charts, percentage retracements, support and resistance angles, and the Master Chart, he is able to reach a conclusion and executes the trade.

Example: The range in fluctuations and the life of the present option of October Eggs is 4485 low and 5025 high, making a range of 540 points. Subtract from 540 and we have the balance of 180. This means that the market had advanced 1½ circles or cycles and was at a 180 degree angle on May 3, 1949. The writer sold October Eggs at 5015 on May 3, 1949.

Although this trade failed to live up to its expectations, I was more inter-ested in the thought process that led to determining the entry level. Studying Gann's first-person account, I discovered the trading techniques that he con-sidered important in determining a trade. When Gann started trading seri-ously, he used a combination of swing charts, percentage retracements, and angles to determine price support, and swing charts and anniversary (cycle) dates to determine timing. Later, he developed master charts of price and time to trade. This technique is beyond the scope of this introductory book because the more simple techniques need to be mastered before they can be used successfully. In addition, specific analysis tools are required that are only available through the Lambert-Gann Publishing Company. Additionally, a deep understanding of cycles and their causes is required.

Generally speaking, however, Gann used a combination of pattern, price, and time to generate his trades. As I said earlier, these are the main parts of Gann analysis that I consider important in developing a trading system. There-fore, although Gann demonstrated an interest and proficiency in many other areas dealing with price and time analysis, pattern, price, and time are the major themes of this book.

THE BASIS OF GANN THEORY

The Law of Vibration

During an interview Gann once revealed that the secret to his trading was un-derstanding the vibration of a commodity. The "Law of Vibration," as he called it, explains the cause of the periodic recurrence of the rise and fall in commodities. The following excerpts are from an article Gann wrote that covers this topic in greater detail.[2]

> I soon began to note the periodical recurrence of the rise and fall in stocks and commodities. This led me to conclude that natural law was the basis of market movements. After exhaustive researches and investigations of the known sciences, I discovered that the Law of Vibration enables me to accu-rately determine the exact points to which stocks or commodities should rise and fall within a given time. The working out of this law determines the cause and predicts the effect long before the Street is aware of either. Most speculators can testify to the fact that it is looking at the effect and ignoring the cause that has produced their losses.
>
> • • •
>
> It is impossible here to give an adequate idea of the Law of Vibration as I apply it to the markets, however, the layman may be able to grasp some of

---

[2]As reprinted in *The W. D. Gann Technical Review*, vol. 1, no. 11, p. 1, November 12, 1982.

the principles when I state that the Law of Vibration is the fundamental law upon which wireless telegraphy, wireless telephone and phonographs are based. Without the existence of this law the above inventions would have been impossible.

• • •

In going over the history of markets and the great mass of related statistics, it soon becomes apparent that certain laws govern the changes and variations in the value of stocks and there exists a periodic or cyclic law, which is at the back of all these movements. Observation has shown that there are regular periods of intense activity on the Exchange followed by periods of inactivity. Mr. Henry Hall, in his recent book, devoted much space to 'Cycles of Prosperity and Depression' which he found recurring at regular intervals of time. The law which I have applied will not only give these long cycles or swings, but the daily and even hourly movements of stocks. By knowing the exact vibration of each individual stock I am able to determine at what point each will receive support and at what point the greatest resistance is to be met.

• • •

Those in close touch with the markets have noticed the phenomena of ebb and flow, or rise and fall in the value of stocks. At certain times a stock becomes intensely active, large transactions being made in it; at other times this same stock will become practically stationary or inactive with a very small volume of sales. I have found that the Law of Vibration governs and controls these conditions. I have also found that certain phases of this law govern the rise in a stock and entirely different rules operate on the decline.

• • •

I have found that in the stock itself exists its harmonic or inharmonic relationship to the driving power or force behind it. The secret of all its activity is therefore apparent. By my method I can determine the vibration of each stock and by also taking certain time values into consideration I can in the majority of cases tell exactly what the stock will do under given conditions.

• • •

The power to determine the trend of the market is due to my knowledge of the characteristics of each individual stock and a certain grouping of different stocks under their proper rates of vibration. Stocks are like electrons, atoms, and molecules, which hold persistently to their own individuality in response to the fundamental Law of Vibration. Science teaches "that an original impulse of any kind finally resolves itself into periodic or rhythmical motion," also, "just as the pendulum returns again in its swing, just as the moon returns in its orbit, just as the advancing year ever brings the rose to spring, so do the properties of the elements periodically recur as the weight of the atoms rises."

• • •

From my extensive investigations, studies and applied tests, I find that not only do the various stocks vibrate, but that the driving forces controlling the stocks are also in the state of vibration. These vibratory forces can only be known by the movements they generate on the stocks and their values in the market. Since all great swings or movements of the market are cyclic they act in accordance with the periodic law.

• • •

If we wish to avert failure in speculation we must deal with causes. Everything in existence is based on exact proportion and perfect relationship. There is no chance in nature, because mathematical principles of the highest order lie at the foundation of all things. Faraday said: "There is nothing in the Universe but mathematical points of force."

• • •

Through the Law of Vibration every stock in the market moves in its own distinctive sphere of activities, as to intensity, volume and direction; all the essential qualities of its evolution are characterized in its own rate of vibration. Stocks, like atoms, are really centers of energies, therefore they are controlled mathematically. Stocks create their own field of action and power; power to attract and repel, which in principle explains why certain stocks at times lead the market and "turn dead" at other times. Thus to speculate scientifically it is absolutely necessary to follow natural law.

• • •

After years of patient study I have proven to my entire satisfaction as well as demonstrated to others that vibration explains every possible phase and condition of the market.

This information helps us to understand a little more about the type of research W. D. Gann did to develop his analysis technique. The article should be read as background material, as it is beyond the scope of the material that is covered in this book. In this book I accept Gann's basis for market movement and that the markets are being influenced by the Law of Vibration. I do not wish to explain how to prove the existence of the Law of Vibration, but find it more useful to write about how to use the techniques Gann used to trade the market. For example, I have assumed that cycles and vibrations exist and, at this point, do not intend to prove either their existence or the existence of their influence on the movement of stock and commodity prices.

Mathematics

Gann was a rare mathematician. He was a student of numbers, number theory, and the progression of numbers. He often said his analysis theory was based on natural law and mathematics.

Since time progresses as the earth turns on its axis, and time is measured by numbers and progressions of numbers, and since prices in their movement upward and downward are measured in numbers, we can understand why Gann had an intense interest in numbers, number theory, and mathematics. And remember . . . he did not have a personal computer, or even a handheld or desktop calculator—just a pencil.

Gann said his trading method was based on natural and mathematical law. For years he refused to reveal any part of this method. The method was based on natural law, but the theory behind it was based on mathematics. Since price and time are denoted in mathematical terms (numbers), his system involved numbers and number progressions. He simply said that he had researched far back into history and even went to India for old pre-Hindu records and philosophies as well as the ancient archives of the pre-Hindu period.

As we study Gann's works, we begin to see that some numbers took a dominant place in his trading method. The square of numbers was an important issue with him, namely: 16, 25, 36, 49, 64, 121, and 144. He thought that markets moved in patterns sensitive to the price movement of these squares in terms of both price and time. For example, a rally in a specific market may have a tendency to find resistance 64 cents or 64 days from a bottom. Similarly, a decline in a market may find support 144 dollars or weeks from a top. This technique was combined with others that he developed, and it became a major part of his analysis tools.

Key Numbers

At this point, some of you may be discounting Gann's methods because of their relative obscurity, but I would ask you to suspend disbelief. Gann found several numbers significant for a variety of reasons, some religious or spiritual, some historical, and some psychological. Whether or not his belief was reasonable or based on provable fact is largely irrelevant here—he used them as the basis for his trading, and they can work if incorporated properly into a technical trading system.

Gann researched numbers and cycles in many unique ways. Much of his research focused on the specific meaning of a number and how it relates to market movement. His research included the study of early Egyptian writings as well as cycle information. He also did extensive research of the cycles highlighted in the Bible. Records indicate that the early Egyptians considered the number seven to be the symbol of both earthly and eternal life. It is thought of as a number symbolizing a complete cycle, for seven is denoted as the number of time and rhythm. This information was used by Gann to develop a seven-day-cycle theory for short-term market moves.

Gann deemed three and one-half important, as it is half of seven, and in the Bible it occurs several times—for example, in the Book of Revelation, where the woman was sent into the wilderness for three and one-half years; during Daniel's vision of 42 months (3½ years); when the Christ child was hidden in Egypt for three and one-half years; and during Christ's public ministry, which lasted for exactly three and one-half years. Gann used this information to study and research the 3½-day, -week, -month, and -year cycle, and applied the knowledge he gained to trade the market.

Gann also considered the number nine important, as it occurs in the nine beatitudes recorded in Matthew's Gospel, and he believed that nine corresponds with the number of stages of a disciple's advance to a higher life. The number 12 was important to Gann, as it denoted space for him. He found it recurring in the twelve tribes of Israel, the 12 disciples, and the 12 houses of the Zodiac.

Other important Gann numbers are derived as follows: One year is 365 days, as this is the time it takes the sun to enter a hemisphere, move to the opposite hemisphere, and then return to the starting point. The movement of the sun produces definite seasons, affects crops and weather, and therefore has a dominant effect on our lives. For this reason the 30-day or sun cycle has dominance. Besides what has already been said about the number seven, it is important because of its link to the lunar cycle.

The number 144 was also important to Gann, whether because of there being 1440 minutes in a day (the decimal point is disregarded), it is 40% of a circle ($360° \times 0.40 = 144°$), or because it is the square of 12. Numbers that occur repeatedly in the different sciences—such as mathematics, geometry, physics—cycles, and other natural studies were very important to Gann.

After studying mathematics and researching number patterns, Gann had to find a practical use for his newly acquired knowledge. Armed with this information Gann turned to the stock and commodity markets. After applying his strong background in mathematics to these markets, he concluded that markets adhere to mathematical law. From this conclusion he was able to develop his trading theory. This theory basically stated that market movement is governed by the forces of pattern, price, and time.

PATTERN

In Gann Theory, pattern is defined as the study of market swings. Swing charts determine trend changes. For example, a trend changes to up when the market crosses swing tops, and it changes to down when the market crosses swing bottoms. The trader can also gain information from swing charts about the size and duration of market movements. This is how price, which is size, and time, which is duration, are linked to a pattern. In addition, the trader can learn about specific characteristics of a market by analyzing the patterns formed by the swing charts. For example, the charts delineate a market's tendency to form double tops and bottoms, signal tops and bottoms, and the tendency to balance previous moves.

PRICE

In Gann theory, price analysis consists of swing-chart price targets, angles, and percentage retracement points.

Swing-chart Price Targets

After constructing a swing chart, the trader creates important price information that can be used to forecast future tops and bottoms. These prices can be referred to as *price balance points*. For example, if the swing chart shows the market has had a recent tendency to rally 7–10 cents before forming a top, then from the next bottom, the forecast will be for a subsequent 7–10 day rally. Conversely, if the market has shown a tendency to break 10–12 points from a top, then following the next top, the trader can forecast a break of 10–12 cents. If the swings equal previous swings, then the market is balanced.

Angles

Geometric angles are another important part of the Gann trading method. The markets are geometric in design and function, so it follows that they will follow geometric laws when charted. Gann insisted on the use of the proper scale for each market when charting, to maintain a harmonic relationship. He therefore chose a price scale that was in agreement with a geometric design or formula. He mainly relied on a 45-degree angle to divide a chart into important price and time zones. This angle is usually referred to as the "1 × 1" angle, because it represents one unit of price with one unit of time. He also used other proportional geometric angles to divide price and time. These angles are known as 1 × 2 and 2 × 1 angles because they represent one unit of price with two units of time and two units of price with one unit of time, respectively. All of the angles are important because they indicate support and resistance. They also have predictive value for future direction and price activity. All of which is necessary to know in order to forecast where the market can be in the future and when it is likely to be there.

Percentage Retracement Points

Just as Gann angles offer the trader price levels that move with time, percentage retracement points provide support and resistance that remain fixed as long as a market remains in a price range. Gann is commonly acknowledged to have formulated the percentage retracement rule, which states that most price moves will correct to 50%. Other percentage divisions are 25% and 75%, with the 50% level occurring the most frequently.

Gann believed traders would become successful if they used price indicators such as swing-chart balance points, angles, and percentage retracement points to find support and resistance. In essence, however, the combination of the two price indicators provide the trader with the best support and resistance with which to work. For example, while the uptrending 1×1 angle from a major bottom and a 50% price level provide strong support individually, the point where these two cross provides the trader with the strongest support on the chart.

TIME

According to Gann, time had the strongest influence on the market because when time is up, the trend changes. Gann used swing charts, anniversary dates, cycles, and the square of price to measure time.

Swing-Chart Timing

A properly constructed swing chart is expected to yield valuable information about the duration of price swings. This information is used to project both the duration of future upmoves from a current bottom and the duration of future downmoves from current tops. The basic premise behind swing-chart timing is that market patterns repeat; this is why it is necessary to keep records of past rallies and breaks. As a swing bottom or top is being formed, the trader must utilize the information from previous swings to project the minimum and maximum duration of the currently developing swing. The basic premise is that price swings balance time with previous price swings. However, in strong upmoves the duration of a rally is greater than the duration of a break, and subsequent upswings are equal to or greater than previous upmoves. Conversely, in strong downmoves the duration of a break is greater than the duration of a rally, and subsequent downswings are equal to or greater than previous downmoves.

Anniversary Dates

Among the timing tools Gann used is a concept he referred to as "anniversary dates." This term refers to the historical dates the market made major tops and bottoms. The information collected in effect reflects the seasonality of the market because often an anniversary date repeats in the future. A cluster of anniversary dates indicates the strong tendency of a market to post a major top and bottom each year at the same time. For example, in order to predict future tops and bottoms in wheat, Gann claimed to have studied prices back to the twelfth century, noting not only the prices, but the dates of the highs and lows. The dates and time spans between these anniversary dates—top to top, top to bottom, bottom to bottom, and bottom to top—were fundamental factors in this thinking. The information he learned from the research was very important to his analysis, and these dates gave obvious clues to another of his approaches to the market: time cycles.

Cycles

As mentioned earlier, Gann tried to build analysis tools that were geometric in design. When looking at anniversary dates he saw a series of one-year cycles. In geometric terms, the one-year cycle represented a circle or 360 degrees. Building on the geometric relationship of the market, Gann also considered the quarterly divisions of the year to be important timing periods. These quarterly divisions are the 90-day cycle, the 180-day cycle, and the 270-day cycle. In using the one-year cycle and the divisions of this cycle, you will find a date where a number of these cycles line up (preferably three or more) on a single point in time in the future. A date where a number of cycles line up is called a *time cluster*. This time cluster is used to predict major tops and bottoms. Time cycles are a major part of Gann analysis, and should be combined with price indicators to develop a valid market forecast.

SQUARING THE PRICE RANGE
WITH TIME

The squaring of price and time was one of the most important and valuable discoveries that Gann ever made. In his trading course he stated "if you stick strictly to the rule, and always watch when price is squared by time, or when time and price come together, you will be able to forecast the important changes in trend with greater accuracy."

The squaring of price with time means an equal number of points up or down, balancing an equal number of time periods—either days, weeks, or months. Gann suggested traders square the range, low prices, and high prices.

Squaring the Range

When Gann angles are drawn inside a range, the angles provide the trader with a graphical representation of the squaring of the range. For example, if a market has a range of 100 and the scale is 1 point, a Gann angle moving up from the bottom of the range at 1 point per time period will reach the top of the range in 100 time periods. A top, bottom, or change in trend is expected during the time period when this occurs. This cycle repeats as long as the market remains inside the range.

Squaring a Low

Squaring a low means an equal amount of time has passed since the low was formed. This occurs when a Gann angle moving up from a bottom reaches the time period equal to the low. For example, if the low price is 100 and the scale is 1, then at the end of 100 time periods an uptrending Gann angle will reach the square of itself. Watch for a top, bottom, or change in trend at this point. The market will continue to square the low as long as the low holds.

A graphical representation of squaring a low price can be seen on a chart Gann called a *zero-angle chart*. This chart starts an uptrending angle from price 0 at the time the low occurred and brings it up at one unit per time period. When this angle reaches the original low price, a top, bottom, or change in trend is expected.

Squaring a High

Squaring a high means an equal amount of time has passed since the high was formed. This occurs when a Gann angle moving down from a top reaches the time period equal to the high. For example, if the high price is 500 and the scale is 5, then at the end of 100 time periods a downtrending Gann angle will reach the square of itself. Watch for a top, bottom, or change in trend at this point. The market will continue to square the high as long as the high holds.

A graphical representation of squaring a high price can be seen on a zero-angle chart. This chart starts an uptrending angle from price 0 at the time the high occurred and brings it up at one unit per time period. When this angle reaches the original high price, a top, bottom, or change in trend is expected.

Time analysis in Gann Theory requires the trader to study market swings, anniversary dates, cycles, and the squaring of price and time to help determine future top, bottom, and change in trend points.

While the previous time studies require the trader to derive the data from actual charts, the basis of much of this analysis is drawn from Gann's fundamental studies of financial astrology and his proprietary master charts. In the next section a brief discussion of the complexity of these two techniques is presented.

ADVANCED PRICE AND TIME TECHNIQUES

Natural Cycles and Financial Astrology

While this book covers the most conventional methods of time analysis, another important tool Gann used to analyze time was the study of natural cycles. A natural cycle is a cycle that cannot be altered by man. For example, although a twenty-eight-day cycle in a market can be discovered through analysis of historical price action, a naturally occurring fourteen-day cycle is the moon cycle. While one cycle may be changed or altered as more data becomes available, the moon cycle cannot change. Since the moon cycle follows a natural law, its position can be predicted well into the future. To Gann the division of time by the natural cycles of the moon, the sun, and the planets was very important. For example, his thirty-day cycle was based on the sun cycle, and the twelve-year and eighty-four-year cycles were based on Jupiter and Uranus cycles, respectively.

The study of natural cycles, their origins, and their influences on the markets led Gann to develop a trading system based on financial astrology. Financial astrology is the study of how planets and their phenomena affect commodity and stock markets. The financial astrologer believes planetary influences are the cause of bull and bear markets.

Gann was often quoted as saying that there was nothing mysterious about his methods of prediction. He also claimed, in effect, that if he had the appropriate data, he could use geometry and algebra along with the theory of cycles to predict when a certain event would happen. This is ultimately the language of the astrologer. Also note that in much of his work Gann used the term *cycle* as did the Greeks (to the Greeks the word "cycle" meant circle, again an astrological term). Astrologers use math, geometry, and algebra to find the locations of the planets and the moon, study past effects when the planets were in certain positions relative to each other, the sun, and the earth, and then use their calculations to make their forecasts.

For years Gann made charts predicting the future of prices, a year in advance (his annual forecasts), and financial astrology was apparently the method he used in making these forecasts. Included in them were the exact price, the time of the day, as well as the day and month.

The fundamental principle behind financial astrology is that the planets' orbits, rulerships, groups of planets, and the sun and moon have an effect on the minds and actions of people and events, and in particular, these planetary effects affect the cycles and prices of stocks and commodities. That in sum is the meaning of financial astrology. While you may wish to reserve judgment on this matter, the fact remains that Gann was expert at financial astrology, that he was totally committed to it, and that he used it as a means of improving his trades.

He was careful not to publish anything whatsoever on his use of financial astrology because he knew such a revelation would receive bad press, and the effect this would have on his status and on his brokerage and advisory business.

Gann certainly broke new ground in financial astrology. Most astrologers are capable of using the longitude readings or time periods only. However, he was able to convert longitude to price, and was thereby able to generate a methodology for support and resistance levels. This was a new advance in financial astrology, and helps to explain how he could allegedly makes calls within one-eighth of a point on stocks for highs and lows. You can begin to see how he was able to make long-range predictions, as well as minute-to-minute forecasts.

Finally, the study of, but not necessarily the belief in, astrology played a major role in the development of Gann's forecasting technique. Rather than try to explain how he used astrology, the following is an excerpt from a rare item[3] that explains in great detail how he converted astrological analysis into price and time analysis and a trading system. Rather than write in his normal veiled language, in which astrological references were replaced with market terms, Gann used terms unique to astrology.

In the first paragraph Gann explains how to convert degrees of the planets to price to find support and resistance

> . . . 67 (cents), add 90 gives 157 or 7 degrees Virgo. Add 135 gives 202 or 22 degrees Libra. Add 120 gives 127 or 7 degrees Leo. Add 180 gives 247 or 7 degrees Sagittarius. Add 225 gives 292 or 22 degrees Capricorn. Add 240 gives 307 or 7 degrees Aquarius. Add 270 gives 337 or 7 degrees Pisces. Add 315 gives 382 or 22 degrees Aries. Add 360 gives 427 or 7 degrees Gemini. Add 271¼ gives 438¼. High on May Beans was 436¾. After that high the next extreme low was 201½. Note that 67 plus 125 gives 202, and that one-half of 405 is 202½, and 180 plus 22½ is 202½, which are the mathematical reasons why May Soy Beans made bottom at 201½.

---

[3]From a missive on Gann letterhead with the title, "Soy Beans: Price Resistance Levels," which originally came with the W. D. Gann Commodities Course, but which was left out of later reprints of the course.

All of the above price levels can be measured in Time Periods of days, weeks and months, and when the time periods come out at these prices, it is important for a change in trend, especially if confirmed by the geometrical angles from highs and lows.

Here, Gann created support and resistance levels using the longitude of the position of the sun. In the next excerpt, Gann used the longitude of the major planets to create support and resistance levels.

Active Angles and Degrees

By live or active angles is meant Prices and Time Periods where the Longitude of the major planets are or where the squares, triangles, oppositions are to these planets.

The averages of the six major planets Heliocentric and Geocentric are the most powerful points for Time and Price Resistance. Also the Geocentric and Heliocentric average of the five major planets with Mars left out, is of great importance and should be watched.

You should also calculate the averages of eight planets which move around the Sun as this is the first most important odd square. The square of "1" is one, and "1" is the Sun. 8 added to "1" gives 9, the square of 3 and completes the first important odd square, which is important for Time and Price.

Examples of live, active angles: At the present writing, January 18, 1954, Saturn Geocentric is 8 to 9 degrees Scorpio. Add the square or 90 degrees gives 8 to 9 degrees Aquarius and equals the price 308–309, for May Beans.

The planet Jupiter is at 21 degrees Gemini, which is 81 degrees in longitude from "0" the square of 9. Subtract 135 degrees from Jupiter gives 306 or 6 degrees Aquarius. This is why Soy Beans have met resistance so many times between 306 and 311¼. The Price Resistance levels come out strong around these degrees and prices and the Geometrical angles come out on daily, weekly and monthly, but the Power of Saturn and Jupiter aspects, working out Time to these Price Resistance Levels, is what halts the advance in Soy Beans.

Example: December 2, 1953, May Soybeans high 311¼. This equaled 18 degrees 45′ in Pisces, close square or 90 degrees of Jupiter, 135 degrees to Saturn and 180 degrees of the averages, and 120 degrees of Uranus.

300 price equals 30 degrees Virgo. 302 equals 30 degrees Libra. 304 equals 30 degrees Scorpio. On January 18, 1954, the planet Saturn Geocentric is 8 degrees 30 hours Scorpio, and 15 degrees Scorpio gives a price of 303, therefore when May Beans decline to 302, they will be below the body or longitude of Saturn and will indicate lower. At the same time, using the Earth's revolution of 365¼ days to move around the Sun, a price of 308½ is 90 degrees or square to Saturn. As long as the price is below 308½ it is within the square and in position to go lower. But by the 24th revolution, when the price breaks below 304, it is in the bear sign of Scorpio, a fixed sign and will indicate lower prices.

Study and analyze all options of all commodities in the same way as we have analyzed May Beans. Remember, when these Resistance Points are met you must give the market time to show that it is making tops or bottoms and getting ready to make a change in trend. Do not guess, wait until you get a definite indication buy or sell against these resistance levels and place a stop loss order. Having before you all the information outlined above, you would certainly have gone short of May Soy Beans on December 2, 1953 and cover your shorts on December 17 at 296 because the price was down to the 45 degree angle from 44 on the Monthly high and low chart.

To a trained astrologer and experienced trader, these excerpts reveal an important link between pattern, price, and time. In addition, they also show that although using financial astrology can be a useful trading tool, a trader should not abandon conventional charting techniques, as both aspects have to be used together. For example, knowledge of astrology is necessary to interpret and convert the degrees of the planets, but knowledge of technical analysis techniques is still needed to build charts, interpret tops and bottoms, find support and resistance, and place stop orders. All of this information may seem complicated to follow, but remember the overwhelming theme in each paragraph is pattern, price, and time.

The Master Charts

Researching and trading required a tremendous amount of time, especially since Gann had to chart everything by hand. At the same time, he sensed the need to simplify his analysis by developing a pattern, price, and time chart that was universal and permanent. This became the motivating force behind the design and invention of the master charts.

Over the years Gann developed a number of master charts, including the Square of Nine, the Square of Four, and the Master 360 Degree Chart. These charts incorporated the best features of his price and time techniques, and provided him with a quick and easy way to forecast a market. The master charts can best be described as permanent charts in the form of circles, squares, and spirals, which represent natural angles and permanent resistance points for either price, time, or volume. Although it is claimed that he used these charts exclusively to trade late in his career, the *Master Egg Course* example demonstrates how he used his master charts in conjunction with his conventional bar charts.

It should be noted that these charts probably represent Gann's life work, and should therefore not be used until the more conventional Gann analysis tools are mastered. Since deep study and research are necessary to learn how to use the master charts, a proper background in Gann analysis is necessary.

This is why I consider the master charts beyond the scope of this book. In addition, the master charts are only available in his trading course.

GANN THEORY AND ITS APPLICATION TO TRADING

Gann theory is based on the principle that price and time must balance. Markets are constantly in a position of change and subject to movement, sometimes with great volatility. Gann Theory states that there is order to this movement. By using the proper tools to analyze this movement, an accurate forecast for future direction can be made.

Finding the balancing points is necessary to predict future prices and movement. Gann developed a number of methods to help determine these balance points. The first method uses patterns created by swing charts to find the balance points. The second method uses angles and the squaring of price and time to find the balance points. The third method uses time.

While the perfect market remains balanced all the time, it also proves to be uninteresting, because major moves occur when price is ahead of time or time is ahead of price. The proper use of the various Gann analysis tools will help you to determine when these major moves are most likely to occur.

Now that the theory has been explained, how can it be applied to trading?

The first step is to create the charts that properly demonstrate the concepts of pattern, price, and time analysis. The second step is to create swing charts or trend indicator charts that provide the trader with a way to analyze the size and duration of the rallies and breaks. The third step is to use the information derived from the swing chart to forecast future price and time targets. In addition to forecasting, this chart is also used to determine the trend of the market.

After the pattern has been analyzed in the form of the swing chart, the trader moves to the fourth step, which is the creation of Gann angle charts. Using the tops and bottoms discovered with the swing chart, the trader draws properly scaled geometric angles up from bottoms and down from tops. Since these angles move at uniform rates of speed, the trader uses the angles as support or resistance, and attempts to forecast the future direction and price potential of the market.

Percentage retracement levels are also created using the information derived from the swing charts. Each paired top and bottom on the swing chart forms a range. Inside of each range are the percentage retracement levels, the strongest being the 50% price level. The fifth step is to draw the percentage retracement level inside of each range. At this point the trader can judge the strength or weakness of the market by relating the current market price with the percentage levels. For example, a strong market will be trading above the 50% price and a weak market will be trading below the 50% price.

Time studies are then applied to the market in the sixth step. Traders should use historical charts to search for anniversary dates and cycles that could indicate the dates of future tops and bottoms. The swing chart is used to forecast the future dates of tops and bottoms based on the duration of previous rallies and breaks. Gann angle charts are used to predict when the market will be squaring price and time. Now the percentage retracement chart indicates the major time divisions of the current range, with 50% in time being the most important.

In the seventh step, the information obtained from the pattern, price, and time charts is combined to create a trading strategy. This is the most important step because it demonstrates where the three charts are linked. For example, the swing chart tells the trader when the trend changes. If the trend changes to up, the trader uses the previous rallies to forecast how far and how long the rally can be expected to last. The Gann angles drawn from the swing chart bottom show the trader uptrending support that is moving at a uniform rate of speed. In addition, the Gann angle chart shows the trader the time that will be required to reach the swing chart objective based on the speed of the Gann angle. The 50% price level acts as support when the market is above it, and as resistance when it is below it. The strongest point on the chart will occur at the intersection of the uptrending Gann angle and the 50% price. Finally, time indicators are used to prove to the trader that the upside target is possible because anniversary dates and cycles can verify the existence of similar market movement in the past.

Combining pattern, price, and time, the trader creates a trading strategy. This trading strategy is based on the principle of price and time balancing at certain points on the chart. The three methods of analysis draw this information out of the chart. Without the proper application of the three analysis tools, valuable information would be lost to the trader. This is the essence of Gann Theory, which states that there is order to the market if the proper tools are used to read the charts.

3   Chart Basics

Throughout this book, many references will be made to charts, and it will become clear to the reader that certain charts are more important than others. It is my intention to make you aware of as many different types of charts as space allows because traders find some charts easier to "read" than others. Such preferences are mainly psychological, probably based on an individual's thought process. These charts use the data generated by the market action and are not created by oscillators or averages, which sometimes smooth out the important price activity taking place in the market. As stated, our primary theme is price, time, and pattern. Each time a chart is created or analyzed, references are created that highlight these three main points. Some traders pick out the key information contained in the swing charts, others find angle charts easier to use, while a small percentage is able to use the information produced by a combination of the two types of charts. Finally, even if you find this type of analysis too difficult to grasp, you should be aware that these types of charts are absolutely necessary in technical analysis.

Charts are the tools of the futures-market analyst. Just like the doctor who relies on special instruments to perform complex medical procedures, the lawyer, who relies on law books and court precedents, and the architect, who uses form and structure to create magnificent buildings, the chartist must have the necessary instruments to correctly analyze, forecast, and trade the futures markets.

GANN-FORMAT CHARTS

The main charts to be used for technical analysis should contain the following data: the open, the high, the low, and the close. The charts can be simple bar or Gann-style that feature a vertical line for the range with a hook to the left on the high, a hook to the left on the low, a dot to the left of the range for the opening, and a dash to left of the range for the close (Figure 3.1). Both charts contain the same data, but since much of charting is perception, some chartists may prefer one look over the other.

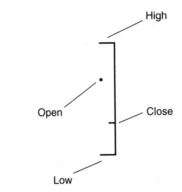

Figure 3.1   Gann-format chart.

Scale

The scale of the chart is important in price and time charting because of the sensitivity of the price movement per time period. Price and time or Gann-format charts need to have a one-to-one scale or an equal number of squares in the grid up and to the right. For example, Gann preferred 8 grid and 12 grid to the inch chart paper (Figure 3.2). This gives the market a square look that is necessary when drawing Gann angles from tops and bottoms. A line drawn diagonally from one corner to the next corner on this type of chart cuts the square exactly in half and produces a true 45 degree angle.

If you do not have the Ganntrader 2 program or have no desire to make your charts by hand, then you will have to use charts created by other charting software. These types of charts often cause problems for Gann analysts because they are created to fit a rectangular screen shape. When using programs such as Omega SuperCharts (Figure 3.3) or Omega TradeStation, it is important for the analyst to adjust the scale of the chart on the screen to the proper price and time scale of the market being analyzed. For example, a soybean chart should be charted at 1 cent per day or a treasury bond should be charted at 4/32nds per day. Although Gann angles drawn from tops and bottoms on a square chart produce 45 degree angles, simply drawing a 45 degree angle from tops or bottoms on an improperly scaled chart does not produce angles at the same points as on a properly scaled chart, which means the market is not likely to follow the up- and downtrending angles. When this occurs, the trader loses the ability to accurately forecast future price movement as well as support and resistance.

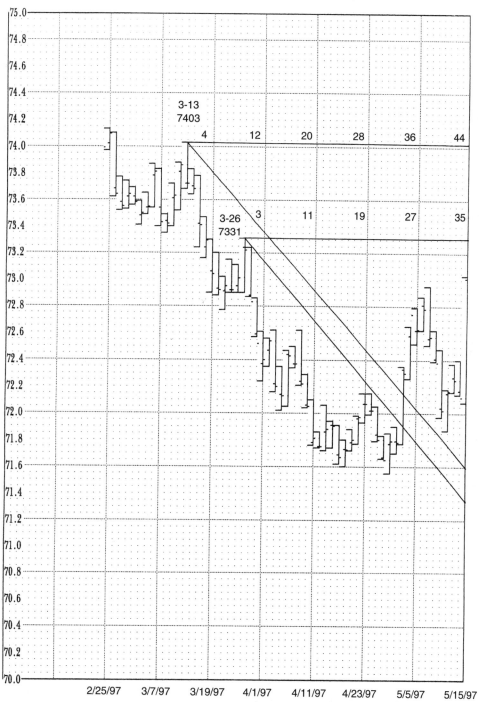

Figure 3.2   Properly scaled Gann-format chart. The angles have a mathematical relationship to the market.

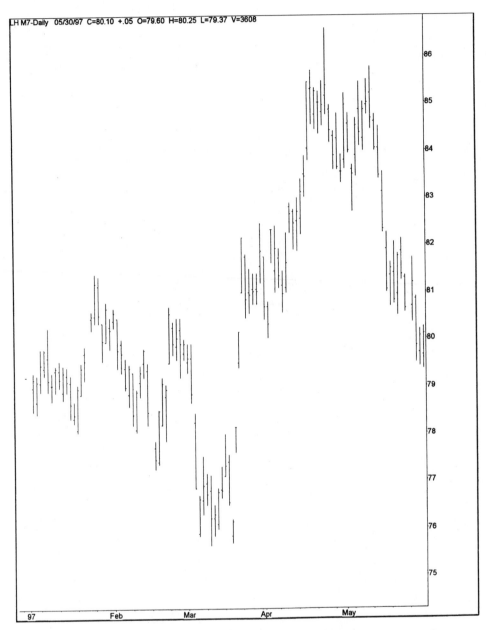

LH M7-Daily 05/30/97 C=80.10 +.05 O=79.60 H=80.25 L=79.37 V=3608

Figure 3.3   Compressed bars make this chart difficult to analyze using Gann techniques. (Chart created with SuperCharts® by Omega Research Inc.)

Size

A small chart tends to cloud the chart pattern, as all of the major support and resistance points are compressed into a compact area. Although many chart programs have the ability to focus on identifiable points on the chart, there are usually too many steps in the process. This is one of the reasons why charting on paper and off the computer is the best way to chart a market using Gann-based price and time analysis. Although it takes time to manually update markets each day, week, or month, the benefits derived by having the ability to give the chart predictive value by drawing support and resistance into the future outweighs by far the time used to update the chart manually.

A large chart is therefore a must. All of the relevant angles must be visible on the chart, not just the nearby angles. This is because angles drawn from historical tops and bottoms often have an effect on current market conditions. Also, simply charting nearby angles can distort the support and resistance levels because the analyst will not be able to note clusters of support and resistance angles. If all of the relevant angles cannot be seen, the analyst may mistakenly perceive chart points as weak support or resistance when they are actually strong points.

PROPER CHART CONSTRUCTION

When making long-term charts the analyst should be aware of variations in the chart format. Gann insisted on the proper construction of the long-term chart. For example, he recommended combining same-contract months as opposed to the very popular nearly market continuation chart. Thus, when the 1995 November Soybean Chart expired, the analyst would begin to chart the 1996 November Soybean Chart on the same long-term chart, and so on with future contracts. This is different from combining near-term charts such as November Soybeans with January Soybeans with March Soybeans and so on.

The reason for long-term charting is to maintain the mathematical relationships of the tops and bottoms of the same contract months. Furthermore, it avoids the mixing of old-crop and new-crop commodity contracts, which often produced large gaps in the chart. Although large gaps also appear in same-contract continuation charts, the market usually begins trading at or near important reference points unique to the specific contract, such as the 50% price of the all-time range. Major tops and bottoms, which may not have shown up in the deferred contracts, may have occurred in nearby contracts. By charting the market same-contract month to same-contract month instead of nearby to nearby, historical tops and bottoms unique to a specific contract can more easily be compared, as also can cycles and trading swings.

At this point I differ somewhat with Gann's charting style. My research suggests that this type of charting is fine for long-term observation of the market, but not necessarily for short-term trading. This is because the majority of the trading public will be focusing on the price action of the current active contract. Furthermore, during Gann's trading days, data were sparse, and most of the time the contract traded for only three to six months. Today a trader is able to create Gann-format charts of over two years for most contracts before the contract becomes actively traded. Valuable information can be lost if these data are combined with data from a previous time period. Research shows that creating monthly, weekly, and daily charts of a contract from its first trading day can yield valuable information in regard to cycle timing as well as the main trend and major support and resistance levels. My research strongly suggests that a specific-year contract be charted from the first day of trading if the data are available for at least twelve months. For example, creating a monthly, weekly, or daily chart of the 1997 November Soybeans from the first trading day in February 1995 can provide more precise and relevant data in terms of both price and time than can combining the 1997 November Soybean chart with the 1996 November Soybean chart from November 1996.

I am not advocating abandoning Gann's style of combining same contract month with same contract month. The trader should continue to do this in order to find historical tops and bottoms as well as major cycle and seasonal dates. In order to produce more precise information for trading, however, it is strongly recommended that the chartist use all of the price and time information available from the currently traded active contract. Additional support for this conclusion can be found by analyzing and trading the 1998 November Soybean contract while the 1997 November Soybean contract is most active.

If you were to trade the 1998 November Soybean contract, why would you need to know what the 1997 November Soybean contract was doing? Because all of the information you would need to trade is contained on the 1998 November Soybean chart. Gann was not wrong in recommending that the same contract roll, because during his day the contract years did not overlap as they do today.

Remember, continue to build same-contract continuation charts for observation for major tops and bottoms and cycles, but use the currently active contract from the first trading day to trigger trading opportunities.

The continuation method is not recommended for markets that do not have an "old crop" or a "new crop," for example, the currencies, stock indices, and treasury bonds. The rollover from one month of a financial contract to the next month does not have as great an impact on the chart pattern as does a rollover from old-crop soybeans to new-crop soybeans. This is not to suggest you not chart the same contract to same contract for the financials. This type of contract may still be used to identify major tops and bottoms that are contract specific. For trading purposes, however, the long-term charting of the current active contract is highly recommended.

One other difficulty of contract-to-contract long-term charting is the rollover. These charts can be rolled on the first notice day or the last trading date or somewhere in between. Often markets get quite active during the delivery month. This activity can lead to high volatility, which can run a market sharply higher or lower. The spike moves that can be produced can distort the chart picture.

Although Gann had good intentions when he suggested rolling over same-contract month to same-contract month, conditions have changed since he was trading. His technique was not wrong, because valuable information can be obtained from the chart style he suggested, but this style is not functional in today's trading markets. Gann encouraged traders to research and experiment and often changed his techniques to fit changes in contract specifications and market activity. In order to keep up with conditions that exist today, the trader must be flexible in his analysis. The chartist is therefore strongly encouraged to use all of the data that are available for each contract. Based on current market conditions, the trader should build monthly, weekly, and daily charts with the most actively traded contract from the first day of trading along with Gann continuation charts.

Price and Time Charting Requirements

Price and time charting also requires the analyst to chart the market on all of the days the futures contract traded (Figure 3.4). Therefore, no spaces are left for holidays or weekends. This is because each day has a specific point value, so allowing space for nontrading days can distort the future value of the angle (Figure 3.5). For example, if today is January 5, a Gann angle drawn from a bottom a few days before Thanksgiving on an improperly spaced chart will give value to holidays such as Thanksgiving, Christmas, and New Year's Day. If the value of the grid is 2 cents per day, the angle will then be off by as much as 6 cents on January 5. By being off this much, a trader may inadvertently buy a market that is 6 cents to high. The main rule to follow is to chart the market on an open trading day and skip the days when the particular exchange is closed from trading. During the early life of a contract, there may only be one price for the open, high, low, and close. On these days, simply mark the close on the proper day.

Time Periods

During Gann's time, many of the markets traded six days a week, while today all of the markets are open only five days. In addition, during the last few years many markets have added overnight trading to the former day-session-only format. It is highly recommended that the chartist not mix a full day's data with the day-session-only data. Charting the day session and overnight trading

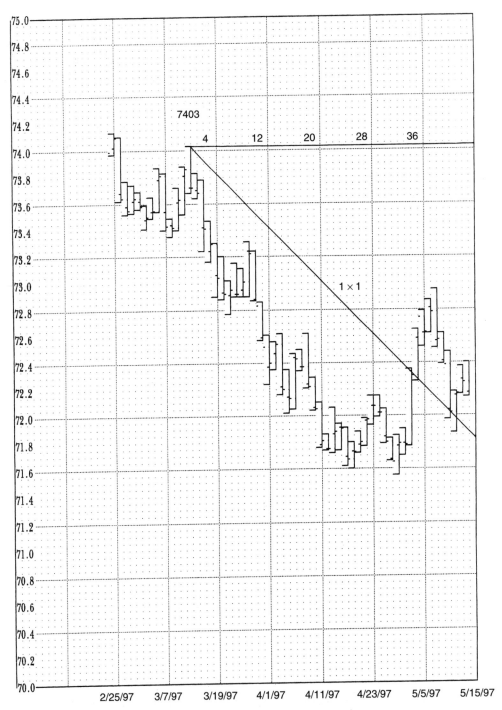

Figure 3.4   Gann chart with market days.

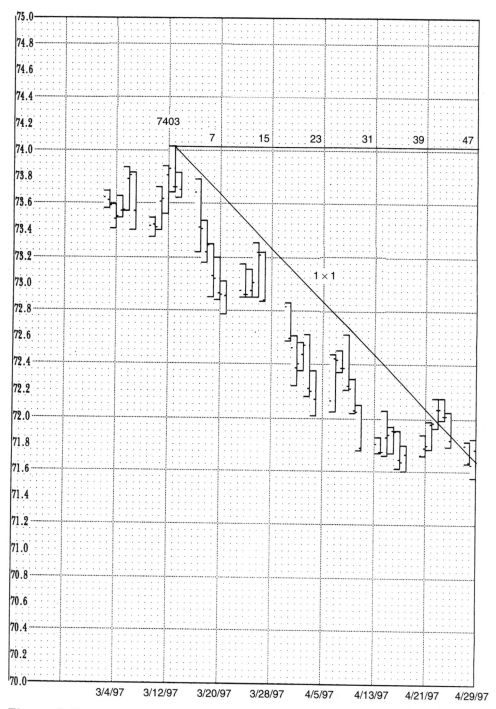

Figure 3.5   Gann chart with calendar days. A calendar-day chart has a different look than a market-day chart. It also distorts the future value of the angle as it will include the value of the nontrade days.

open, high, low, and close on a chart made up primarily of day-session-only ranges will yield improperly constructed ranges, percentage retracement points, swing charts, and Gann angles. If an ambitious chartist creates a full-day chart and a day-session-only chart, he must designate the difference between the two charts. Although the day-session range may be the same as the full-day range, it is very important not to mix the two time periods.

Intraday Charting Techniques

An intraday chart poses a similar time-period problem. The chartist must designate an intraday chart "full-session" or "day session." Incorrectly charting the intraday full session and day-session will yield improperly constructed ranges, percentage retracement points, swing charts, and Gann angles. If the chartist chooses full session only, then she must connect the data properly when combining the overnight session with the day session. There should be no spaces on the charts for periods when thinly traded markets did not post a price during overnight action when the market was open. This is in keeping with the rule that each grid has a point value when the market is required to be open. On days when the trading session ends early, such as the day before a holiday in the financial markets, the chartist must end the chart when the market stops trading for the day and begin the chart on the very next bar when trading resumes. The basic idea is to avoid leaving holes in the intraday chart unless the data are unavailable because they are corrupted or, in the case of computer charts, off-line at the time of retrieval.

CHARTING PROGRAMS

As mentioned before, the larger the chart, the better. A program such as Gann-trader 2 can produce very large Gann-format charts. This program reads CSI (Commodity Systems, Inc.) data and can easily create charts with or without Gann techniques applied to the body of the chart. Chartists using this program have the option of creating either charts with full details already applied at printing time or bare Gann-format charts. Charts printed with full analysis techniques applied are fine for observation of the market, but at some point the charts will have to be recreated each time a bar changes. These charts can also be created with plenty of room to update. When using Gann-format charts on programs such as SuperCharts or TradeStation, the chartist has the ability to save the angles on the chart for future use. These chart programs may also be able to update the angles as the market trades into the future. A large chart enables the chartist to see all of the relevant information and also allows for the ability to draw Gann angles, percentage retracement points, and tops and bottoms into the future. This is one of the major benefits of a program such as Ganntrader 2, which allows the chartist to extend all of his important analysis tools into the future, thus making it possible for him to forecast future market activity.

At this point the chartist should note that the programs mentioned for creating Gann charts and Gann analysis tools simply place the information on the charts where instructed. For example, Ganntrader 2 has the ability to draw angles from charts once the desired top or bottom is identified. There are functions that allow for the automatic generation of swing charts and Gann angles, but at some point these points must be filtered to make the data obtained relevant to the current market conditions.

In addition, SuperCharts and TradeStation simply draw Gann angles from the places on the chart where the user tells them to begin drawing. These points are not predetermined by the program. It is therefore necessary to have a strong background in Gann Theory if these programs are to be utilized to their fullest extent.

These programs provide the analyst with quick snapshots of the market with Gann techniques applied, but they cannot replace the need to study and practice Gann Theory on charts generated manually. Nonetheless, I strongly recommend that the serious Gann student purchase these programs.

TYPES OF CHARTS

Yearly and quarterly charts can be constructed primarily to show major long-term tops, bottoms, and percentage retracement points for the purpose of long-term forecasting. Trading using these charts is not recommended because the trend changes take too long to develop. Since most of this book is dedicated to developing trading techniques and strategies, I chose to focus on the monthly, weekly, and daily charts for developing a trading system.

Monthly Charts

The monthly chart (Figure 3.6) is an important chart to observe if the database contains at least five years of data. The monthly chart consists of the open, high, low, and close of each month of the year. With this chart the trader can observe the major tops, bottoms, and percentage retracement points. In addition, traders can note the dates of tops and bottoms in order to track the cyclical and seasonal movement of a market. Using this chart, the trader will have an excellent opportunity to track the size and duration of the swings of the market from top-to-bottom, bottom-to-top, top-to-top, and bottom-to-bottom. Finally, traders can see where and how major moves begin and end.

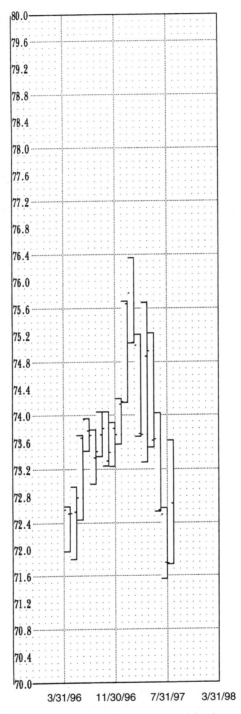

Figure 3.6   Gann-format monthly chart.

Weekly Charts

The weekly chart (Figure 3.7) is an important chart to observe if the database contains at least two years of data. The weekly chart consists of the open, high, low, and close on a weekly basis. With this chart the trader can observe the major tops, bottoms, and percentage retracement points. In addition, traders can note the dates of tops and bottoms in order to track the cyclical and seasonal movement of a market. Using this chart, the trader will have an excellent opportunity to track the size and duration of the swings of the market from top-to-bottom, bottom-to-top, top-to-top, and bottom-to-bottom. Finally, traders can see where and how major moves begin and end.

Daily Charts

The daily chart (Figure 3.8) is an important chart to observe if the database contains at least 1 year of data. The daily chart consists of the open, high, low, and close. With this chart the trader can observe the major tops, bottoms and percentage retracement points. In addition, traders can note the dates of tops and bottoms in order to track the cyclical and seasonal movement of a market. Using this chart, the trader will have a great opportunity to track the size and duration of the swings of the market from top-to-bottom, bottom-to-top, top-to-top, and bottom-to-bottom. Finally, traders can see where and how major moves begin and end.

The Trend Indicator or Swing Charts

After observing the trading pattern of a market, the analyst has to work on the chart to produce useful information. The first chart the analyst must construct is the trend indicator or swing chart (Figure 3.9). All other charts are based on the information created and observed on this chart. The swing chart, which follows the up and down movements of the market, can be created for all time periods—that is, monthly, weekly, daily, and intraday. This is because all markets make swings and all markets have trends. The swing chart is necessary because when properly constructed it provides the trader with valuable price and time information that can be useful in forecasting future price movement, cycle tops and bottoms, and for building mechanical trading systems.

Swings can be created in terms of both price and time. The most popular forms of swing charting are the one-time-period or minor-swing chart, the

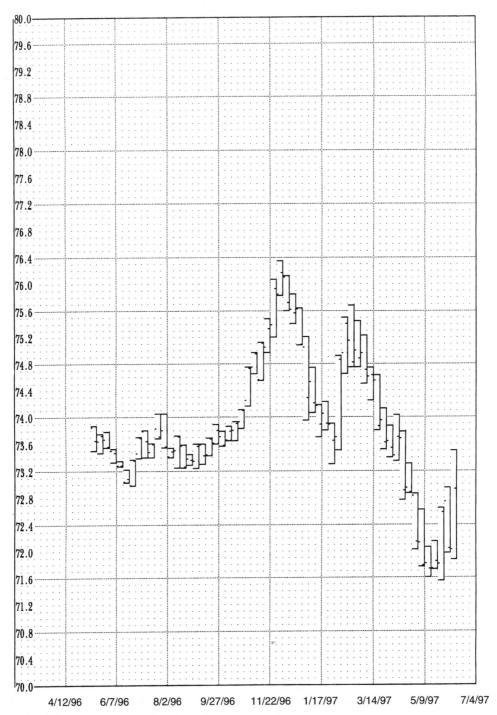

Figure 3.7   Gann-format weekly chart.

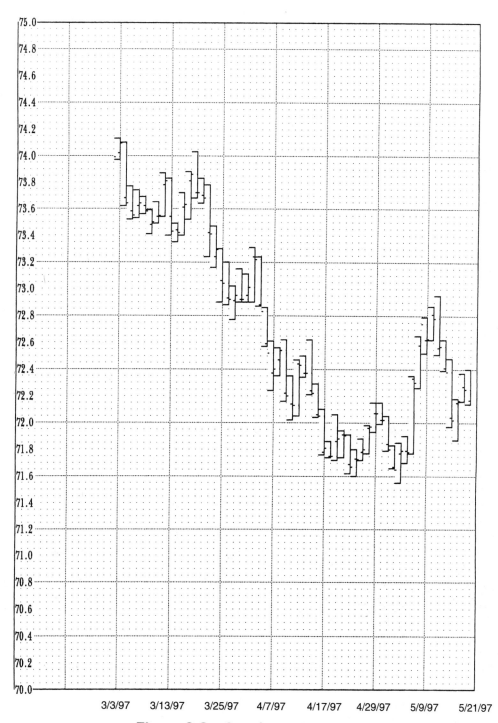

Figure 3.8   Gann-format daily chart.

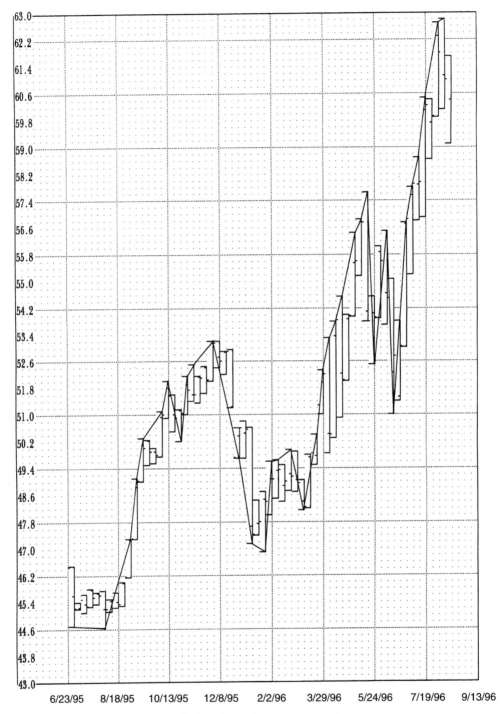

Figure 3.9 Gann-format swing chart.

two-time-period or intermediate swing chart, and the three-time-period or main-trend swing chart. Some analysts also refer to the daily chart as the minor-trend chart, the weekly as the intermediate-trend chart, and the monthly as the main-trend chart. Either way, all charts make swings and all swings can be traced and marked on a chart regardless of the time period charted.

Pattern Charts

After observing the market and creating the three swing charts, the trader will begin to learn the characteristics of a market. These characteristics include which markets have a tendency to make double or triple tops and bottoms, which markets have a tendency to post signal tops (closing price reversal tops) or signal bottoms (closing price reversal bottoms), and which markets can be pyramided. In addition to the support and resistance (price information) that are contained on the swing chart, the trader will also find time information readily available. This time information includes anniversary dates (cycle dates), length of swings up and down, and the seasonality of the market. It is important to derive all of the pattern, price, and time information the market is offering, so a properly constructed swing chart must be maintained at all times.

Besides the pattern, price, and time information that appear on the swing chart, the trader must know that this information is what the author refers to as "horizontal and vertical" information (Figure 3.10). The horizontal information are the tops and bottoms. This is because a line drawn into the future from these tops and bottoms is always horizontal. These lines move out to infinity. On the other hand, time is always expressed as a vertical line on the chart, and traces the dates of important tops and bottoms into the future. The points at which these lines cross are important support, resistance, and timing zones into infinity.

Gann-Angle Charts

Inside the horizontal and vertical zones the market also moves diagonally (Figure 3.11). These diagonal lines or angles represent both price and time and create patterns that have to be judged to determine the strength and direction of the market. Because of the price and time nature of these angles, they have predictive value, which gives the trader the ability to forecast future price movement.

The angles are drawn from tops and bottoms. Each angle drawn from a top or bottom carries the characteristics of that top or bottom. For example,

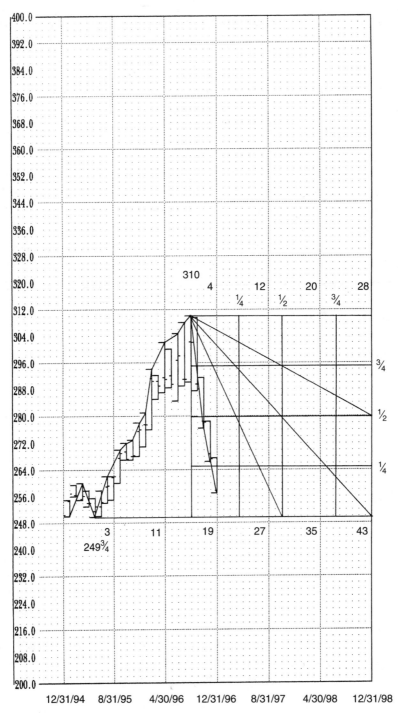

Figure 3.10   Gann-format square chart.

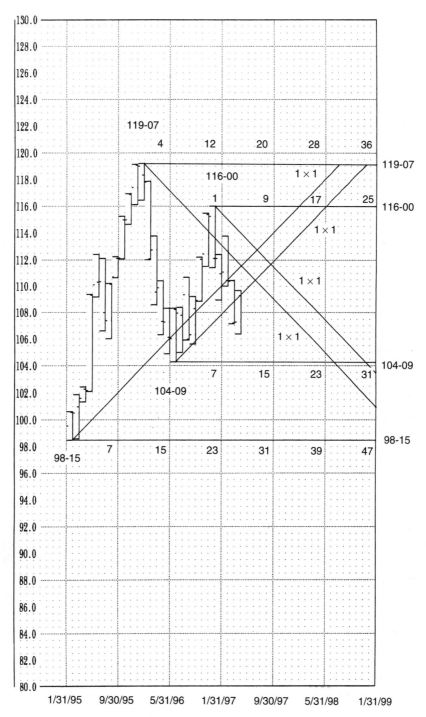

Figure 3.11   Gann-format angle chart.

an angle drawn from a three-day main bottom will have more strength than an angle drawn from a minor bottom, and an angle on a monthly chart will be stronger than an angle from a weekly or daily chart. This is another reason why the major tops and bottoms have to be identified properly on the swing charts. Missing or failing to update just one swing top or bottom can have future ramifications. This is because the past, present, and future all exist on the angle at the same time: they are drawn from the past, we know where they are currently, and can extend them into the future. This is in keeping with Gann's statement from his Master Egg Course that was quoted earlier:

> Years of this research and experience have proved that the first advance from which a reaction runs more than 3 days will set an angle for an important top later. This rule works on weekly and monthly charts also. After there is a second or third top and when there is a decline from the third top, an angle from that top must call bottoms and tops of the next advance.

In order to have a properly constructed angle chart, the chartist must know the correct scale for each market traded. Without the correct scale, price and time will be incorrect and predictive information will be lost. Finally, the crossing of two or more independently determined support and resistance points must be noted, as these price levels become the strongest support and resistance zones on the chart. These support and resistance points can come from the same chart, for example, the daily main trend-indicator chart with angles, or they can be combinations of time periods such as support angles from the monthly and daily charts.

Percentage Retracement Charts

The final chart to be observed and constructed in this chapter is the percentage retracement chart (Figure 3.12). This chart is also constructed from the swing chart. The swing chart tops and bottoms form ranges. Inside these ranges are percentage retracement points such as 33%, 50%, and 67%. These points alone represent important support and resistance points. When these percentage retracement points are combined with former tops and bottoms and angles, they create very strong impact points that can turn a market or change a trend.

The range created by a top and bottom also forms important timing points such as the end of the range and the percentage retracement points of time inside the range. The combination of the strong price and time points forms a tool that is useful in predicting and easily identifying support and resistance points.

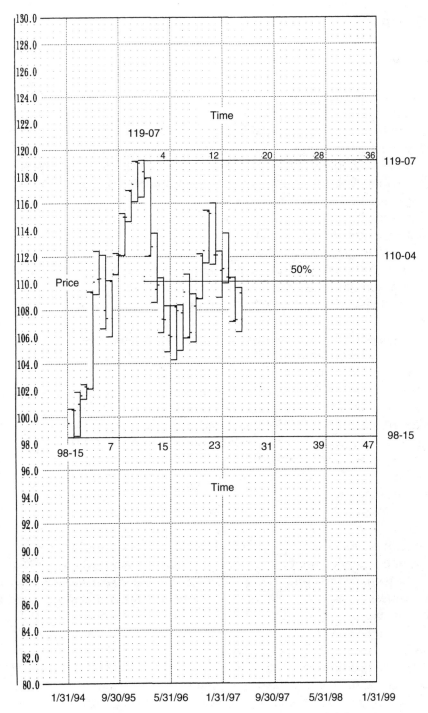

Figure 3.12   Percentage retracement chart.

SUMMARY

Price and time data come in two forms: (1) tabular data and (2) visual data. The first type is the raw data that are contained in computer files, which list the date, open, high, low, close, volume, and open interest. Anyone with a computer is most familiar with this type of data. The second is a graph representation of these tabular data. The three main elements of tabular and graphic data are price, time, and volume. The main topics in this book are price and time and the combination of the two, which forms pattern. Volume and open interest, which can be major determinants of pattern, trend, and trading, are not discussed in this book.

Price can be charted in various increments: dollars/pound, dollars/bushel, or dollars/ounce, to name a few. When it comes to price and time analysis, the price scale used on a chart is most important because the trader must have control of the chart, and using the correct price scale per grid helps the chartist accomplish this task. Studying the market movement on a chart can help the chartist determine quite accurately which price scale to use. An incorrect price scale will make a trade use incorrect support and resistance points as well as force the chartist to mistime the market while looking for specific price and time matchups. It cannot be overemphasized how important it is to properly scale a chart.

Time is another important factor that must be considered when constructing charts. The chartist must give herself an opportunity to observe the market in as many time periods as possible. These time periods should range from long-term (yearly) to short-term (five minutes). Creating charts in various time periods can help the trader to understand the nature of the market being analyzed. This can then help her determine when the market will turn with reasonable accuracy.

A properly constructed chart consists of price and time factors that, when combined, produce easily identifiable patterns that can help a person trade with reasonable accuracy. In addition, successful trade-system design and money-management techniques are better applied when the trader is working with a consistently designed chart. Records are necessary in a well-run business, and without them, the business will fail. Charts are records that must be designed and maintained properly or the trader will fail. Care should be taken to create usable charts. The past must be studied to determine the future, and the charts are the records of past market action. Just as markets take time to develop, the chartist must take time to develop the necessary charts to study the development of bull or bear markets. In order to move on and learn some of the finer points of pattern, price, and time analysis, the trader must make a commitment to maintaining first-rate charts.

From the simple bar chart the trader can create the swing chart that identifies the trend, tops, and bottoms. The swing chart also creates patterns that the trader can use to identify when and how a trend is likely to begin or end. In addition, the swing chart offers the trader a chance to discover the important timing points of the current contract that can be used for future trading, and it records the horizontal support and resistance points in a market. Angle charts created from the swing charts show diagonal movement in a market and carry the characteristics of the bottom or top from which the angle was drawn. In other words, the stronger the original top or bottom, the stronger the angle from which it was drawn. Each set of swings forms a range, inside of which are percentage retracement points. The combination of the horizontal and diagonal points form impact points that can turn a market or change a trend. These points can be created by the various analysis tools or by combining time periods. Time can also be combined in the same manner to provide the trader with key cycle dates. Finally, combining pattern, price, and time can become the basis for the development of a trading system.

4　Minor Trend Indicator Charts

While studying commodity market charts the trader will inevitably discover the small fluctuations of the market. These small fluctuations collectively make up the minor trend. Although they are minor in nature, these trends provide useful information the trader can use to determine what the minor trend of a market is and when it will change.

The fascination with the minor trend makes this indicator quite popular, as traders envision vast profits seemingly available from capturing the minor swings of the market. Unfortunately, traders who attempt to make a "quick buck" at trading the minor trend find the situation to be the opposite because of the numerous false signals and prohibitive costs of doing business. While this chart is necessary to construct to become aware of the role the minor trend plays in the intermediate- and long-term trends, it is not recommended to be the sole source of trend information.

Traders accustomed to a gambling mentality can find themselves in a situation where they are hooked on the pure emotion of trading the minor swings, the greed stemming from capturing the "whole move," and the fear of missing out on the "big move." The trader who relies exclusively on the minor swings of the market is likely to develop doubts in his trading ability, and most often will abandon or fade his system after a series of losses or missed moves. This loss of confidence can have major ramifications on the future of his trading, as there will always be doubt lurking in his head as he develops more sophisticated systems.

The pitfalls of trading exclusively with the minor trend have to be addressed, not to discourage the use of the minor trend as an indicator of future market movement, but to make the trader aware of the part the minor trend has in creating successful trading tools. At this time it should be noted that the minor trend should be used to learn more about the intermediate and main trends. This is its most beneficial use unless the trader is forced because of her career decision to trade the minor trend on an intraday or day-to-day basis. While it can be shown that more money is made over the long run by trading the major market swings, those who can afford the risk, have low trading costs, instantaneous access to the market, and the time to develop an optimized trading system can have positive results.

Trading the minor trend is a full-time job. The trader has to maintain a properly constructed chart at all times. This is because a major move can occur at any time, and the trader has to be ready. Those who find success at trading the minor trend are those who can control risk and are willing to take a series of losses in exchange for a few trades whose profits are far greater than the losses. Traders who cannot handle the prospect of having more losing trades than winning trades, who have a closed mind, and the inability to accept changes in trend quickly should avoid trading the minor trend.

Given the noted pitfalls of using the minor trend as the sole indicator of future market direction, the reader invariably asks: "Why the minor trend indicator chart?" Following the proper construction of this chart, the trader will have before him a chart depicting each minor top and minor bottom and the date each one occurred. In addition, the trader will also be able to determine when minor trend changes have taken place and the duration of the swings in terms of price and time.

DEFINITION

Since the minor swing chart can be used to identify the minor tops and bottoms for any time period, in order to avoid confusion about whether we are speaking exclusively of the monthly, weekly, daily, or intraday charts, we call each trading time period a bar.

The minor swing chart, or one-bar chart, follows the one-bar movement of the market. From a low price each time the market makes a higher-high than the previous bar, a minor trend line moves up from the recent low to the new high. This action makes the previous low price a minor bottom (Figure 4.1). From a high price each time the market makes a lower-low than the previous bar, a minor trend line moves down from the recent high to the new low. This action makes the previous high price a minor top (Figure 4.2). The combination of a minor trend line from a bottom and a minor trend line from a top forms a minor swing. This is important information, because when stop placement is discussed, traders will be told to place stops under minor swing bottoms, not under lows, and over minor swing tops, not over highs. Learn and know the difference between a low and a minor swing bottom, and a high and a minor swing top.

Once the first minor swing is formed, the trader can anticipate a change in minor trend. If the minor swing chart begins from the first trading month, week, or day and the minor trend line moves up to a new high, this does not mean that the minor trend has turned up. Conversely, if the first move is down, this does not mean the minor trend is down. The only way for the minor trend to turn up is to cross a minor top, and the only way for the minor trend to turn down is to cross a minor bottom. In addition, if the minor trend

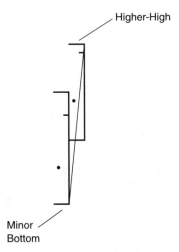

Figure 4.1   Gann price bar, minor bottom. A low price becomes a minor bottom when the market posts a higher-high.

is up and the market makes a minor swing down that does not take out the previous minor swing bottom, this is a correction. If the minor trend is down and the market makes a minor swing up that does not take out the previous minor swing top, this is also a correction. A market is composed of two types of up and down moves. The minor swing chart draws attention to these types of moves by identifying trending up moves and correcting up moves, as well as trending down moves and correcting down moves.

In summary, when implementing the minor swing chart, the analyst is merely following the one-bar up and down movements of the market. The intersection of an established downtrending line with a new uptrending line is a minor swing bottom. The intersection of an established uptrending line with

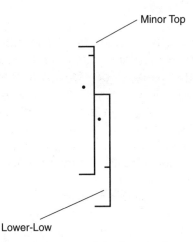

Figure 4.2   Gann price bar, minor top. A high price becomes a minor top when the market posts a lower-low.

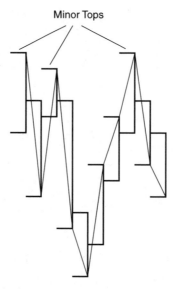

Figure 4.3 Minor trend indicator bars from a high price. Minor tops are formed by the one-bar down swings of the market. From a high, the minor trend line moves down to the lower-low.

a new downtrending line is a minor swing top. The combination of minor swing tops and bottoms forms the minor trend indicator chart (Figure 4.3). The crossing of a minor swing top changes the minor trend to up. The penetration of a minor trend bottom changes the minor trend to down. The market is composed of uptrends, downtrends, and corrections.

CONSTRUCTION

In order to properly construct the minor trend indicator chart the following must be available: a bar chart, price and time data, a red pen, a green pen, a black pen, and a ruler. The black pen is used to update the chart, the green pen is used to track the upward movement of the trend line, and the red pen is used to track the downward movement of the trend line. Since a poorly drawn line may be misinterpreted, the ruler is used to keep the lines straight. Use the price and time data to ensure the proper marking of highs and lows, as relying on visual estimation invites faulty identification, which can also have an adverse affect on the research.

   It is best to start the minor trend indicator chart (Figure 4.4) from the first trading bar of the contract, because by the time the contract being analyzed becomes the actively traded market, the analyst will have constructed all of the minor swings of the contract and derived valuable information about price

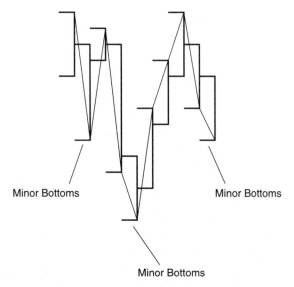

Minor Bottoms   Minor Bottoms

Minor Bottoms

Figure 4.4 Minor trend indicator bars from a low price. Minor bottoms are formed by the one-bar upswings of the market. From a low, the minor trend line moves up to the higher-high.

and time from the activity charted. This chart serves as a "fingerprint" of the market, because each individual market has unique patterns contained in the total chart by which it can be identified. This is why precise and accurate data must be maintained at all times.

The Minor Trend and the Monthly Chart from a Low Price

On a monthly chart, start the indicator during the first month of trading, then each month simply follow the movement of the market. From a low price if the market makes a higher-high, use the green pen to move the minor trend line up from the low of one bar back to the high on the current bar. This action makes the low of one bar back a minor bottom. Each month that the market posts a subsequent higher-high, move the minor trend line up to the succeeding higher price. Continue to move the minor trend line from high to high until the market makes a lower-low. At this point, use the red pen to move the minor trend line down from the high of one bar back to the low of the current bar. This action makes the high of one bar back a minor top. Each month that the market posts a subsequent lower-low, move the minor trend line down to the succeeding lower price. Continue to move the minor trend line from low to low until the market makes a higher-high.

The Minor Trend and the Monthly Chart
from a High Price

On a monthly chart (Figure 4.5), start the indicator during the first month of trading, then each month simply follow the movement of the market. From a high price if the market makes a lower-low, use the red pen to move the minor trend line down from the high of one bar back to the low of the current bar. This action makes the high of one bar back a minor top. Each month that the market posts a subsequent lower-low, move the minor trend line down to the succeeding lower price. Continue to move the minor trend line from low to low until the market makes a higher-high. At this point, use the green pen to move the minor trend line up from the low of one bar back to the high of the current bar. This action makes the low of one bar back a minor bottom. Each month that the market posts a subsequent higher-high, move the minor trend line up to the succeeding higher price. Continue to move the minor trend line from high to high until the market makes a lower-low.

The Minor Trend and the Weekly Chart
from a Low Price

On a weekly chart (Figure 4.6), start the indicator during the first week of trading, then each week simply follow the movement of the market. From a low price if the market makes a higher-high, use the green pen to move the minor trend line up from the low of one bar back to the high of the current bar. This action makes the low of one bar back a minor bottom. Each week that the market posts a subsequent higher-high, move the minor trend line up to the succeeding higher price. Continue to move the minor trend line from high to high until the market makes a lower-low. At this point, use the red pen to move the minor trend line down from the high of one bar back to the low of the current bar. This action makes the high of one bar back a minor top. Each week that the market posts a subsequent lower-low, move the minor trend line down to the succeeding lower price. Continue to move the minor trend line from low to low until the market makes a higher-high.

The Minor Trend and the Weekly Chart
from a High Price

On a weekly chart start the indicator during the first week of trading, then each week simply follow the movement of the market. From a high price if the market makes a lower-low, use the red pen to move the minor trend line

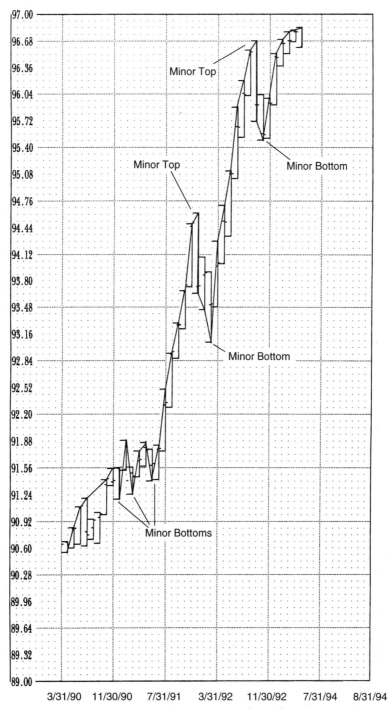

Figure 4.5 Monthly minor trend indicator chart from a high price.

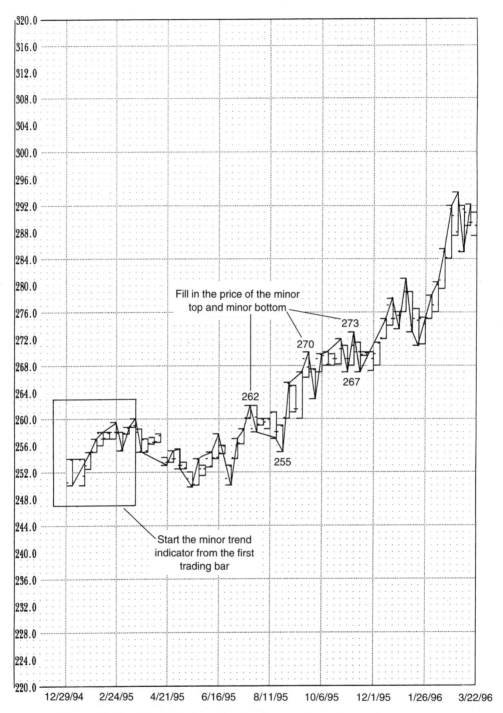

Figure 4.6   Weekly minor trend indicator chart from a low price.

down from the high of one bar back to the low of the current bar. This action makes the high of one bar back a minor top. Each week that the market posts a subsequent lower-low, move the minor trend line down to the succeeding lower price. Continue to move the minor trend line from low to low until the market makes a higher-high. At this point, use the green pen to move the minor trend line up from the low of one bar back to high of the current bar. This action makes the low of one bar back a minor bottom. Each week that the market posts a subsequent higher-high, move the minor trend line up to the succeeding higher price. Continue to move the minor trend line from high to high until the market makes a lower-low.

The Minor Trend and the Daily Chart from a Low Price

On a daily chart, start the indicator on the first day of trading, then each day simply follow the movement of the market. From a low price if the market makes a higher-high, use the green pen to move the minor trend line up from the low of one bar back to the high of the current bar. This action makes the low of one bar back a minor bottom. Each day that the market posts a subsequent higher-high, move the minor trend line up to the succeeding higher price. Continue to move the minor trend line from high to high until the market makes a lower-low. At this point, use the red pen to move the minor trend line down from the high of one bar back to the low of the current bar. This action makes the high of one bar back a minor top. Each day that the market posts a subsequent lower-low, move the minor trend line down to the succeeding lower price. Continue to move the minor trend line from low to low until the market makes a higher-high.

The Minor Trend and the Daily Chart from a High Price

On a daily chart, start the indicator on the first day of trading, then each day simply follow the movement of the market. From a high price if the market makes a lower-low, use the red pen to move the minor trend line down from the high of one bar back to the low of the current bar. This action makes the high of one bar back a minor top. Each day that the market posts a subsequent lower-low, move the minor trend line down to the succeeding lower price. Continue to move the minor trend line from low to low until the market makes a higher-high. At this point, use the green pen to move the minor trend line up from the low of one bar back to the high of the current bar. This action makes the low of one bar back a minor bottom. Each day that the market posts a subsequent higher-high, move the minor trend line up to the succeeding higher price. Continue to move the minor trend line from high to high until the market makes a lower-low.

This completes the explanation of how to begin building a minor trend indicator chart. Continue this process on the monthly, weekly, and daily charts until the chart is up to date with the current market. After each minor swing has been identified, go back to write above the minor tops the price and the date of occurrence. Do the same for the minor bottoms, but write the price and the date of occurrence below the minor bottom.

The Inside Bar

An important fact to note when tracking the minor swings of the market is the occurrence of the inside move and the outside move. Since this chart pattern holds true for all time periods (monthly, weekly, and daily), we refer to it as an *inside bar* (Figure 4.7). The inside bar occurs when the high is lower than the previous high and the low is higher than the previous low. When charting the minor swings of the market, the analyst ignores the inside bar and waits to see the trading range of the next bar. Since the inside bar is ignored, the analyst must always look at the preceding bar to determine if the minor trend line should be moved up or down. This bar is known as the *last active bar*. If the trend line was moving up before the inside bar and the current rally takes out the high of the last active bar, then the minor trend line moves up. If the trend line was moving up before the inside bar and the market moves below the low of the last active bar, then the minor trend line moves down. If the trend line was moving down before the inside bar and the break takes out the low of the last active bar, then the minor trend line moves down. If the trendline was moving down before the inside bar and the mar-

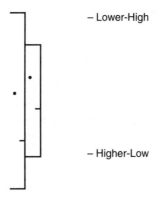

– Lower-High

– Higher-Low

Figure 4.7   Inside bar chart. Note that the high is lower than the previous high and the low is higher than the previous low.

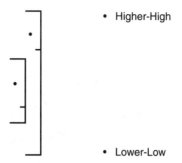

Figure 4.8   Outside bar chart. Note that the high is higher than the previous high and the low is lower than the previous low. The order of the events is important.

ket moves above the high of the last active bar, then the minor trend line moves up. In summary, the trader ignores the inside bar and refers to the last active bar to find the direction of the minor trend line's movement.

The Outside Bar

The outside time period (outside bar; see Figure 4.8) occurs when the high of the current time period is higher than the previous time period and the low of the current time period is lower than the low of the current time period. Contrary to the inside bar, the order of occurrence of the high and low on an outside move day are critical and should be noted. If the minor trend line is moving up and the first move of the outside move day is to the high, the minor trend line moves up to the high, then down to the low on the same bar (Figure 4.9). If the minor trend line is moving up and the first move of the outside move day

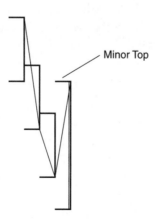

Figure 4.9   Minor trend indicator outside bar chart. The minor top is formed first. The minor trend indicator moves lower as the outside bar occurs. If a high precedes a low, move the trend line to high, then down to low.

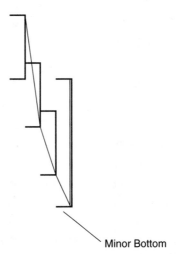

Minor Bottom

Figure 4.10   Minor trend indicator outside bar chart. The minor trend bottom is formed first. The minor trend indicator moves lower as the outside bar occurs. If a low precedes a high, move the trend line to low, then up to high.

is to the low, the minor trend line moves down to the low, then up to the high (Figure 4.10). Furthermore, if the minor trend line is moving down and the first move of the outside move day is to the high, the minor trend line moves to the high, then to the low. Finally, if the minor trend line is moving down and the first move of the outside move day is to the low, the minor trend line moves to the low, then to the high.

It is critical that the correct order of the high and low of an outside move day be recorded properly, because the market will either be continuing the trend or the trader will be forced to move the stop to a new level. When back-testing the minor trend indicator on historical data and the order of an outside day cannot be confirmed, it is safe to assume that the price closest to the opening occurred first and the price closest to the close occurred last.

STOP ORDERS

Although stop orders are discussed later in the book with more specific examples, the general rule to follow is to place them under minor bottoms (Figure 4.11) and above minor tops. This is because when the stop is hit, the minor trend will change. On the other hand, stops that are placed under lows and above highs are caught more often and simply take the trader out of the market. Another, more basic reason this type of popular stop should be avoided is that the trader is simply placing the stop within the normal swing of the market. When using the minor swing chart to enter a market never

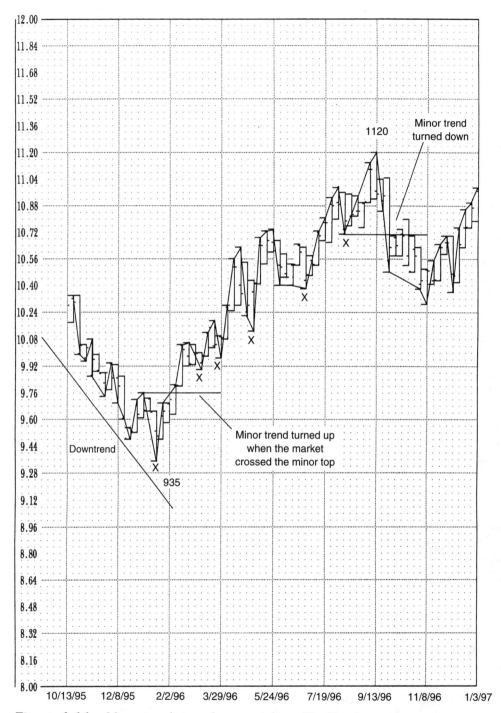

Figure 4.11   Minor trend stop placement chart. The X indicates that stops are placed under minor bottoms during an uptrend. The stops follow the uptrend. "Dollar" stops are not considered.

consider using a stop set at a specific dollar amount, as it will almost certainly get taken out during the normal course of trading.

The stop points established are set by the market. The construction and study of the minor swing chart in advance will therefore help a trader determine if the specific market he wants to trade creates price swings he can afford to trade. If the trader cannot afford the stop generated, then he is undercapitalized to trade the specific market and should find another one he can afford to trade in with his limited capital.

The price level the market is trading at often determines the size of the swing and ultimately the size of the stop. For example, markets trading near highs have wider swings than markets trading near low prices. Stops should be placed one, two, or three price units above or below minor swing tops and bottoms. Which stop placement is indicated depends on the position of the market relative to the price level and the current market volatility. For example, when the market is trading at a historically low level, a stop should be placed closer to the minor top or minor bottom than when a market is trading at a historically high level. Use the long-term charts to determine the position of the market and place the stop accordingly.

When specific markets are discussed rules are given for determining the proper stop placement relative to the minor top or minor bottom and in accordance with the current trading level of the market.

USING THE INFORMATION GENERATED

Keep a record of these swings, as these points can become important support and resistance points during the life of the current market or historical support and resistance points in future years. Besides being important price points, the dates of the minor tops and bottoms can become important timing points during the life of the current market or historical timing points in future years.

Now that the minor tops and bottoms have been identified, record the swings in terms of price and time from top-to-top, top-to-bottom, bottom-to-top, and bottom-to-bottom. This information can be used to determine whether or not a market is expanding or contracting. Minor swings should also be grouped by price levels and calendar dates. This will give the trader an idea of the behavior of the market at various price levels during particular periods. In addition to cyclical information, this chart contains important seasonal data. Traders should also analyze the strength of up moves from various price levels as well as their corresponding corrections. Conversely, traders should study the strength of down moves from various price levels and their corresponding corrections. A spreadsheet program can be used to organize this information so the changes in price and time can be easily calculated. It is important to keep a record of these swings because they can become valuable in forecasting future price and time swings.

Depending on the trader's perspective, all of these charts should be created in order to determine the minor trend of the time period studied. Further analysis will show that all of these charts are interrelated. Thus, creating all of them will not be wasted effort. By creating these charts the trader is given a top-down perspective: a minor top or bottom on the monthly chart is the most important, followed by a minor top or bottom on the weekly chart, then a minor top and bottom on the daily chart, and finally a minor top and bottom on the hourly chart (not discussed here).

After creating the minor trend chart and studying the tops and bottoms, the following should be strongly noted in order to understand the interrelationship of the charts. This concept is addressed again when percentage retracements and Gann angles are discussed.

1. A minor top on a monthly chart is always a minor top on the weekly, daily, or hourly charts.
2. A minor top on a weekly chart is always a minor top on the daily and hourly charts, but not always on the monthly chart.
3. A minor top on the daily chart is always a minor top on the hourly chart, but not always on the weekly or monthly charts.
4. A minor top on the hourly chart is not always a minor top on the daily, weekly, or monthly charts.
5. A minor bottom on a monthly chart is always a minor bottom on the weekly, daily, or hourly charts.
6. A minor bottom on a weekly chart is always a minor bottom on the daily and hourly charts, but not always on the monthly chart.
7. A minor bottom on the daily chart is always a minor bottom on the hourly chart, but not always on the weekly or monthly charts.
8. A minor bottom on the hourly chart is not always a minor bottom on the daily, weekly, or monthly charts.
9. A minor uptrend and a minor downtrend on the monthly chart are composed of a series of swings from the weekly, daily, and hourly charts. Study how many weekly, daily, or hourly swings on average it takes to form a monthly uptrend or downtrend.
10. A minor uptrend and a minor downtrend on the weekly chart are composed of a series of swings from the daily and hourly charts. Study how many daily or hourly swings on average it takes to form a weekly uptrend or downtrend.
11. A minor uptrend and a minor downtrend on the daily chart are composed of a series of swings from the hourly chart. Study how many

hourly swings on average it takes to form a daily uptrend or downtrend.

12. A minor uptrend and a minor downtrend on the hourly chart are composed of a series of swings from the other intraday time periods, such as the 30-minute, 15-minute, or 5-minute chart. Study how many time period swings on average it takes to form an hourly uptrend or downtrend.

SUMMARY

The minor trend indicator chart simply follows the minor or one-bar swings of the market. Traders simply follow the up and down movements of the market by raising or lowering the minor trend line. The crossing of the minor top and the minor bottom change the trend to up or to down, not the movement of the trend line. This action creates uptrends, downtrends, and corrections. Changes in direction turn lows into bottoms and highs into tops. Inside bars should be ignored during the construction of the minor trend indicator chart. In contrast, outside-bar moves should be watched carefully, as the order of the high or low of the outside bar is critical to the structure of the minor trend indicator chart. When an outside bar occurs, traders should note which came first, the high or the low.

Avoid placing stops over highs and under lows; instead, place them over tops and under bottoms. The placement of the stop should also be relative to the historical trading position of the market. Studying and analyzing the data created by the minor swing chart can help the trader determine the duration of the swings in terms of price and time from top-to-top, top-to-bottom, bottom-to-top, and bottom-to-bottom. This information can then be used to judge whether a market is expanding or contracting. In addition, market behavior at various price levels and time periods can help a trader determine the nature of a market. Finally, the trader should have a working knowledge of the interrelationships of the monthly, weekly, daily, and intraday charts to gain a better understanding of support and resistance.

5 Intermediate Trend Indicator Charts

After studying the minor swing chart and learning some of its disadvantages, the analyst may naturally be drawn to the intermediate swing chart (Figure 5.1). After being made aware of the exigencies relating to the minor trend chart, the trader may feel that trading the intermediate swing chart offers a better opportunity to trade successfully. In addition, the intermediate trend chart offers the trader more "true" changes in trend and is less likely to whipsaw. Finally, the cost of trading is decreased considerably because fewer signals are generated by the intermediate trend chart as compared to the minor trend chart.

Following are some of the major benefits of trading using the intermediate swing chart:

1. Intermediate trend opportunities occur less frequently than minor trend opportunities. This keeps the cost of trading to a minimum.
2. Trading less frequently than the minor trend indicator makes the trader less likely to be whipsawed and also makes the possibility of a long series of losses less likely.
3. Intermediate trend trading opportunities develop more slowly and more predictably than minor trend opportunities. This gives the trader time to watch the formation and to make adjustments when necessary.
4. Although the same technique is required to create the intermediate trend chart, and the minor trend chart, the amount of time devoted can be less especially if the market is currently in a steep uptrend or downtrend.
5. The mental exhaustion caused by frequently changing direction, over-trading, and taking a series of losses is not as common for the intermediate trend trader as it is for the minor trend trader.
6. Study of the minor trend chart is helpful in determining upcoming trend changes on the intermediate trend chart. Additionally, study of the intermediate trend chart is helpful in determining trend changes in the main trend chart (see Chapter 6).

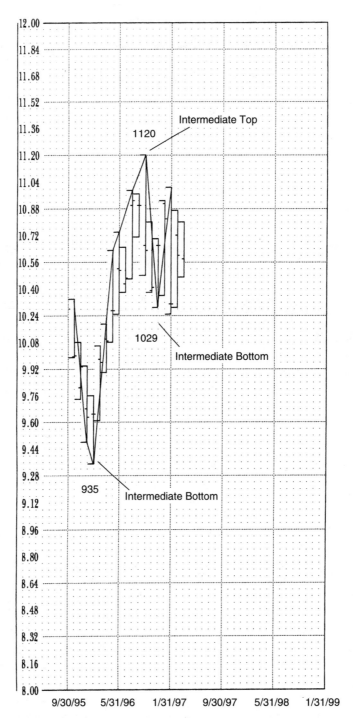

Figure 5.1   Intermediate trend chart in which the trend-line indicator moves up or down according to the two-bar movement of the market.

After learning the disadvantages of the minor trend chart and learning some of the advantages of the intermediate trend chart, the trader often chooses the intermediate trend chart as her sole source of trend data and information. Following the proper construction of this chart, the trader will have before her a chart depicting each intermediate top and intermediate bottom and the date on which each of them occurred. In addition, she will be able to determine when intermediate trend changes have taken place and the duration of the intermediate swings in terms of price and time. From this information a simple trading system can be developed.

DEFINITION

Since the intermediate swing chart can be used to identify the intermediate tops and bottoms for any time period, in order to avoid confusion about whether we are speaking exclusively of the monthly, weekly, daily, or intraday charts, we call each trading time period a bar.

The intermediate swing chart, or two-bar chart, follows the two-bar movements of the market (Figure 5.2). From a low price each time the market makes a higher-high than the previous bar for two consecutive time periods, an intermediate trend line moves up from the low two bars back to the new high. This action makes the low price from two bars back an intermediate bottom. From a high price each time the market makes a lower-low than the previous bar for two consecutive time periods, an intermediate trend line moves down from the high two bars back to the new low. This action makes the high price from two bars back an intermediate top. The combination of an intermediate trend line from an intermediate bottom and an intermediate trend line from an intermediate top forms an intermediate swing. This is important information, because when stop placement is discussed, traders will be told to place stops under intermediate swing bottoms, not under lows, and over intermediate swing tops, not over highs. Learn and know the difference between a low and an intermediate swing bottom, and a high and an intermediate swing top.

Once the first intermediate swing is formed, the trader can anticipate a change in the intermediate trend. If the intermediate swing chart begins from the first trading month, week, or day and the intermediate trend line moves up to a new high, this does not mean that the intermediate trend has turned up. Conversely, if the first move is down, this does not mean the intermediate trend is down. The only way for the intermediate trend to turn up is to cross an intermediate top, and the only way for the intermediate trend to turn down is to cross an intermediate bottom. In addition, if the intermediate trend is up and

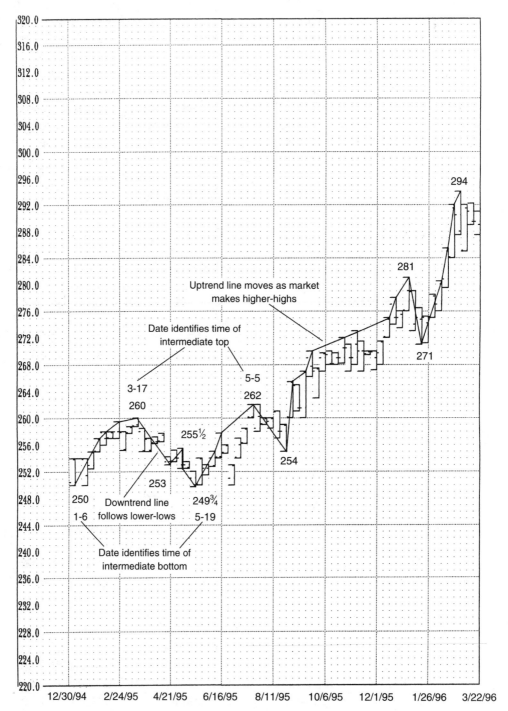

Figure 5.2   Intermediate trend indicator chart. The intermediate chart follows two-bar swings of the market. Each price is an intermediate bottom or an intermediate top.

the market makes an intermediate swing down that does not take out the previous intermediate swing bottom, this is a correction. If the intermediate trend is down and the market makes an intermediate swing up that does not take out the previous intermediate swing top, this is also a correction. A market is composed of two types of up and down moves. The intermediate swing chart draws attention to these types of moves by identifying trending up moves and correcting up moves, as well as trending down moves and correcting down moves.

In summary, when implementing the intermediate swing chart, the analyst is merely following the two-bar up and down movements of the market. The intersection of an established downtrending line with a new uptrending line is an intermediate swing bottom. The intersection of an established uptrending line with a new downtrending line is an intermediate swing top. The combination of intermediate swing tops and bottoms forms the intermediate trend indicator chart (Figure 5.3). The crossing of an intermediate swing top changes the intermediate trend to up. The penetration of an intermediate trend bottom changes the intermediate trend to down. The market is composed of intermediate uptrends, intermediate downtrends, and intermediate trend corrections.

CONSTRUCTION

In order to properly construct the intermediate trend indicator chart the following must be available: a bar chart, price and time data, a red pen, a green pen, a black pen, and a ruler. The black pen is used to update the chart, the green pen is used to track the upward movement of the intermediate trend line, and the red pen is used to track the downward movement of the intermediate trend line. Since a poorly drawn line may be misinterpreted, the ruler is used to keep the lines straight. Use the price and time data to ensure the proper marking of highs and lows, as relying on visual estimation invites faulty identification, which can also have an adverse affect on the research.

It is best to start the intermediate trend indicator chart (Figure 5.4) from the first trading bar of the contract because by the time the contract being analyzed becomes the actively traded market, the analyst will have constructed all of the intermediate swings of the contract and derived valuable information about price and time from the activity charted. This chart serves as a "fingerprint" of the market, because each individual market has unique patterns contained in the total chart by which it can be identified. This is why precise and accurate data must be maintained at all times.

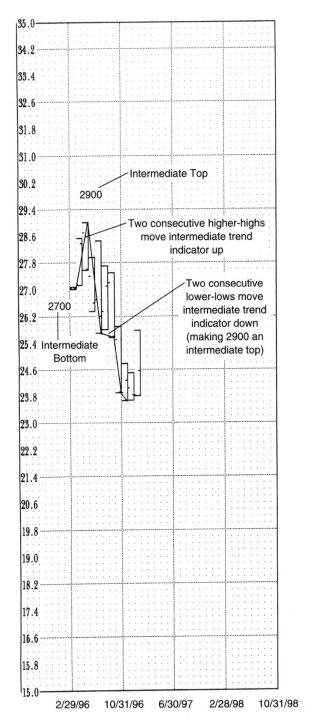

Figure 5.3   Intermediate trend chart showing an intermediate top and bottom.

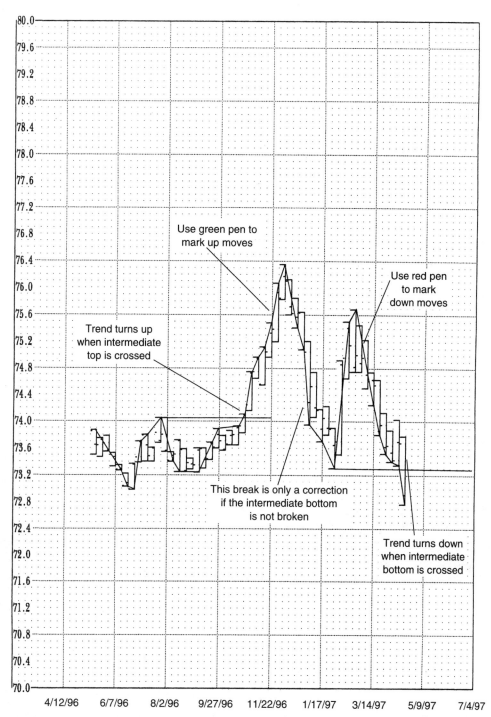

Figure 5.4   Example of an intermediate trend chart for 1997 weekly Canadian dollar.

The Intermediate Trend and the Monthly Chart from a Low Price

On a monthly chart, start the indicator during the first month of trading, then each month simply follow the movement of the market. From a low price if the market makes two consecutive higher-highs, use the green pen to move the intermediate trend line up from the low of two bars back to the high on the current bar. This action makes the low of two bars back an intermediate bottom. Once the two-bar indicator has triggered upward motion it is no longer necessary to have two consecutive higher-highs to move the intermediate trend line up. Each month that the market posts a subsequent higher-high, move the intermediate trend line up to the succeeding higher price. Continue to move the intermediate trend line from high to high until the market makes two consecutive lower-lows. At this point, use the red pen to move the intermediate trend line down from the high of two bars back to the low on the current bar. This action makes the high of two bars back an intermediate top. Once the two-bar indicator has triggered downward motion it is no longer necessary to have two consecutive lower-lows to move the intermediate trend line down. Each month that the market posts a subsequent lower-low, move the intermediate trend line down to the succeeding lower price. Continue to move the intermediate trend line from low to low until the market makes two consecutive higher-highs.

The Intermediate Trend and the Monthly Chart from a High Price

On a monthly chart, start the indicator during the first month of trading, then each month simply follow the movement of the market. From a high price if the market has two consecutive lower-lows, use the red pen to move the intermediate trend line down from the high of two bars back to the low on the current bar. This action makes the high of two bars back an intermediate top. Once the two-bar indicator has triggered downward motion it is no longer necessary to have two consecutive lower-lows to move the intermediate trend line down. Each month that the market posts a subsequent lower-low, move the intermediate trend line down to the succeeding lower price. Continue to move the intermediate trend line from low to low until the market makes two consecutive higher-highs. At this point, use the green pen to move the intermediate trend line up from the low of two bars back to the high on the current bar. This action makes the low of two bars back an intermediate bottom. Once the two-bar indicator has triggered upward motion it is no longer necessary to have two consecutive higher-highs to move the intermediate trend line up. Each month that the market posts a subsequent higher-high, move the intermediate trend line up to the succeeding higher price. Continue to move the intermediate trend line from high to high until the market makes two consecutive lower-lows.

The Intermediate Trend and the Weekly Chart from a Low Price

On a weekly chart, start the indicator during the first week of trading, then each week simply follow the movement of the market. From a low price if the market has two consecutive higher-highs, use the green pen to move the intermediate trend line up from the low of two bars back to the high on the current bar. This action makes the low of two bars back an intermediate bottom. Once the two-bar indicator has triggered upward motion it is no longer necessary to have two consecutive higher-highs to move the intermediate trend line up. Each week that the market posts a subsequent higher-high, move the intermediate trend line up to the succeeding higher price. Continue to move the intermediate trend line from high to high until the market makes two consecutive lower-lows. At this point, use the red pen to move the intermediate trend line down from the high of two bars back to the low on the current bar. This action makes the high of two bars back an intermediate top. Once the two-bar indicator has triggered downward motion it is no longer necessary to have two consecutive lower-lows to move the intermediate trend line down. Each week that the market posts a subsequent lower-low, move the intermediate trend line down to the succeeding lower price. Continue to move the intermediate trend line from low to low until the market makes two consecutive higher-highs.

The Intermediate Trend and the Weekly Chart from a High Price

On a weekly chart, start the indicator during the first week of trading then each week simply follow the movement of the market. From a high price if the market has two consecutive lower-lows, use the red pen to move the intermediate trend line down from the high of two bars back to the low on the current bar. This action makes the high of two bars back an intermediate top. Once the two-bar indicator has triggered downward motion it is no longer necessary to have two consecutive lower-lows to move the intermediate trend line down. Each week that the market posts a subsequent lower-low, move the intermediate trend line down to the succeeding lower price. Continue to move the intermediate trend line from low to low until the market makes two consecutive higher-highs. At this point, use the green pen to move the intermediate trend line up from the low of two bars back to the high on the current bar. This action makes the low of two bars back an intermediate bottom. Once the two-bar indicator has triggered upward motion it is no longer necessary to have two consecutive higher-highs to move the intermediate trend line up. Each week that the market posts a subsequent higher-high, move the intermediate trend line up to the succeeding higher price. Continue to move the intermediate trend line from high to high until the market makes two consecutive lower-lows.

The Intermediate Trend and the Daily Chart from a Low Price

On a daily chart, start the indicator on the first day of trading, then each day simply follow the movement of the market. From a low price if the market has two consecutive higher-highs, use the green pen to move the intermediate trend line up from the low of two bars back to the high on the current bar. This action makes the low of two bars back an intermediate bottom. Once the two-bar indicator has triggered upward motion it is no longer necessary to have two consecutive higher-highs to move the intermediate trend line up. Each day that the market posts a subsequent higher-high, move the intermediate trend line up to the succeeding higher price. Continue to move the intermediate trend line from high to high until the market makes two consecutive lower-lows. At this point, use the red pen to move the intermediate trend line down from the high of two bars back to the low on the current bar. This action makes the high of two bars back an intermediate top. Once the two-bar indicator has triggered downward motion it is no longer necessary to have two consecutive lower-lows to move the intermediate trend line down. Each day that the market posts a subsequent lower-low, move the intermediate trend line down to the succeeding lower price. Continue to move the intermediate trend line from low to low until the market makes two consecutive higher-highs.

The Intermediate Trend and the Daily Chart from a High Price

On a daily chart, start the indicator on the first day of trading, then each day simply follow the movement of the market. From a high price if the market has two consecutive lower-lows, use the red pen to move the intermediate trend line down from the high of two bars back to the low on the current bar. This action makes the high of two bars back an intermediate top. Once the two-bar indicator has triggered downward motion it is no longer necessary to have two consecutive lower-lows to move the intermediate trend line down. Each day that the market posts a subsequent lower-low, move the intermediate trend line down to the succeeding lower price. Continue to move the intermediate trend line from low to low until the market makes two consecutive higher-highs. At this point, use the green pen to move the intermediate trend line down from the low of two bars back to the high on the current bar. This action makes the low of two bars back an intermediate bottom. Once the two-bar indicator has triggered upward motion it is no longer necessary to have two consecutive higher-highs to move the intermediate trend line up. Each day that the market posts a subsequent higher-high, move the intermediate trend line up to the succeeding higher price. Continue to move the intermediate trend line from high to high until the market makes two consecutive lower-lows.

This completes the explanation of how to begin building an intermediate trend indicator chart. Continue this process on the monthly, weekly, and daily charts until the chart is up to date with the current market. After each intermediate swing has been identified, go back to write above the intermediate tops the price and the date of occurrence. Do the same for the intermediate bottoms, but write the price and the date of occurrence below the intermediate bottom (Figure 5.5).

The Inside Bar

An important fact to note when tracking the intermediate swings of the market is the occurrence of the inside move and the outside move. Since this chart pattern holds true for all time periods (monthly, weekly, and daily), we refer to it as an inside bar (Figure 5.6). The inside bar occurs when the high is lower than the previous high and the low is higher than the previous low. When charting the intermediate swings of the market, the analyst ignores the inside bar and waits to see the trading range of the next bar. Since the inside bar is ignored, the analyst must always look at the preceding bar to determine if the intermediate trend line should be moved up or down. This bar is known as the last active bar. If the intermediate trend line was moving up before the inside bar and the current rally takes out the high of the last active bar, then the intermediate trend line moves up. If the trend line was moving up before the inside bar and the market moves below the low of the last active bar, then the intermediate trend line moves down. If the trend line was moving down before the inside bar and the break takes out the low of the last active bar, then the intermediate trend line moves down. If the intermediate trend line was

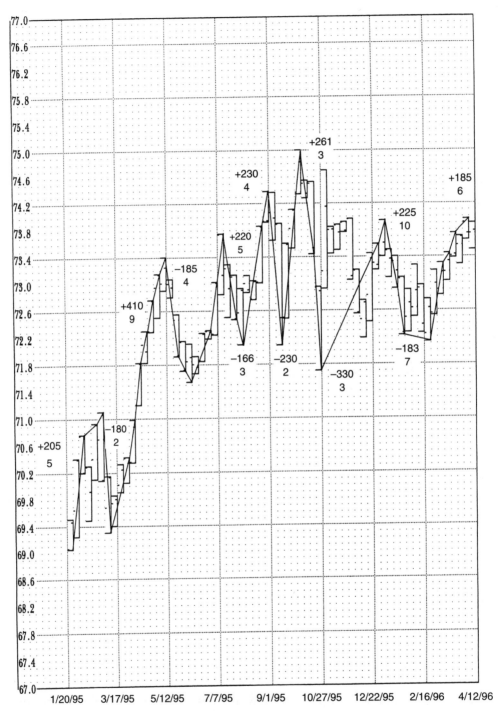

Figure 5.5   Chart showing an intermediate trend swinging up and down. After recording the size of the moves in terms of price, look for common swings, average rallies, and average breaks.

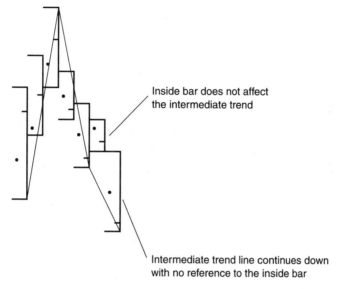

Inside bar does not affect
the intermediate trend

Intermediate trend line continues down
with no reference to the inside bar

Figure 5.6   Inside bar chart showing an intermediate trend.

moving down before the inside bar and the market moves above the high of the last active bar, then the intermediate trend line moves up. In summary, the trader ignores the inside bar and refers to the last active bar to find the direction of the intermediate trend line.

The Outside Bar

The outside time period (outside bar; see Figure 5.7) occurs when the high of the current time period is higher than the previous time period and the low of the current time period is lower than the low of the current time period. Contrary to the inside bar, the order of occurrence of the high and low on an outside move day are critical and should be noted. If the intermediate trend line is moving up and the first move of the outside move day is to the high, the intermediate trend line moves up to the high. If the intermediate trend line is moving up and the first move of the outside move day is to the low, the intermediate trend line ignores the move to the low and moves to the high. Furthermore, if the intermediate trend line is moving down and the first move of the outside move day is to the high, the intermediate trend line ignores the move to the high and moves to the low. Finally, if the intermediate trend line is moving down and the first move of the outside move day is to the low, the intermediate trend line moves to the low.

It is critical that the correct order of the high and low of an outside move day be recorded properly, because the market will either be continuing the

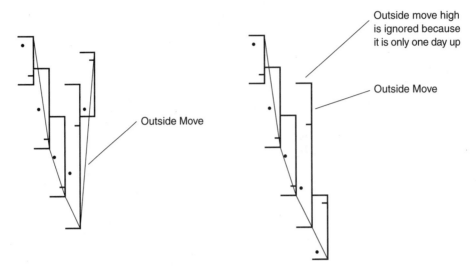

Figure 5.7   Outside bar charts showing an intermediate trend and outside moves. *Left:* the trend indicator moving down. The low of the outside day occurs before the high. The intermediate trend indicator moves down, then up to high. *Right:* the trend indicator moves down in resumption of the downtrend, which ignores the outside move.

intermediate trend or the trader will be forced to move the stop to a new level. When back-testing the intermediate trend indicator on historical data and the order of an outside day cannot be confirmed, it is safe to assume that the price closest to the opening occurred first and the price closest to the close occurred last.

STOP ORDERS

Although stop orders are discussed later in the book with more specific examples, the general rule to follow is to place them under intermediate bottoms (Figure 5.8) and above intermediate tops. This is because when the stop is hit, the intermediate trend will change. On the other hand, stops that are placed under lows and above highs are caught more often and simply take the trader out of the market. Another, more basic reason this type of popular stop should be avoided is that the trader is simply placing the stop within the normal swing of the market. When using the intermediate swing chart to enter a market never consider using a stop set at a specific dollar amount, as it will almost certainly get taken out during the normal course of trading.

The stop points established are set by the market. The construction and study of the intermediate swing chart in advance will therefore help a trader determine if the specific market he wants to trade creates price swings he can

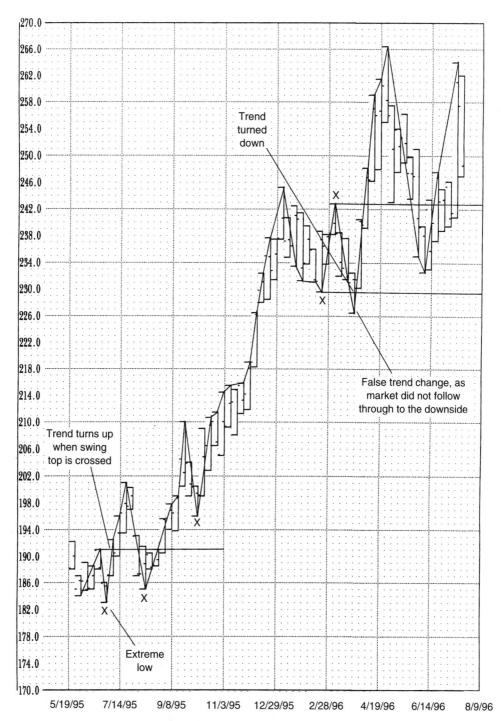

Figure 5.8   Intermediate trend chart and stop placement.

afford to trade. If the trader cannot afford the stop generated, then he is undercapitalized to trade the specific market and should find another one he can afford to trade in with his limited capital.

The price level the market is trading at often determines the size of the swing and ultimately the size of the stop. For example, markets trading near highs have wider intermediate swings than markets trading near low prices. Stops should be placed one, two, or three price units above or below intermediate swing tops and bottoms. Which stop placement is indicated depends on the position of the market relative to the price level and the current market volatility. For example, when the market is trading at a historically low level, a stop should be placed closer to the intermediate top or intermediate bottom than when a market is trading at a historically high level. Use the long-term charts to determine the position of the market and place the stop accordingly.

When specific markets are discussed rules are given for determining the proper stop placement relative to the intermediate top or intermediate bottom and in accordance with the current trading level of the market.

USING THE INFORMATION GENERATED

Keep a record of these swings, as these points can become important support and resistance points during the life of the current market or historical support and resistance points in future years. Besides being important price points, the dates of the intermediate tops and bottoms can become important timing points during the life of the current market or historical timing points in future years.

Now that the intermediate tops and bottoms have been identified, record the intermediate swings in terms of price and time from top-to-top, top-to-bottom, bottom-to-top, and bottom-to-bottom. This information can be used to determine whether or not a market is expanding or contracting. Intermediate swings should also be grouped by price levels and calendar dates. This will give the trader an idea of the way the market is behaving at various price levels during particular periods. In addition to cyclical information, this chart contains important seasonal data. Traders should also analyze the strength of up moves from various price levels as well as their corresponding corrections. Conversely, traders should study the strength of down moves from various price levels and their corresponding corrections. A spreadsheet problem can be used to organize this information so the changes in price and time can be easily calculated. It is important to keep a record of these swings because they can become valuable in forecasting future price and time swings.

Depending on the trader's perspective, all of these charts should be created in order to determine the intermediate trend of the time period studied.

Further analysis will show that all of these charts are interrelated. Thus, creating all of them will not be wasted effort. By creating these charts the trader is given a top-down perspective: an intermediate top or bottom on the monthly chart is the most important, followed by an intermediate top or bottom on the weekly chart, then an intermediate top and bottom on the daily chart, and finally an intermediate top and bottom on the hourly chart (not discussed here).

After creating the intermediate trend chart and studying the tops and bottoms, the following should be strongly noted in order to understand the interrelationship of the charts. This concept is addressed again when percentage retracements and Gann angles are discussed.

1. An intermediate top on a monthly chart is always an intermediate top on the weekly, daily, or hourly charts.
2. An intermediate top on a weekly chart is always an intermediate top on the daily and hourly charts, but not always on the monthly chart.
3. An intermediate top on the daily chart is always an intermediate top on the hourly chart, but not always on the weekly or monthly charts.
4. An intermediate top on the hourly chart is not always an intermediate top on the daily, weekly, or monthly charts.
5. An intermediate bottom on a monthly chart is always an intermediate bottom on the weekly, daily, or hourly charts.
6. An intermediate bottom on a weekly chart is always an intermediate bottom on the daily and hourly charts, but not always on the monthly chart.
7. An intermediate bottom on the daily chart is always an intermediate bottom on the hourly chart, but not always on the weekly or monthly charts.
8. An intermediate bottom on the hourly chart is not always an intermediate bottom on the daily, weekly, or monthly charts.
9. An intermediate uptrend and an intermediate downtrend on the monthly chart are composed of a series of intermediate swings from the weekly, daily, and hourly charts. Study how many weekly, daily, or hourly intermediate swings on average it takes to form a monthly uptrend or downtrend.
10. An intermediate uptrend and an intermediate downtrend on the weekly chart are composed of a series of intermediate swings from the daily and hourly charts. Study how many daily or hourly intermediate swings on average it takes to form a weekly uptrend or downtrend.
11. An intermediate uptrend and an intermediate downtrend on the daily chart are composed of a series of intermediate swings from the hourly chart. Study how many hourly intermediate swings on average it takes to form a daily uptrend or downtrend.

12. An intermediate uptrend and an intermediate downtrend on the hourly chart are composed of a series of intermediate swings from the other intraday time periods, such as the 30-minute, 15-minute, or 5-minute chart. Study how many time period intermediate swings on average it takes to form an hourly uptrend or downtrend.

13. An intermediate uptrend is made up of upswings and corrections.

14. An intermediate downtrend is made up of downswings and corrections.

15. An intermediate uptrend is made up of minor uptrends and minor downtrends.

16. An intermediate downtrend is made up of minor uptrends and minor downtrends.

17. An intermediate top is always a minor top, but a minor top is not always an intermediate top.

18. An intermediate bottom is always a minor bottom, but a minor bottom is not always an intermediate bottom.

SUMMARY

The intermediate trend indicator chart simply follows the intermediate or two-bar swings of the market. Traders follow the up and down movements of the market by raising or lowering the intermediate trend line. The crossing of the intermediate top and the intermediate bottom change the intermediate trend to up or to down, not the movement of the intermediate trend line alone. This action creates uptrends, downtrends, and corrections. Changes in direction turn lows into bottoms and highs into tops. Inside bars should be ignored during the construction of the intermediate trend indicator chart. In contrast, outside-bar moves should be watched carefully, as the order of the high or low of the outside bar is critical to the structure of the intermediate trend indicator chart. Traders should note which came first, the high or the low when an outside bar occurs.

Stops must be placed over intermediate tops and under intermediate bottoms, not over highs and under lows. The placement of the stop should also be relative to the historical trading position of the market. Studying and analyzing the data created by the intermediate swing chart can help the trader determine the duration of the swings in terms of price and time from top-to-top, top-to-bottom, bottom-to-top, and bottom-to-bottom. This information can then be used to judge whether a market is expanding or contracting. In addition, market behavior at various price levels and time periods can help a trader determine the nature of a market. Finally, the trader should have a working knowledge of the interrelationships of the monthly, weekly, daily, and intraday charts to gain a better understanding of support and resistance.

6   Main Trend Indicator Charts

After studying the minor and intermediate swing charts and learning some of their advantages and disadvantages, the analyst may naturally be drawn to the main swing chart. After being made aware of the exigencies relating to trading the minor trend chart and experiencing the relative ease of using the intermediate trend chart, the trader may want to develop an indicator for a longer-term view of the market. While the minor trend indicator is the most active, followed by the intermediate trend indicator, the main trend indicator is the least active. This does not necessarily make it better, however, as the objective of creating these charts is to trade for profits. The minor trend chart has too many sudden changes in trend along with high trading costs, while the main trend chart has low trading costs in terms of commissions, but high costs in terms of missed opportunities. The best way to use this chart is in conjunction with the intermediate trend indicator. For example, in a bull market as determined by the main trend chart, it is better to use the intermediate trend indicator for buying opportunities following corrections. Conversely, in a bear market as determined by the main trend indicator, it is better to use the intermediate trend indicator to enter the market following corrections. The construction of the main trend chart should not be treated lightly, as the main trend of every market should be the trader's primary concern.

To be able to analyze a market and trade successfully, the analyst must construct the main trend chart, the intermediate trend chart, and the minor trend chart. The swings of the shorter-term charts make up the swings of the longer-term charts. While each chart has its advantages and disadvantages, combining the charts to generate trades is the best use of these charts. The best way to use these charts is to always trade in the direction of the main trend; use the intermediate trend chart to enter and exit the market in the direction of the main trend; and the more aggressive traders can use the minor trend chart to trigger buys and sells in the direction of the intermediate and main trends. Do not use any one chart as the sole reference for trading. Use a combination of the charts in the direction of the main trend. Following the proper construction of the main trend chart, the trader will have before him a chart that shows each main top and main bottom and the date each main top and main bottom occurred (Figure 6.1). In addition, he will be able to determine when main trend

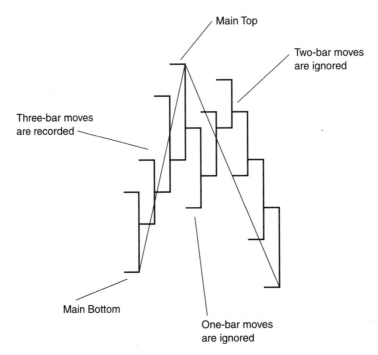

Figure 6.1   Basic construction of the main trend indicator chart.

changes have taken place and the duration of the main swings in terms of price and time. From this information a simple trading system can be developed.

DEFINITION

Since the main swing chart can be used to identify the main tops and bottoms for any time period, in order to avoid confusion about whether we are speaking exclusively of the monthly, weekly, daily, or intraday charts, we call each trading time period a bar.

The main swing chart follows the three-bar movements of the market (Figure 6.2). From a low price each time the market makes a higher-high than the previous bar for three consecutive time periods, a main trend line moves up from the low three bars back to the new high. This action makes the low price from three bars back a main bottom. From a high price each time the market makes a lower-low than the previous bar for three consecutive time periods, a main trend line moves down from the high three bars back to the new low. This action makes the high price from three bars back a main top. The combination of a main trend line from a main bottom and a main trend

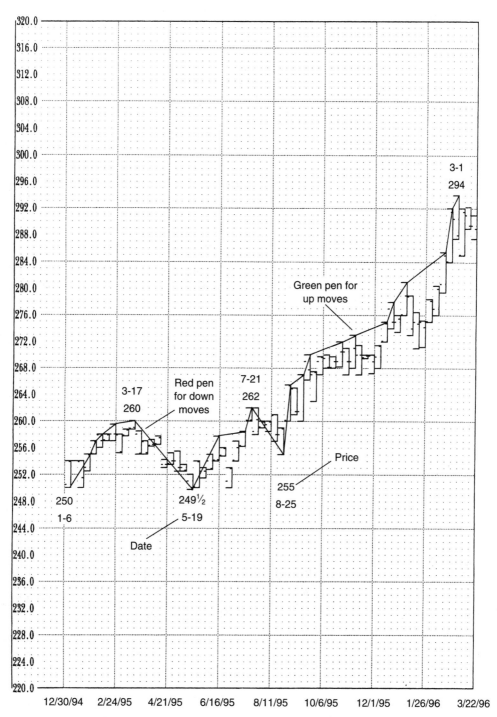

Figure 6.2   Example of a main trend indicator chart.

line from a main top forms a main swing. This is important information, because when stop placement is discussed, traders will be told to place stops under main swing bottoms, not under lows, and over main swing tops, not over highs. Learn and know the difference between a low and a main swing bottom, and a high and a main swing top.

Once the first main swing is formed, the trader can anticipate a change in the main trend. If the main swing chart begins from the first trading month, week, or day and the main trend line moves up to a new high, this does not mean that the main trend has turned up. Conversely, if the first move is down, this does not mean the main trend is down. The only way for the main trend to turn up is to cross a main top, and the only way for the intermediate trend to turn down is to cross a main bottom. In addition, if the main trend is up and the market makes a main swing down that does not take out the previous main swing bottom, this is a correction. If the main trend is down and the market makes a main swing up that does not take out the previous main swing top, this is also a correction. A market is composed of two types of up and down moves. The main swing chart draws attention to these types of moves by identifying trending up moves and correcting up moves, as well as trending down moves and correcting down moves.

In summary, when implementing the main swing chart, the analyst is merely following the three-bar up and down movements of the market. The intersection of an established downtrending line with a new uptrending line is a main swing bottom. The intersection of an established uptrending line with a new downtrending line is a main swing top. The combination of main swing tops and bottoms forms the main trend indicator chart. The crossing of a main swing top changes the main trend to up. The penetration of a main trend bottom changes the main trend to down. The market is composed of main uptrends, main downtrends, and main trend corrections.

CONSTRUCTION

In order to properly construct the main trend indicator chart the following must be available: a bar chart, price and time data, a red pen, a green pen, a black pen, and a ruler. The black pen is used to update the chart, the green pen is used to track the upward movement of the main trend line, and the red pen is used to track the downward movement of the main trend line. Since a poorly drawn line may be misinterpreted, the ruler is used to keep the lines straight. Use the price and time data to ensure the proper marking of highs and lows, as relying on visual estimation invites faulty identification, which can also have an adverse effect on the research.

It is best to start the main trend indicator chart (Figure 6.3) from the first trading bar of the contract because by the time the contract being analyzed becomes the actively traded market, the analyst will have constructed all of the main swings of the contract and derived valuable information about price and time from the activity charted. This chart serves as a "fingerprint" of the market, because each individual market has unique patterns contained in the total chart by which it can be identified. This is why precise and accurate data must be maintained at all times.

The Main Trend and the Monthly Chart from a Low Price

On a monthly chart, start the indicator during the first month of trading, then each month simply follow the movement of the market. From a low price if the market makes three consecutive higher-highs, use the green pen to move the main trend line up from the low of three bars back to the high on the current bar. This action makes the low of three bars back a main bottom. Once the three-bar indicator has triggered upward motion it is no longer necessary to have three consecutive higher-highs to move the main trend line up. Each month that the market posts a subsequent higher-high, move the main trend line up to the succeeding higher price. Continue to move the main trend line from high to high until the market makes three consecutive lower-lows. At this point, use the red pen to move the main trend line down from the high of three bars back to the low on the current bar. This action makes the high of three bars back a main top. Once the three-bar indicator has triggered downward motion it is no longer necessary to have three consecutive lower-lows to move the main trend line down. Each month that the market posts a subsequent lower-low, move the main trend line down to the succeeding lower price. Continue to move the main trend line from low to low until the market makes three consecutive higher-highs.

The Main Trend and the Monthly Chart from a High Price

On a monthly chart, start the indicator during the first month of trading, then each month simply follow the movement of the market. From a high price if the market has three consecutive lower-lows, use the red pen to move the main trend line down from the high of three bars back to the low on the current bar. This action makes the high of three bars back a main top. Once the three-bar indicator has triggered downward motion it is no longer necessary

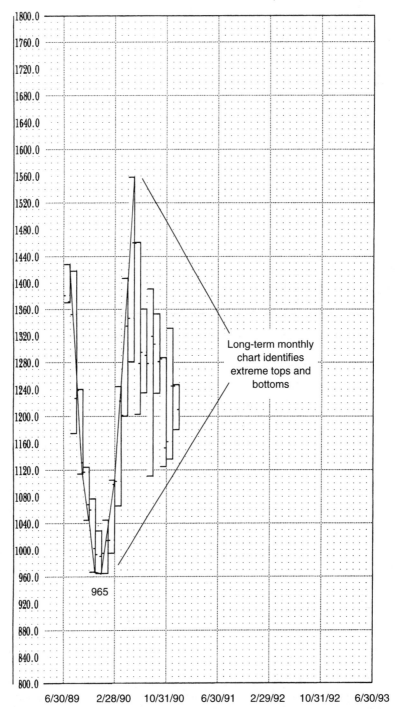

Figure 6.3   Monthly main trend indicator chart from a low price.

to have three consecutive lower-lows to move the main trend line down. Each month that the market posts a subsequent lower-low, move the main trend line down to the succeeding lower price. Continue to move the main trend line from low to low until the market makes three consecutive higher-highs. At this point, use the green pen to move the main trend line up from the low of three bars back to the high on the current bar. This action makes the low of three bars back a main bottom. Once the three-bar indicator has triggered upward motion it is no longer necessary to have three consecutive higher-highs to move the main trend line up. Each month that the market posts a subsequent higher-high, move the main trend line up to the succeeding higher price. Continue to move the main trend line from high to high until the market makes three consecutive lower-lows.

The Main Trend and the Weekly Chart from a Low Price

On a weekly chart, start the indicator during the first week of trading, then each week simply follow the movement of the market. From a low price if the market has three consecutive higher-highs, use the green pen to move the main trend line up from the low of three bars back to the high on the current bar. This action makes the low of three bars back a main bottom. Once the three-bar indicator has triggered upward motion it is no longer necessary to have three consecutive higher-highs to move the main trend line up. Each week that the market posts a subsequent higher-high, move the main trend line up to the succeeding higher price. Continue to move the main trend line from high to high until the market makes three consecutive lower-lows. At this point, use the red pen to move the main trend line down from the high of three bars back to the low on the current bar. This action makes the high of three bars back a main top. Once the three-bar indicator has triggered downward motion it is no longer necessary to have three consecutive lower-lows to move the main trend line down. Each week that the market posts a subsequent lower-low, move the main trend line down to the succeeding lower price. Continue to move the main trend line from low to low until the market makes three consecutive higher-highs.

The Main Trend and the Weekly Chart from a High Price

On a weekly chart (Figure 6.4), start the indicator during the first week of trading, then each week simply follow the movement of the market. From

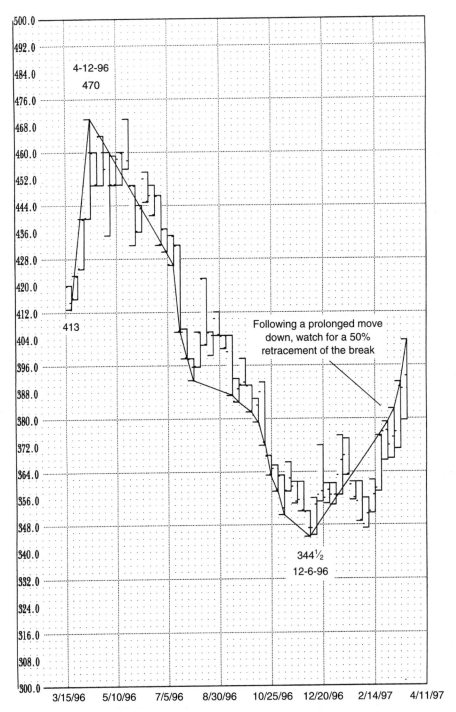

Figure 6.4   Weekly main trend indicator chart from a high price. Once the main trend indicator starts in a down direction on the weekly chart, it often lasts for several weeks.

a high price if the market has three consecutive lower-lows, use the red pen to move the main trend line down from the high of three bars back to the low on the current bar. This action makes the high of three bars back a main top. Once the three-bar indicator has triggered downward motion it is no longer necessary to have three consecutive lower-lows to move the main trend line down. Each week that the market posts a subsequent lower-low, move the main trend line down to the succeeding lower price. Continue to move the main trend line from low to low until the market makes three consecutive higher-highs. At this point, use the green pen to move the main trend line up from the low of three bars back to the high on the current bar. This action makes the low of three bars back a main bottom. Once the three-bar indicator has triggered upward motion it is no longer necessary to have three consecutive higher-highs to move the main trend line up. Each week that the market posts a subsequent higher-high, move the main trend line up to the succeeding higher price. Continue to move the main trend line from high to high until the market makes three consecutive lower-lows.

The Main Trend and the Daily Chart from a Low Price

On a daily chart (Figure 6.5), start the indicator on the first day of trading, then each day simply follow the movement of the market. From a low price if the market has three consecutive higher-highs, use the green pen to move the main trend line up from the low of three bars back to the high on the current bar. This action makes the low of three bars back a main bottom. Once the three-bar indicator has triggered upward motion it is no longer necessary to have three consecutive higher-highs to move the main trend line up. Each day that the market posts a subsequent higher-high, move the main trend line up to the succeeding higher price. Continue to move the main trend line from high to high until the market makes three consecutive lower-lows. At this point, use the red pen to move the main trend line down from the high of three bars back to the low on the current bar. This action makes the high of three bars back a main top. Once the three-bar indicator has triggered downward motion it is no longer necessary to have three consecutive lower-lows to move the main trend line down. Each day that the market posts a subsequent lower-low, move the main trend line down to the succeeding lower price. Continue to move the main trend line from low to low until the market makes three consecutive higher-highs.

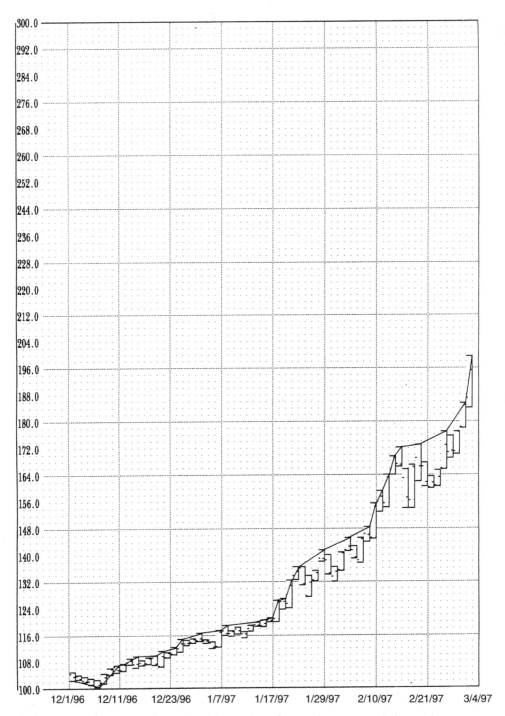

Figure 6.5   Daily main trend indicator chart from a low price, showing the importance of the three-day main trend indicator. Observe that this chart does not show a three-day correction over a three-month time period. Also note that trading ranges are narrow near lows and expand near highs.

The Main Trend and the Daily Chart
from a High Price

On a daily chart, start the indicator on the first day of trading, then each day simply follow the movement of the market. From a high price if the market has three consecutive lower-lows, use the red pen to move the main trend line down from the high of three bars back to the low on the current bar. This action makes the high of three bars back a main top. Once the three-bar indicator has triggered downward motion it is no longer necessary to have three consecutive lower-lows to move the main trend line down. Each day that the market posts a subsequent lower-low, move the main trend line down to the succeeding lower price. Continue to move the main trend line from low to low until the market makes three consecutive higher-highs. At this point, use the green pen to move the main trend line up from the low of three bars back to the high on the current bar. This action makes the low of three bars back a main bottom. Once the three-bar indicator has triggered upward motion it is no longer necessary to have three consecutive higher-highs to move the main trend line up. Each day the market posts a subsequent higher-high, move the main trend line up to the succeeding higher price. Continue to move the main trend line from high to high until the market makes three consecutive lower-lows.

This completes the explanation of how to begin building a main trend indicator chart (Figure 6.6). Continue this process on the monthly, weekly, and daily charts until the chart is up to date with the current market. After each main swing has been identified, go back to write above the main tops the price and the date of occurrence. Do the same for the main bottoms, but write the price and the date of occurrence below the main bottom.

The Inside Bar

An important fact to note when tracking the main swings of the market is the occurrence of the inside move and the outside move. Since this chart pattern holds true for all time periods (monthly, weekly, and daily), we refer to it as an inside bar (Figure 6.7). The inside bar occurs when the high is lower than the previous high and the low is higher than the previous low. When charting the main swings of the market, the analyst ignores the inside bar and waits to see the trading range of the next bar. Since the inside bar is ignored, the analyst must always look at the preceding bar to determine if the main trend line should be moved up or down. This bar is known as the last active bar. If the main trend line was moving up before the inside bar and the current rally takes out the high of the last active bar, then the main trend line moves up. If the trend line was moving up before the inside bar and the market moves below the low of the last active bar, then the main trend line moves down. If

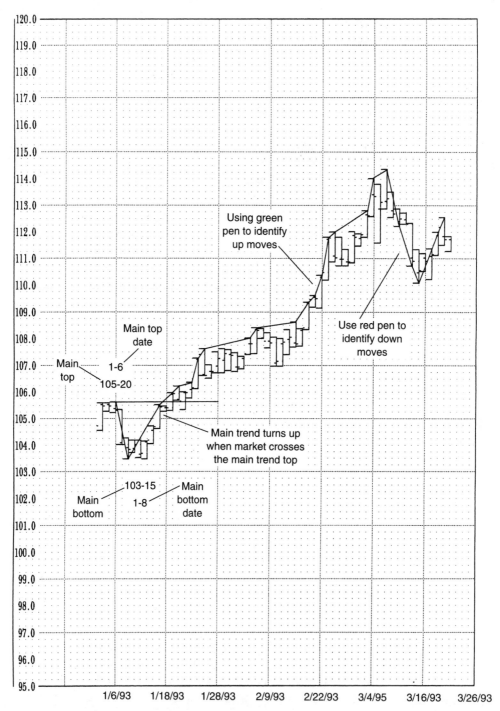

Figure 6.6   Main trend indicator chart showing the up and down movement of the market. The chart follows the market's main (three-bar) swings.

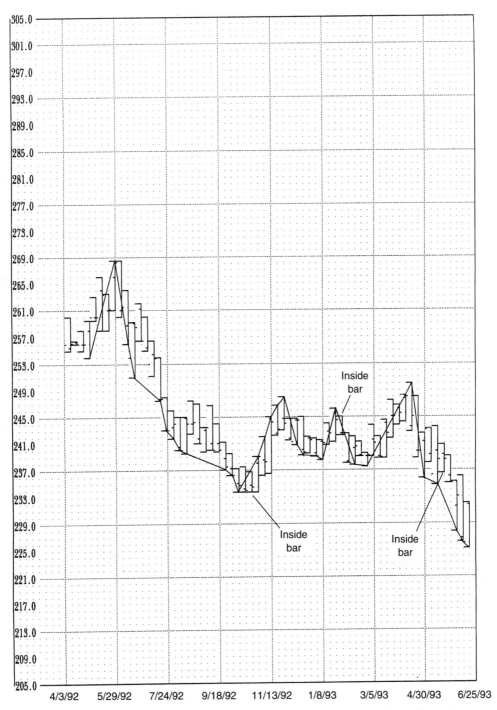

Figure 6.7   An inside bar chart showing that the inside bar does not affect the main trend indicator; the main trend indicator ignores the inside bar.

the trend line was moving down before the inside bar and the break takes out the low of the last active bar, then the main trend line moves down. If the trend line was moving down before the inside bar and the market moves above the high of the last active bar, then the main trend line moves up. In summary, the trader ignores the inside bar and refers to the last active bar to find the direction of the main trend line.

The Outside Bar

The outside time period (outside bar; see Figure 6.8) occurs when the high of the current time period is higher than the previous time period and the low of the current time period is lower than the low of the current time period. Contrary to the inside bar, the order of occurrence of the high and low on an outside move day are critical and should be noted. If the main trend line is moving up and the first move of the outside move day is to the high, the main trend line moves up to the high. If the main trend line is moving up and the first move of the outside move day is to the low, the main trend line ignores the move to the low and moves to the high. Furthermore, if the main trend line is moving down and the first move of the outside move day is to the high, the main trend line ignores the move to the high and moves to the low. Finally, if the main trend line is moving down and the first move of the outside move day is to the low, the main trend line moves to the low.

It is critical that the correct order of the high and low of an outside move day be recorded properly, because the market will either be continuing the main trend or the trader will be forced to move the stop to a new level. When back-testing the main trend indicator on historical data and the order of an outside day cannot be confirmed, it is safe to assume that the price closest to the opening occurred first and the price closest to the close occurred last.

STOP ORDERS

Although stop orders are discussed later in the book with more specific examples, the general rule to follow is to place them under main bottoms (Figure 6.9) and above main tops. This is because when the stop is hit, the main trend will change. On the other hand, stops that are placed under lows and above highs are caught more often and simply take the trader out of the market. Another, more basic reason this type of popular stop should be avoided is that the trader is simply placing the stop within the normal swing of the market. When using the main swing chart to enter a market never consider using a stop set at a specific dollar amount, as it will almost certainly get taken out during the normal course of trading.

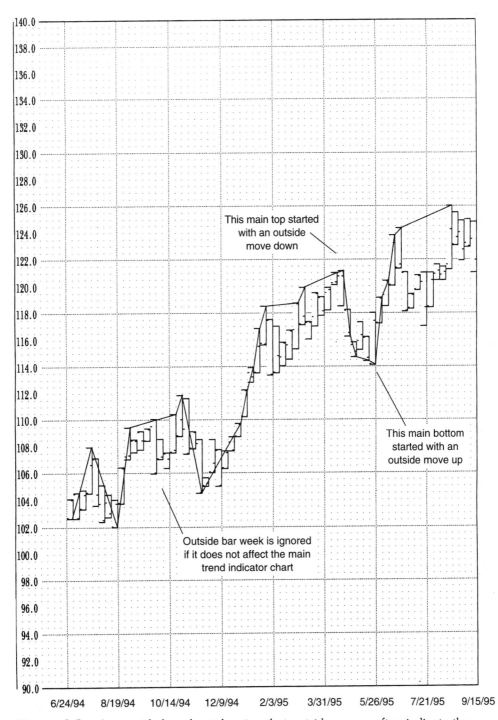

Figure 6.8 An outside bar chart showing that outside moves often indicate the formation of a future main top or main bottom.

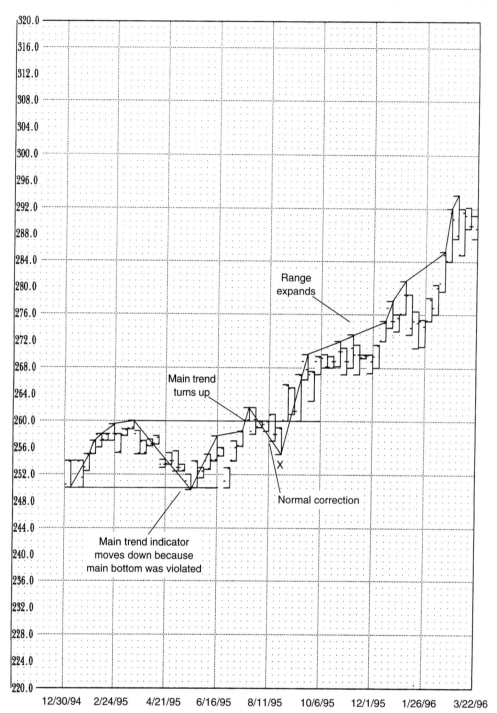

Figure 6.9   Main trend indicator chart and stop placement chart. The X indicates that stops are placed under main bottoms, not at fixed dollar amounts. Stops are set by the market movement. A move stops with the three-bar swings created by the market movement.

The stop points established are set by the market. The construction and study of the main swing chart in advance will therefore help a trader determine if the specific market he wants to trade creates price swings he can afford to trade. If the trader cannot afford the stop generated, then he is undercapitalized to trade the specific market and should find another one he can afford to trade in with his limited capital.

The price level the market is trading at often determines the size of the swing and ultimately the size of the stop. For example, markets trading near highs have wider swings than markets trading near low prices. Stops should be placed one, two, or three price units above or below main swing tops and bottoms. Which stop placement is indicated depends on the position of the market relative to the price level and the current market volatility. For example, when the market is trading at a historically low level, a stop should be placed closer to the main top or main bottom than when a market is trading at a historically high level. Use the long-term charts to determine the position of the market and place the stop accordingly.

When specific markets are discussed rules are given for determining the proper stop placement relative to the main top or main bottom and in accordance with the current trading level of the market.

USING THE INFORMATION GENERATED

Keep a record of these swings, as these points can become important support and resistance points during the life of the current market or historical support and resistance points in future years. Besides being important price points, the dates of the main tops and bottoms can become important timing points during the life of the current market or historical timing points in future years.

Now that the main tops and bottoms have been identified, record the main swings in terms of price and time from top-to-top, top-to-bottom, bottom-to-top, and bottom-to-bottom. This information can be used to determine whether or not a market is expanding or contracting. Main swings should also be grouped by price levels and calendar dates. This will give the trader an idea of the way the market is behaving at various price levels during particular periods. In addition to cyclical information, this chart contains important seasonal data. Traders should also analyze the strength of up moves from various price levels as well as their corresponding corrections. Conversely, traders should study the strength of down moves from various price levels and their corresponding corrections. A spreadsheet problem can be used to organize this information so the changes in price and time can be easily calculated. It is important to keep a record of these swings because they can become valuable in forecasting future price and time swings.

Depending on the trader's perspective, all of these charts should be created in order to determine the main trend of the time period studied. Further analysis will show that all of these charts are interrelated. Thus, creating all of them will not be wasted effort. By creating these charts the trader is given a top-down perspective: a main top or bottom on the monthly chart is the most important, followed by a main top or bottom on the weekly chart, then a main top and bottom on the daily chart, and finally a main top and bottom on the hourly chart (not discussed here).

After creating the main trend chart and studying the tops and bottoms, the following should be strongly noted in order to understand the interrelationship of the charts. This concept is addressed again when percentage retracements and Gann angles are discussed.

1. A main top on a monthly chart is always a main top on the weekly, daily, or hourly charts.
2. A main top on a weekly chart is always a main top on the daily and hourly charts, but not always on the monthly chart.
3. A main top on the daily chart is always a main top on the hourly chart, but not always on the weekly or monthly charts.
4. A main top on the hourly chart is not always a main top on the daily, weekly, or monthly charts.
5. A main bottom on a monthly chart is always a main bottom on the weekly, daily, or hourly charts.
6. A main bottom on a weekly chart is always a main bottom on the daily and hourly charts, but not always on the monthly chart.
7. A main bottom on the daily chart is always a main bottom on the hourly chart, but not always on the weekly or monthly charts.
8. A main bottom on the hourly chart is not always a main bottom on the daily, weekly, or monthly charts.
9. A main uptrend and a main downtrend on the monthly chart are composed of a series of main swings from the weekly, daily, and hourly charts. Study how many weekly, daily, or hourly main swings on average it takes to form a monthly uptrend or downtrend.
10. A main uptrend and a main downtrend on the weekly chart are composed of a series of main swings from the daily and hourly charts. Study how many daily or hourly main swings on average it takes to form a weekly uptrend or downtrend.
11. A main uptrend and a main downtrend on the daily chart are composed of a series of main swings from the hourly chart. Study how many hourly main swings on average it takes to form a daily uptrend or downtrend.
12. A main uptrend and a main downtrend on the hourly chart are composed of a series of main swings from the other intraday time periods, such as the 30-minute, 15-minute, or 5-minute chart. Study how many

time period main swings on average it takes to form an hourly uptrend or downtrend.

13. A main uptrend is made up of main trend upswings and main trend corrections.

14. A main downtrend is made up of main trend downswings and main trend corrections.

15. A main uptrend is made up of minor and intermediate uptrends and minor and intermediate downtrends.

16. A main downtrend is made up of minor and intermediate uptrends and minor and intermediate downtrends.

17. A main top is always an intermediate and minor top, but an intermediate top or minor top is not always a main top.

18. A main bottom is always an intermediate and minor bottom, but an intermediate or minor bottom is not always a main bottom.

SUMMARY

The main trend indicator chart simply follows the main or three-bar swings of the market. Traders follow the up and down movements of the market by raising or lowering the main trend line. The crossing of the main top and the main bottom changes the main trend to up or to down, not the movement of the main trend line alone. This action creates uptrends, downtrends, and corrections. Changes in direction for three consecutive bars turn lows into main bottoms and highs into main tops. Inside bars should be ignored during the construction of the main trend indicator chart. In contrast, outside-bar moves should be watched carefully, as the order of the high or low of the outside bar is critical to the structure of the main trend indicator chart. When an outside bar occurs, traders should note which came first, the high or the low.

Avoid placing stops over highs and under lows as stops must be placed over main tops and under main bottoms. The placement of the stop should also be relative to the historical trading position of the market. Studying and analyzing the data created by the main swing chart can help the trader determine the duration of the swings in terms of price and time from top-to-top, top-to-bottom, bottom-to-top, and bottom-to-bottom. This information can then be used to judge whether a market is expanding or contracting. In addition, market behavior at various price levels and time periods can help a trader determine the nature of a market. Finally, the trader should have a working knowledge of the interrelationships of the monthly, weekly, daily, and intraday charts to gain a better understanding of support and resistance. The interrelationships between minor, intermediate, and main trend charts should also be noted.

7 Exceptions to the Trend Indicator Rules

In chapters 4, 5, and 6, covering the construction of the trend indicator charts and using them for trading, stop placement was discussed in a simplified manner. The method explained was mechanical and assumed the trader would follow the swings of the market exclusively. Because conditions change based on market conditions, the trader must be aware of certain situations that give her the option to ignore the trend indicator stops and move the stops prematurely. The following are examples of the times the trend indicator may be overruled. These situations include double bottoms and tops, prolonged moves in price, swing balancing, and signal tops and signal bottoms.

THE DOUBLE BOTTOM

After making a trend indicator chart, the analyst will notice that this swing chart makes some common chart patterns more easily identifiable. One of the easiest patterns to recognize is the double-bottom formation. Buying against a double bottom is often safest, because a stop placed under a double bottom is caught less often. This is especially true if the double bottom was formed at an extremely low level or following a prolonged move down in terms of both price and time. An exact match of the bottoms is not necessary to form a double bottom, for example, the second bottom may be slightly above the first bottom. Studying historical charts on how a double bottom is formed on each trend indicator chart can provide the chartist with the correct amount of tolerable price difference. A double bottom that has the second bottom slightly above the first bottom is known as a *secondary higher bottom*, and it often indicates that higher markets are to follow (Figures 7.1–7.3). This is a very common pattern before the start of a big rally, especially after the first bottom was followed by a large spike to the upside.

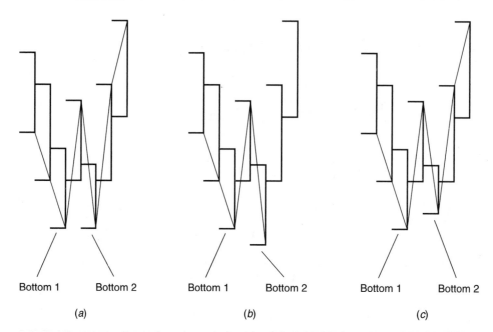

Figure 7.1   Minor trend charts showing double bottoms. The second bottom can be equal to the first bottom (*a*), lower than the first bottom (*b*), or higher than the first bottom (*c*).

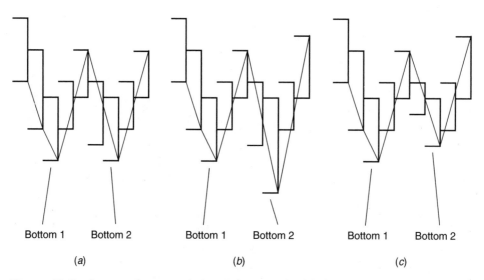

Figure 7.2   Intermediate trend charts showing double bottoms. The second bottom can be equal to the first bottom (*a*), lower than the first bottom (*b*), or higher than the first bottom (*c*).

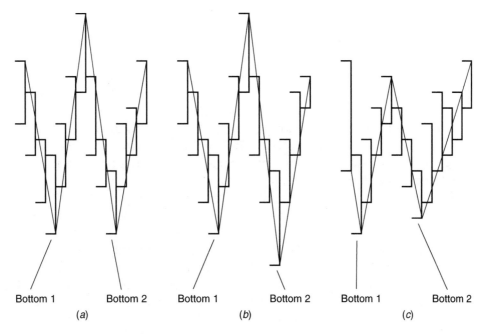

Figure 7.3 Main trend charts showing double bottoms. The second bottom can be equal to the first bottom (*a*), lower than the first bottom (*b*), or higher than the first bottom (*c*).

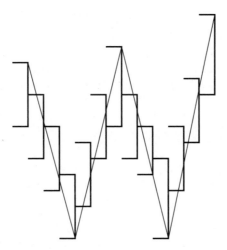

Figure 7.4 A double-bottom formation. The pattern is also referred to as a "W" bottom because the combination of a trend indicator bottom, top, and bottom forms a W.

The double-bottom pattern is also referred to as a "W" bottom (Figure 7.4) because the combination of a trend indicator bottom, trend indicator top, and trend indicator bottom forms a W. This pattern can trigger two trading opportunities: a countertrend buy following the formation of the second bottom and after a breakout over the last swing top. In each trade, stop-loss protection is placed under the last trend indicator bottom.

When deciding to use the double-bottom formation to trigger trading signals, the trader must remember that although this formation can be described the same way for each time indicator from minor to main, the strength of each bottom is different.

Double bottoms on the minor trend indicator chart (Figure 7.5) occur more frequently than on the intermediate and main trend indicator charts. They are also not as strong compared to this formation on the intermediate and main trend indicator charts due to the frequency of the indicator.

Double bottoms on the intermediate trend indicator chart (Figure 7.6) occur less frequently than on the minor trend indicator chart, but more frequently than on the main trend indicator chart. A double-bottom on the intermediate chart is stronger than the same formation on the minor trend indicator chart, but weaker than the same formation on the main trend indicator chart.

Double-bottom formations on the main trend indicator chart (Figure 7.7) occur less frequently than on the minor trend indicator chart and the intermediate trend indicator chart, and are stronger than on these other charts.

The strength of the double bottom is once again a function of time. The greater the distance between double bottoms, the more important the formation. This is especially true if the double bottom has started after a prolonged move down in terms of price and time or at a historically low level. A double bottom formed at an extremely high price level often sets up the first selling opportunity when penetrated. Traders should watch for elongated double-bottom formations, and pay particular attention to where they are taking place.

THE DOUBLE TOP

Another formation easily recognizable following a properly constructed trend indicator chart is the double-top formation (Figures 7.8–7.10). Selling against a double top is often safest, because a stop placed over a double top is caught less often. This is especially true if the double top was formed at an extremely high level or following a prolonged move up in terms of both price and time. An exact match of the tops is not necessary to form a double top, for example, the second top may be slightly below the first top. Studying historical

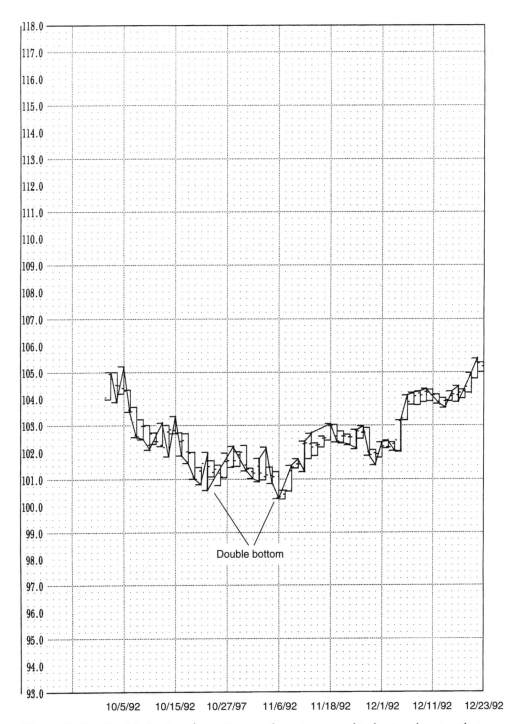

Figure 7.5   Double-bottom formation on the minor trend indicator showing that the second bottom can be lower than the first bottom.

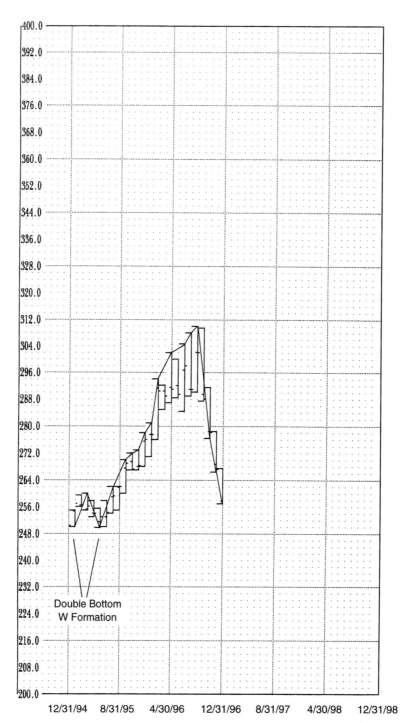

Figure 7.6   Double-bottom formation on the intermediate trend indicator.

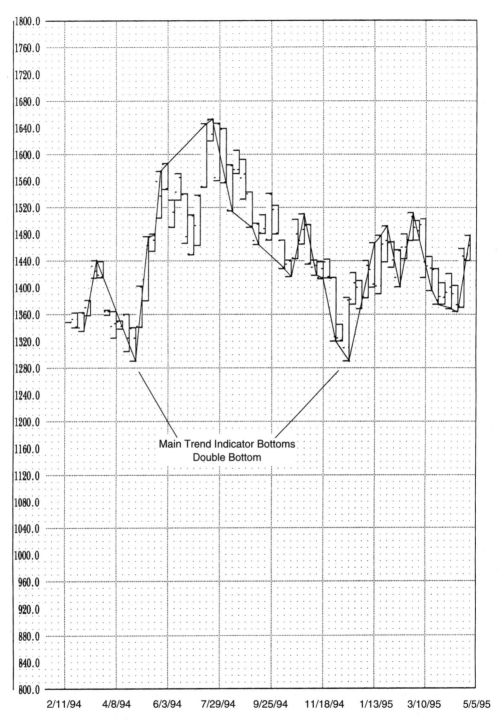

Figure 7.7   Double-bottom formation on the main trend indicator showing that the second bottom can be equal to the first bottom.

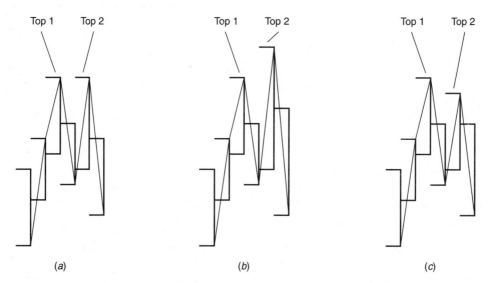

Figure 7.8   Minor trend charts showing double tops. The second top can be equal to the first top (*a*), higher than the first top (*b*), or lower than the first top (*c*).

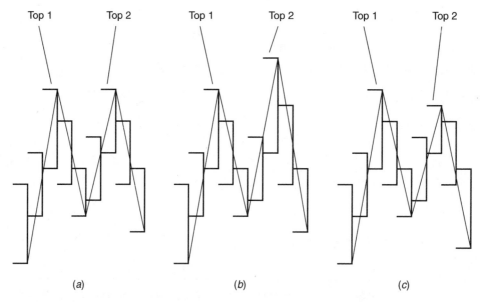

Figure 7.9   Intermediate trend charts showing double tops. The second top can be equal to the first top (*a*), higher than the first top (*b*), or lower than the first top (*c*).

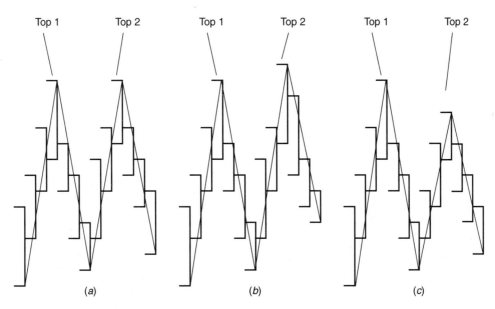

Figure 7.10   Main trend charts showing double tops. The second top can be equal to the first top (*a*), higher than the first top (*b*), or lower than the first top (*c*).

charts on how a double top is formed can provide the chartist with the correct amount of tolerable price difference. A double top that has the second top slightly below the first top is known as a *secondary lower top*, and it often indicates that lower markets are to follow (Figure 7.11). This is a very common pattern before the start of a large break, especially after the first top was followed by a large spike to the downside.

The double-top pattern is also referred to as an "M" top because the combination of a trend indicator top, trend indicator bottom, and trend indicator top forms an M. This pattern can trigger two trading opportunities: a countertrend sell following the formation of the second top and after a breakout under the swing bottom. In each trade, stop-loss protection is placed over the last trend indicator top.

When deciding to use the double-top formation to trigger trading signals, the trader must remember that although this formation can be described the same way for each time indicator from minor to main, the strength of each top is different.

Double tops on the minor trend indicator chart occur more frequently than on the intermediate and main trend indicator charts. They are also not as strong compared to this formation on the intermediate and main trend indicator charts due to the frequency of the indicator.

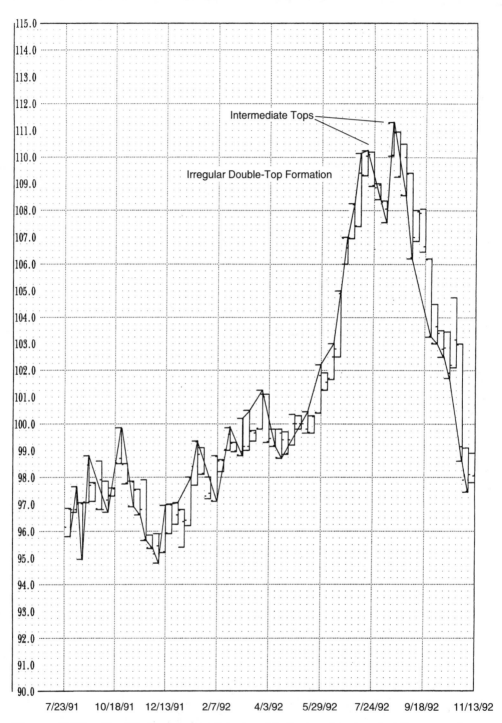

Figure 7.11 Double-top intermediate trend indicator showing that the second top can be higher than the first top.

Double tops on the intermediate trend indicator chart occur less frequently than on the minor trend indicator chart, but more frequently than on the main trend indicator chart. A double-top on the intermediate chart is stronger than the same formation on the minor trend indicator chart, but weaker than the same formation on the main trend indicator chart.

Double-top formations on the main trend indicator chart occur less frequently than on the minor trend indicator chart and the intermediate trend indicator chart, and are stronger than on these other charts.

The strength of the double top is once again a function of time. The greater the distance between double tops, the more important the formation. This is especially true if the double top has started after a prolonged move up in terms of price and time or at a historically high level. A double top formed at an extremely low price level often sets up the first buying opportunity when penetrated. Traders should watch for elongated double-top formations, and pay particular attention to where they are taking place.

PROLONGED RALLY OR BREAK RULE

Although trading using the trend Indicator charts is rule-based and almost completely mechanical, at times existing market conditions overrule these factors. This is especially true when placing trailing stops following a prolonged move up in terms of price and time, for example, seven consecutive bars of trading in the same direction.

Gann suggested that after seven consecutive bars of higher-highs and higher-lows, traders should move the sell stop from below the last trend indicator bottom to below the low of the seventh day up (Figure 7.12). Conversely, he suggested that following seven consecutive bars of lower-highs and lower-lows, traders should move the buy stop from over the last trend indicator top to above the high of the seventh day down.

The stop selection can vary depending on the personal preferences of the trader (Figure 7.13). For example, following a seven-day rally the trader may want to enter a stop close only under the close of the 7th day instead of the low. In the case of a seven-day break, the trader may want to enter a stop close only over the close of the seventh day instead of the high.

Each market has specific characteristics. For example, some markets have a tendency to rally only five consecutive days instead of seven before topping, or five consecutive days instead of seven before bottoming. By studying the historical swing charts of a specific market, a trader can determine the optimal stop required. The number of completed swings a market has made may also trigger the early movement of a stop. For example, the swing action of a market may have a tendency to move in groups of three or five. In this case, a trader

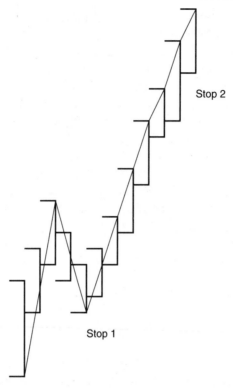

Figure 7.12   Prolonged rally chart. Following a seven-day rally, traders should consider moving the stop from below the swing bottom to below the low of the seventh day up.

may elect to move the stop up to under a low instead of a swing bottom following a three or five swing up move or over a high instead of a swing top following a three or five swing down move.

BALANCING SWINGS

There is another exception to the stop placement rule, the balanced swing chart, which involves the calculation of previous swing moves (Figure 7.14). For example, if the last swing was 9 cents up and 4 cents down, then following the next 9-cent rally, the stop would be moved up from below the last swing bottom to just under a 4-cent correction from the last high price. This type of trailing stop would require the trader to constantly monitor a market making new highs in order to move the stop to the correct place. This stop is designed to get caught after a rally equals or exceeds a previous rally and breaks more than the previous break.

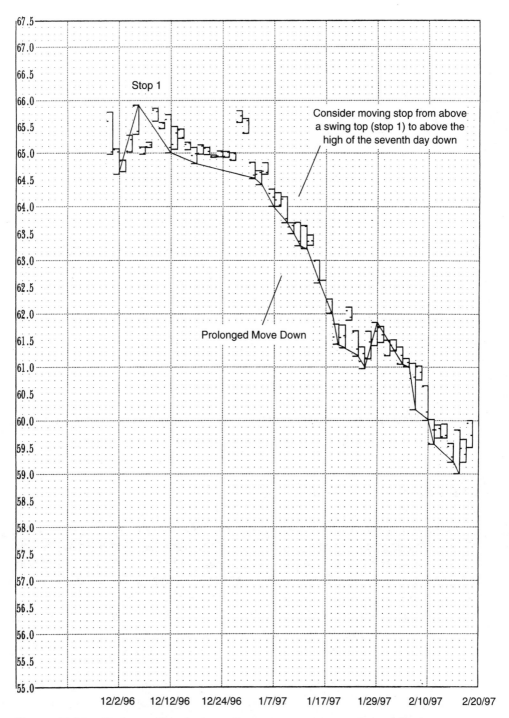

Figure 7.13 text labels:
Stop 1

Consider moving stop from above
a swing top (stop 1) to above the
high of the seventh day down

Prolonged Move Down

Figure 7.13 Prolonged break chart. This is an exception to the trend indicator stop rule. The stop, when elected, does *not* change the trend, but is used to lock in profits.

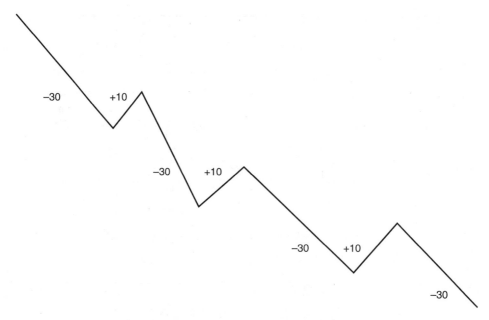

Figure 7.14   A perfectly balanced swing chart.

The situation is reversed for sell stops. For example, if the last swing was 50 points down and 20 up, then following the next 50-point break, the stop would be moved down from above the last swing top to just over a 20-point correction from the last low price.

Overbalancing Price and Time

From the swing charts, the trader should calculate the size and duration of the swings. In a declining market, by definition the declines tend to grow longer and the rallies shorter in terms of both price and time. As a market nears a bottom, the frequency of the swings begin to increase, as do the duration of the rallies in terms of both price and time. This action should be observed and noted as a clue to when a market will bottom; it should be watched particularly when a market has reached a historically low price level.

Often the first clue to a bottom is an expanded range day to the upside. This move may occur in one, two, or three days from the bottom. Even before it crosses a swing top, the market shows signs of a bottom. Traders should keep a record of the first swing up from a bottom. This information often repeats from year to year and could be called a characteristic of a particular market, each market having its own. Records should be kept of these characteristics, as they are often a clue to the size and duration of an impending rally. This type of move often occurs seasonally or cyclically. This is why historical dates of bottoms must be kept. The longer the first rally from a bottom in terms of price and time, the stronger the impending rally. Confidence can be gained by knowing that the size of the rally from a bottom often determines the strength of the next rally. This is important for trading against the trend, when buying the next break in anticipation of a double bottom.

Overbalancing means the current rally has exceeded the previous rally in terms of price and time (Figure 7.15). An overbalance of time is the most important indicator of a change in trend. Although the price movement of a market from a bottom is a good indicator of a near-term change in trend, the longer the market spends above the last swing bottom in terms of time, the greater the probability of a change in trend in the near term. This is known as building a support base of time instead of using price alone to build it.

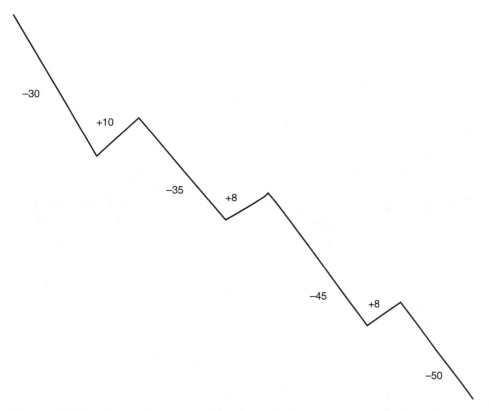

Figure 7.15   Chart showing overbalancing. Rallies in a downtrending market are less than the breaks and are often less than the previous rally. On the other hand, downswings are greater in price than rallies and previous breaks in a downtrending market.

A quick rally that overbalances or crosses a swing top fails more often if a solid time base has not been formed. Sometimes this is called a *quiet market*. Traders are often quoted as saying, "Never short a quiet market." When setting up the bottom for the next rally, it is better for the market to build a support base over several time periods with small ranges rather than with one large move over a short period of time.

Although it was noted earlier that inside bars should be ignored when building a swing chart, it does not mean that they have no importance. Disregarding the inside bar is only valid during the construction phase of the swing chart, as valuable information can be obtained from a series of inside days (Figure 7.16).

The same is true for a top. Following a strong, long-lasting uptrend in terms of both price and time, a market often has a day when the first break from the high exceeds the previous break from a high in terms of both price and time. If the first break from a top is an expanded range day, or if the last day of a two- or three-day break from an extreme high is an expanded range day, then watch for a series of inside days to overbalance time in order to set up the impending break that is likely to lead to a change in trend. Remember that despite a sharp break from a top that exceeds a previous break in terms of price, the market needs to overbalance time in order to trigger an acceleration to the downside, which can change the trend.

This agrees with what was said about support-base building (Figure 7.17). Inside days usually follow an expanded range day. An expanded range day from an extreme bottom is often indicative of a major bottoming formation. This may not be enough, however, to attract new buying that can change the trend to up and cause an acceleration to the upside. This is because the market needs to overbalance time. The series of inside days that usually follow an expanded range day from an extreme bottom help accomplish this formation. It is important that the trader watch for a series of inside days near a bottom for a sign that the main trend is getting ready to turn higher and that the market is getting ready to accelerate to the upside.

Outside moves (Figure 7.18) can be used to indicate impending trend changes. An outside move tends to temporarily stop a rally or break, thus allowing time or price to "catch up" with the current trading situation. Often a series of inside moves occurs within the framework of the outside range. This formation should be watched carefully for indications of base building, which could lead to the start of a rally, or top building, which could trigger a decline. Crossing the high end of the outside move day can lead to the start of an uptrend, while crossing the low of the outside move day can lead to the start of a downtrend. Once again, the position of the market in terms of price and time often determines the strength of the breakout move.

In summary, the height of the market is often determined by the length of the base, and vice versa for tops. Following a prolonged move down in

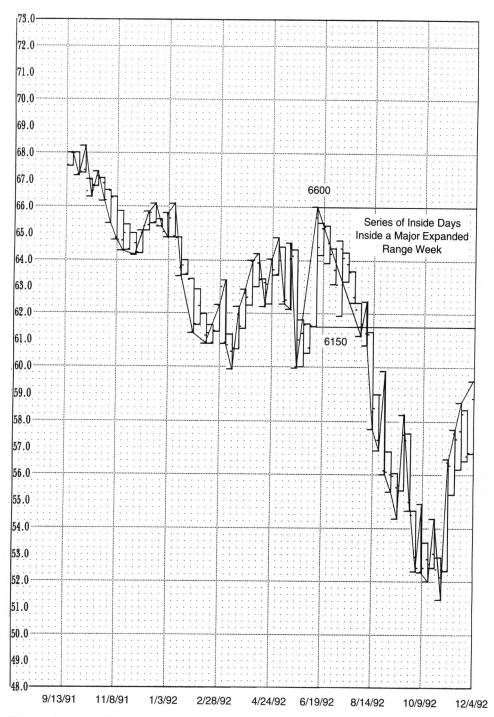

Figure 7.16 Chart showing a series of inside days. Following a series of inside days, the market often accelerates in the direction of the move.

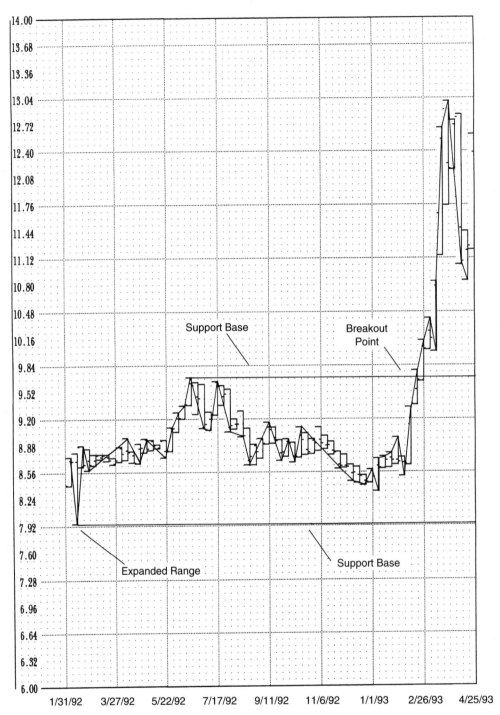

Figure 7.17   Chart showing a support base.

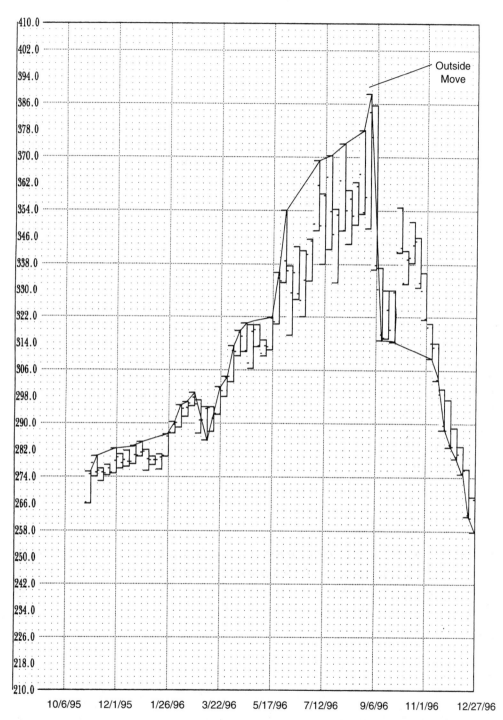

Figure 7.18   Chart showing an outside move. Outside moves often indicate tops, bottoms, or changes in trends.

terms of price and time, especially following an expanded range down, watch for a series of inside moves to signal bottoming action. Conversely, following a prolonged move up in terms of price and time, watch for a series of inside moves to signal topping action. The same is true of a series of inside moves following an outside move.

It should be noted here that buying and selling based on breakouts over these types of tops or bottoms do not change the trend to up or down, but are actually exceptions to the strict trend indictor rules. Buying or selling breakouts in the direction of the trend most often leads to a successful trade; however, totally ignoring the formation is not recommended. To make it successful, this formation needs to be studied and practiced.

Forecasting Price Moves

Learning how to read the swings of a market can also be an important forecasting tool (Figure 7.19). Forecasts started from major tops and bottoms can use previous swing price data to determine with reasonable accuracy where a market could go and when. This technique also helps the trader identify whether a market is behind and has to catch up with the trading pattern, or if it is behind and has to make an adjustment to once again balance the formation.

For example, if the last rally was 40 points in 5 days, then from a bottom, the trader can anticipate a 40-point move in 5 days. If the market moves 60 points in 2 days, then the trader can anticipate a 20 point correction over the next 3 days, before the trend resumes. In addition, if a market rallies only 30 points in 4 days, then the trader can anticipate a 10-point rally the last day of the swing so the market can balance. It takes time to make this type of analysis, because the trader has to know the swing characteristics of the market being traded, and these can only be discerned from records of the swings.

Once a trader becomes proficient with this form of analysis, he should be able to forecast expanded range days or inside days. In other words, he should be able to forecast when a market is likely to move and when it is likely to sit in a range. This can be accomplished either by trading on active days, or by sitting in a range before the market takes off.

SIGNAL TOPS AND SIGNAL BOTTOMS

The two most important exceptions to the trend indicator rules are the signal top (Figure 7.20) and the signal bottom (Figure 7.21). I have studied this formation extensively and have concluded that this is a universal pattern. In other words, it does not matter which market is traded, at some point they all post either a signal top or signal bottom at major tops or major bottoms.

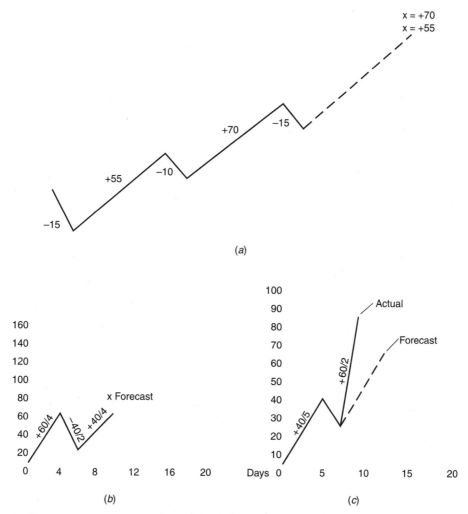

Figure 7.19 (a) Use the swing chart to forecast the next rally. (b) This chart indicates a possible top or change in trend. Note that the first rally was 60 points in 4 days and the second rally was 40 points in 4 days. Time has balanced the previous rally; however, price was short. (c) With an actual rally that was greater than the forecasted rally, this chart points to a correction back to the forecasted level because the swing balances on that date.

The Signal Top

A signal top (Figure 7.22) can be defined as follows: following a prolonged move up in terms of both price and time, a market has a higher-high than the previous time period, a lower-close, a close below the time period's midpoint, and a close below the opening. If this occurs, consider it as a sign that the market has topped and that the trend is getting ready to turn down.

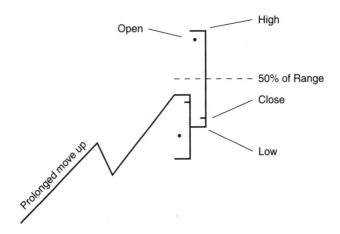

Figure 7.20   Signal top chart. Conditions: (1) a prolonged move up in price and time; (2) a higher-high; (3) a lower-close; (4) a close below opening; and (5) a close below 50% of the time period's range.

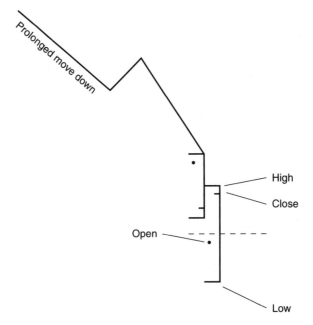

Figure 7.21   Signal bottom chart. Conditions: (1) a prolonged move down in price and time; (2) a lower-low; (3) a higher-close; (4) a close above opening, and (5) a close above 50% of the time period's range.

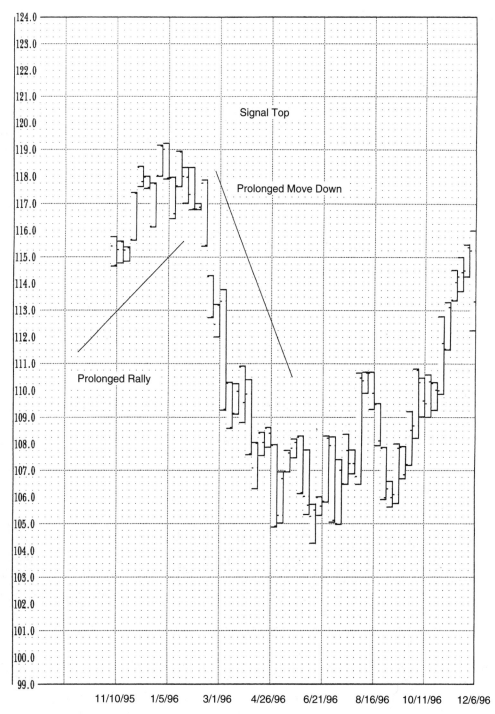

Figure 7.22   A signal top chart showing that a prolonged move up and a signal top often lead to a prolonged move down.

The signal top is one of the most powerful indicators of a major top formation. It most often occurs at or near historical tops and often becomes the contract high, which is why it is important to chart, observe, and note the historical tops of a commodity market. As was said earlier, this is accomplished using the yearly, quarterly, monthly, and weekly continuation charts of the same contract month. These charts come into play most often when a market has had a strong vertical rally and is trading at an area that has not yet been identified as resistance on the current active chart. In other words, this type of top most often occurs following a breakout over an old contract high and at a new contract high.

This signal alone may not be enough to trigger a sell, because often there is no follow-through break and the uptrend resumes. The follow-through break is necessary, as it confirms the signal top formation. The signal top is often called a *closing price reversal top* or a *key reversal top*, but these terms are not as specific as signal top, as neither mentions the close below the day's midpoint, the close below the opening, or the follow-through break, nor the prolonged move up in price and time.

To understand its importance, we need to break the signal top down to its components.

A prolonged move in price is an important part of determining the significance of a signal top. This type of signal must occur following a strong rally in terms of price. As stated earlier, a record should be kept of the size of past rallies in terms of price, because a market often repeats them. Study the past to see if the current rally equals or exceeds a previous rally at the time of the signal top day. Knowing these historical swings in advance can help the trader anticipate the signal top day. In addition to studying the size of the price swings, a trader should know if the market is approaching a historically high price level.

A prolonged move in terms of time is also an important indication of an impending signal top day. As stated earlier, time is most important in determining a change in trend or a top, so knowing the past history of a market's rallies in terms of time can provide important information as to when or if a valid signal top is or will be taking place. Historical swing chart data such as the duration of bottoms to tops and tops to tops can provide this information. If a market is approaching a swing level in terms of time, which has stopped a rally before, then anticipate a signal top.

A higher-high and a lower-close occur quite often even in the midst of a strong rally. Without a prolonged move in price or time and a follow-through break, this pattern may trigger a false topping signal. Research will show that when this pattern fails it is because the market has failed to achieve at least one of the following: a balancing of a price swing, a balancing of a time swing, a follow-through to the downside the next time period.

Although a reversal down can occur following a prolonged move up in terms of price and time, a higher-high and a lower-close, and a follow-through the next time period, there can be different degrees of strength to this signal. For example, the market may have all of the preceding factors, and a close below the day's midpoint, but not be below the opening price. While the best signal top is called a *triple-signal top*, a higher-high and lower-close, with only a close below the midpoint or only below the opening price, are called a *double-signal top*.

Tops with this type of formation should be studied to determine the strength of the signal in predicting major top formations. The same is true for the signal top days that close lower and below the opening price, but not below the day's midpoint.

The following is a list of the various strengths of signal tops, from strongest to weakest, and assuming a prolonged rally in terms of price and time:

1. A higher-high and a lower-close, a close below the opening, and a close below the day's midpoint.
2. A higher-high and a lower-close, and a close below the day's midpoint.
3. A higher-high and a lower-close, and a close below the opening.
4. A higher-high and a lower-close.

The main thing to watch for is a higher-high and a lower-close following a prolonged move up in terms of price and time and a follow-through break. The degree of strength of the top should be determined by whether or not the close is below the midpoint and/or below the opening. Once again, records of how a major top was formed should be kept. These tops should be referred to frequently to determine the strength and reliability of the expected break.

Remember also that while there is an important signal as to the top of the market, it does not automatically change the trend to down, but only temporarily freezes the market and puts it in a position to break to the downside. This break is not a change in trend, although it can lead to one. Records should be maintained to determine how much penetration of the low at the time of the signal top is needed to confirm a valid signal top. This amount varies by market and must be known to avoid false sell signals.

When using the trend indicators to enter and exit positions, traders should move the stops up from under swing bottoms to just below the low of the signal top bar to lock in any profit and to get taken out when the market confirms the signal top with a follow-through break.

Variations in the signal top formation can provide different results. For example, a close below the period's midpoint is suggested, but further filtering of the strength of this signal can be determined if the market closed in the lower 25% or 10% of the day's range. To make this signal more useful in forecasting major tops, the signal should be observed and tested using a program such as *Super Charts* or *Trade Station*.

Time indicators can also be strengthened. Besides looking at the duration of the rally in terms of price, a trader may want to compare signal tops that occur at cyclical or seasonal times. Price analysis may also be filtered by observing and testing signal tops that occur at historical price levels, major percentage retracement points, and major Gann-angle formations.

Although a signal top does not actually change the trend to down mechanically, countertrend traders who are comfortable with their market research on this signal can enter into a countertrend short-term position by selling weakness upon confirmation of the signal top. This often carries a large dollar risk because it is against the trend and because a stop-loss has to be placed above the signal top.

An additional countertrend selling strategy is to sell a 50% retracement of the first leg down from the signal top. This move may take two or more days to develop, but is one of the most common trading patterns. This strategy can be altered to include 33% or 67% retracements. Combined with former main tops, balance points, or Gann angles, retracement sells can produce major entry or exit points that can turn a market or change the trend from up to down.

The Signal Bottom

A signal bottom (Figure 7.23) can be defined as follows: following a prolonged move down in terms of both price and time, a market has a lower-low than the previous time period, a higher-close, a close above the time period's midpoint, and a close above the opening. If this occurs consider this a sign that the market has bottomed and that the trend is getting ready to turn up.

The signal bottom is one of the most powerful indicators of a major bottom formation. It most often occurs at or near historical bottoms and often becomes the contract low, which is why it is important to chart, observe, and note the historical bottoms of a commodity market. As was said earlier, this is accomplished using the yearly, quarterly, monthly, and weekly continuation charts of the same contract month. These charts come into play most often when a market has had a strong vertical break and is trading at an area that has not yet been identified as support on the current active chart (Figure 7.24). In other words, this type of bottom most often occurs following a breakout under an old contract low and at a new contract low.

This signal alone may not be enough to trigger a buy, because often there is no follow-through rally and the downtrend resumes. The follow-through rally is necessary, as it confirms the signal bottom formation. The signal bottom is

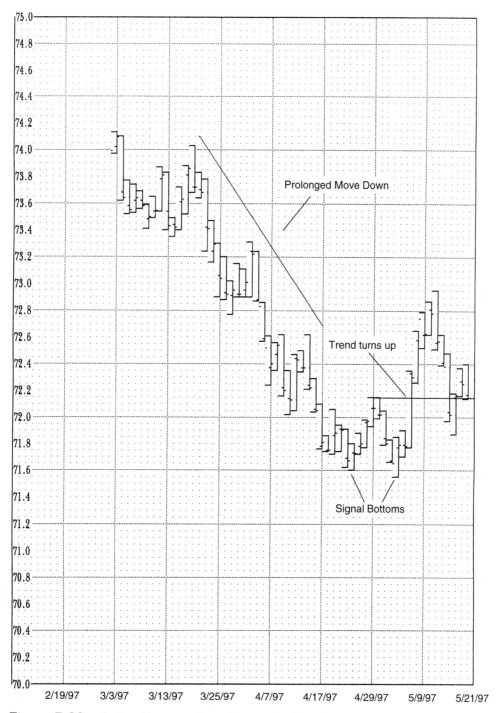

Figure 7.23   A signal bottom chart showing back-to-back signal bottoms, which is a strong sign that the trend is getting ready to turn up.

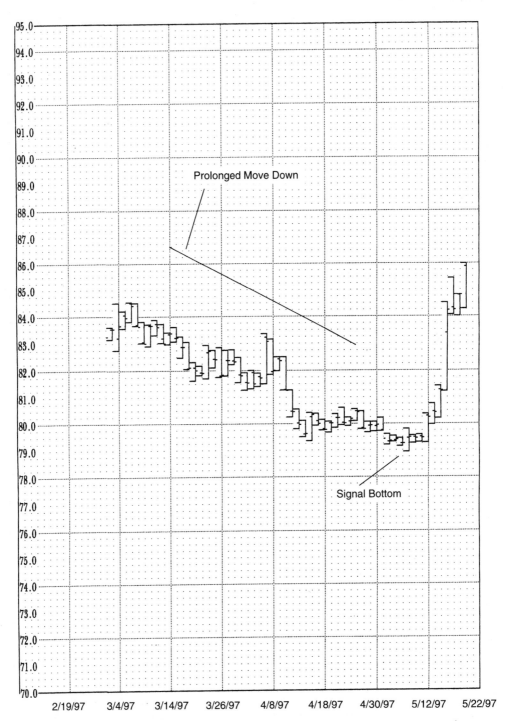

Figure 7.24   A signal bottom chart showing that an outside signal bottom often leads to a strong rally.

often called a *closing price reversal bottom* or a *key reversal bottom*, but these terms are not as specific as signal bottom, as neither mentions the close above the day's midpoint, the close above the opening, or the follow-through rally, nor the prolonged move down in price and time.

To understand its importance, we need to break the signal bottom down to its components.

A prolonged move in price is an important part of determining the significance of a signal bottom. This type of signal must occur following a strong break in terms of price. As stated earlier, a record should be kept of the size of past breaks in terms of price, because a market often repeats them. Study the past to see if the current break equals or exceeds a previous break at the time of the signal bottom day. Knowing these historical swings in advance can help the trader anticipate the signal bottom day. In addition to studying the size of the price swings, a trader should know if the market is approaching a historically low price level.

A prolonged move in terms of time is also an important indication of an impending signal bottom day. As stated earlier, time is most important in determining a change in trend or a bottom, so knowing the past history of a market's breaks in terms of time can provide important information as to when or if a valid signal bottom is or will be taking place. Historical swing chart data such as the duration of bottoms to tops and bottoms to bottoms can provide this information. If a market is approaching a swing level in terms of time, which has stopped a rally before, then anticipate a signal bottom.

A higher-high and a higher-close occur quite often even in the midst of a strong break. Without a prolonged move in price or time and a follow-through rally, this pattern may trigger a false bottoming signal. Research will show that when this pattern fails it is because the market has failed to achieve at least one of the following: a balancing of a price swing, a balancing of a time swing, a follow-through to the upside the next time period.

Although a reversal up can occur following a prolonged move down in terms of price and time, a lower-low and a higher-close, and a follow-through the next time period, there can be different degrees of strength to this signal. For example, the market may have all of the preceding factors, and a close above the current range's midpoint, but not be above the opening price. While the best signal bottom is called a *triple-signal bottom*, a lower-low and higher-close, with only a close above the midpoint or only above the opening price, are called a *double-bottom top*.

Bottoms with this type of formation should be studied to determine the strength of the signal in predicting major bottom formations. The same is true for the signal bottom days that close higher and above the opening price, but not above the current range's midpoint.

The following is a list of the various strengths of signal bottoms from strongest to weakest, and assuming a prolonged break in terms of price and time:

1. A lower-low and a higher-close, a close above the opening, and a close above the day's midpoint.
2. A lower-low and a higher-close, and a close above the day's midpoint.
3. A lower-low and a higher-close, and a close above the opening.
4. A lower-low and a higher-close.

The main thing to watch for is a lower-low and a higher-close following a prolonged move down in terms of price and time and a follow-through rally. The degree of strength of the bottom should be determined by whether or not the close is above the midpoint and/or above the opening. Once again, records of how a major bottom was formed should be kept. These bottoms should be referred to frequently to determine the strength and reliability of the expected rally.

Remember also that while there is an important signal as to the bottom of the market, it does not automatically change the trend to up, but only temporarily freezes the market and puts it in a position to break to the downside. This break is not a change in trend, although it can lead to one. Records should be maintained to determine how much penetration of the high at the time of the signal bottom is needed to confirm a valid signal bottom. This amount varies by market and must be known to avoid false buy signals.

When using the trend indicators to enter and exit positions, traders should move the stops down from above swing tops to just above the high of the signal bottom bar to lock in any profit and to get taken out when the market confirms the signal bottom with a follow-through rally.

Variations in the signal bottom formation can provide different results. For example, a close above the signal bottom range's midpoint is suggested, but further filtering of the strength of this signal can be determined if the market closed in the upper 25% or 10% range of the signal bottom time period. To make this signal more useful in forecasting major bottoms, the signal should be observed and tested using a program such as *Super Charts* or *Trade Station*.

Time indicators can also be strengthened. Besides looking at the duration of a break in terms of price, a trader may want to compare signal bottoms that occur at cyclical or seasonal times. Price analysis may also be filtered by observing and testing signal bottoms that occur at historical price levels, major percentage retracement points, and major Gann-angle formations.

Although a signal bottom does not actually change the trend to up mechanically, countertrend traders who are comfortable with their market research on this signal can enter into a countertrend short-term position by buying strength upon confirmation of the signal bottom. This often carries a large dollar risk because it is against the trend and because a stop-loss has to be placed below the signal bottom.

An additional countertrend buying strategy is to buy a 50% retracement of the first leg up from the signal bottom. This move may take two or more days to develop, but is one of the most common trading patterns. This strategy can be altered to include 33% or 67% retracements. Combined with former main bottoms, balance points, or Gann angles, retracement sells can produce major entry or exit points that can turn a market or change the trend from down to up.

These two exceptions, signal tops and signal bottoms, to the standard stop rule are designed for aggressive traders who want to lock in profits before the market retraces all the way up over a swing top or through a swing bottom. It should be noted that these stops when executed do not represent a change in trend, but are often important indicators of changes in trend that are going to take place in the very near future. These stops are also very effective in active, fast-moving markets when the market makes several large swings over a short period of time.

OTHER IMPORTANT FORMATIONS

In addition to the signal top and signal bottom formations, the market often indicates an impending change in trend by closing on or near a low or high.

Closing Near a Low

Following a prolonged move down in terms of price and time, or when the market is trading near a historically low level, the market will often have an expanded range bar down and settle on the low or within one or two price units of the low (Figure 7.25). The next period the market opens higher and never trades under the close of the low day.

This action does not change the trend, but is a strong sign the market is getting ready to change trend or build a support zone.

Closing Near a High

Following a prolonged move up in terms of price and time, or when the market is trading near a historically high level, the market will often have an expanded range bar up and settle on the high or within one or two price units of the high (Figure 7.26). The next period the market opens lower and never trades over the close of the high day.

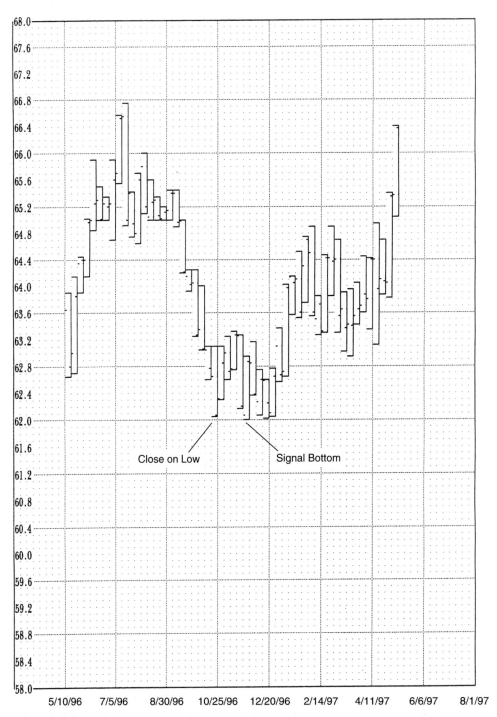

Figure 7.25   Chart showing a closing near a low. Despite a weekly close on the low, the market started a rally. The final bottom was a signal bottom.

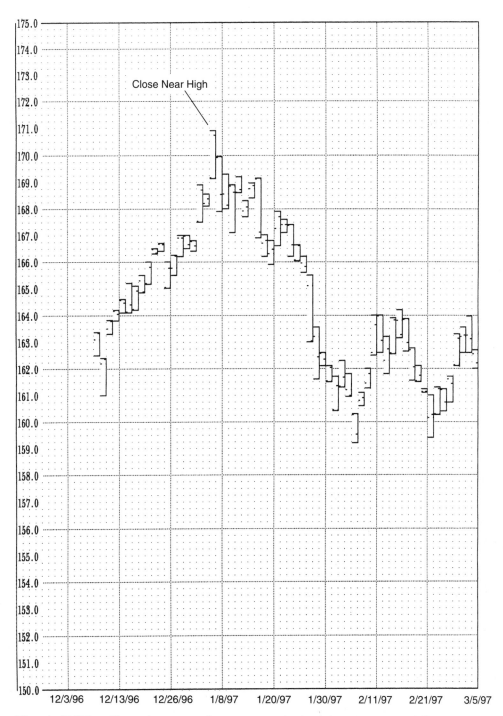

Figure 7.26   Chart showing a closing near a high. A lower opening following a close near a high does not change the trend, but is a strong sign that the market is getting ready to change it or begin a decline.

This action does not change the trend, but is a strong sign the market is getting ready to change trend or build a resistance zone. These top formations should be researched and studied for the accuracy of their forecasting ability.

SUMMARY

Although many traders would like to create purely mechanical trading systems to trade the trend, sometimes conditions exist that may help the trader maximize trading profits and minimize risk. In my opinion, this is exactly what the exceptions to the trend indicator rules accomplish. While a trader often gets caught up in the art of trading using the trend indicator only, he or she must realize that trading successfully involves making strategic adjustments. The ability to identify certain signals such as double bottoms and tops, prolonged moves in price, swing balancing, and signal tops and bottoms will help the trader to determine impending changes in trend before the trend indicator is activated.

This concludes the chapter on chart patterns that are the exceptions to the swing chart rules. In learning about both the chart and the exceptions, pay particular attention to the signal tops and signal bottoms, as the majority of major tops and bottoms formed will occur in this fashion.

8   Swing Chart Trading

After building a trend indicator chart and watching how the market performs, the next step is learning how to build a simple trading system. The simplest system to build is one that places the trader in the trade mechanically. Learning the characteristics of a market and each trend indicator is the key to success when using the swing trading method to enter and exit the market. This chapter focuses on the techniques for building trading strategies using the swing charts. Initiating trades from extreme levels, initiating a trade on a reversal stop, and various methods of pyramiding are discussed.

REVIEWING THE INDICATOR CHARTS

Minor Trend Indicator Charts

The minor or one-day trend indicator chart (Figure 8.1) is easy to construct, as it simply follows the one-day up and down movement of the market.

The minor trend line moves up from a low price following a higher-high than the previous bar. When this occurs a line is drawn from the low one bar back to the high price on the current bar. This action makes the low one bar back a minor bottom. As the market continues to move higher, the trend line moves up to each new high. This process continues until the market posts a price lower than the previous low. When that happens, the minor trend line moves down from the high on the previous bar to the low on the current bar, which makes the last high a minor top. This is the basic formation needed for trading the one-day or minor trend indicator.

Intermediate Trend Indicator Charts

The intermediate or two-day trend indicator chart (Figure 8.2) is also easy to construct. It is very similar to the minor or one-day trend indicator chart except that it follows the two-day movement of the market.

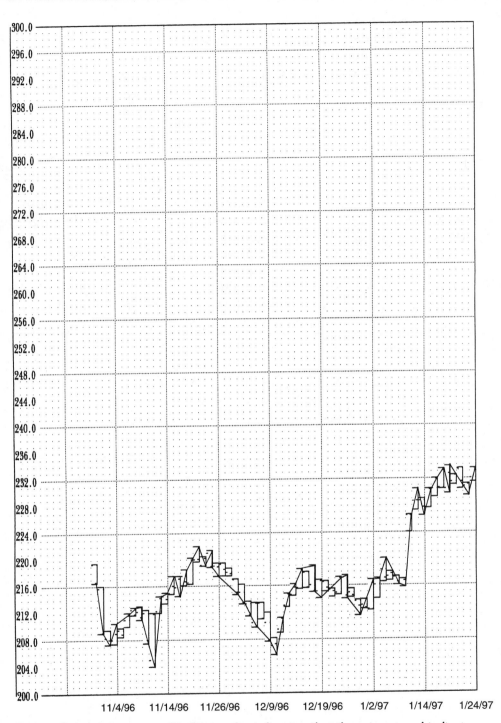

Figure 8.1   A minor trend indicator chart showing that the minor trend indicator or one-day swing chart tracks the one-day movement of the market.

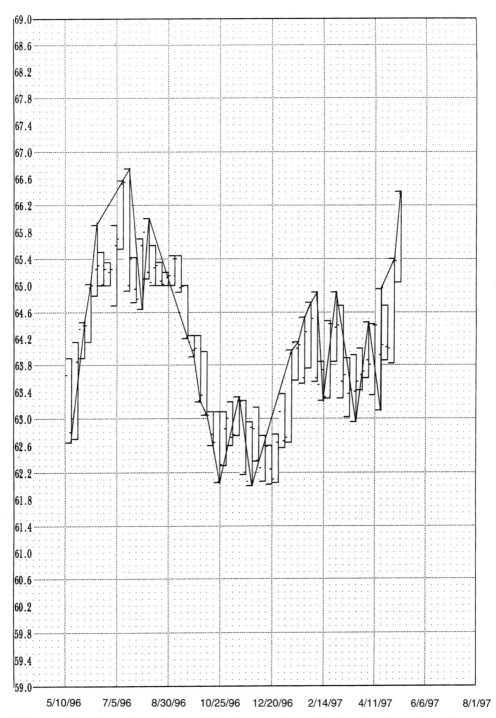

Figure 8.2   An intermediate trend indicator chart showing that the intermediate trend indicator or two-day swing chart tracks the two-day movement of the market.

The intermediate trend line moves up from a low price following two consecutive higher-highs than the previous bar. When this occurs a line is drawn from the low two bars back to the high price on the current bar. This action makes the original low two bars back an intermediate bottom. At this point it is no longer necessary to have two-consecutive higher-highs to move the trend line up. As the market continues to move higher, the trend line moves up to each new high. This process continues until the market posts two consecutive lower-lows. When that happens, the intermediate trend line moves down to the lower-low on the current bar, which makes the high two bars back an intermediate top. This is the basic formation needed for trading the two-day or intermediate trend indicator.

Main Trend Indicator Charts

The main or three-day trend indicator chart (Figure 8.3) is built in a similar fashion to the one-day and two-day trend indicator charts except that it follows the three-day movement of the market.

The main trend line moves up from a low price following three consecutive higher-highs than the previous bar. When this occurs a line is drawn from the low three bars back to the high price on the current bar. This action makes the original low three bars back a main bottom. At this point it is no longer necessary to have three-consecutive higher-highs to move the trend line up. As the market continues to move higher, the trend line moves up to each new high. This process continues until the market posts three consecutive lower-lows. When that happens, the intermediate trend line moves down to the lower-low on the current bar, which makes the high three bars back a main top. This is the basic formation needed for trading the three-day or main trend indicator.

Common Characteristics

It is best to start the three trend indicators from the first day the contract comes on the board. This way the trader charts all of the price swings, and the trend will be known before the contract becomes active. During periods of inactivity or light trading, such as during the first few months of trading, the market sometimes only has a closing price. Treat this price as a high or a low, depending on whether it is above or below the last trading day's range. As this chart is being developed, write in the prices and their dates above the swing tops and below the swing bottoms. This information is necessary because it provides the trader with a permanent history of the contract's main tops and bottoms.

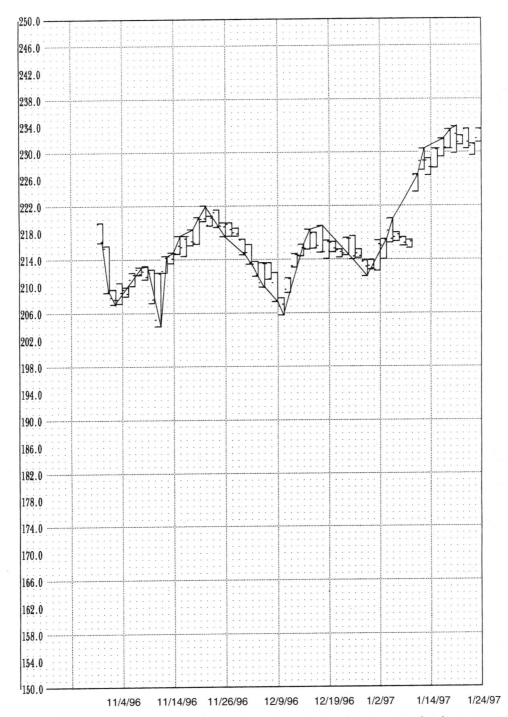

Figure 8.3   A main indicator trend chart showing that the main trend indicator or three-day swing chart tracks the three-day movement of the market.

Enter the history on a spreadsheet where the distance in terms of price and time can be calculated. It is important to record this information so that the trader can see the changes from top-to-bottom, bottom-to-top, top-to-top, and bottom-to-bottom. This information should be maintained in terms of both price and time so that the trader learns the duration and distance of each swing, which she needs to know for forecasting future market swings. In addition a permanent record of the tops and bottoms can be used for cycles and historical tops and bottoms.

The trader should also be aware of market activity at various price levels. For example, the size and duration of the swings at both low and high levels should be noted. The most likely observation is that trading activity is tight and narrow at lows and wide at high levels. This information helps the trader determine in which section of the move the market is trading. By gathering swing data and studying the size and duration of the swings from top-to-top, the analyst can learn from the characteristics of a market at a top when a rally is coming to an end, which can prevent him from entering a new position at a very high level or at the end of a major swing. Conversely, similar information can be gleaned from studying the size and duration of bottoms-to-bottoms, and can prevent the trader from initializing a position at an extremely low level or at the end of a major down cycle.

In regard to these three trend indicators, the same rules govern when a trader enters and exits a market. For instance, the trader enters the market on the long side when the market crosses the last swing top. She continues to maintain her long position as long as the market continues to make higher tops and higher bottoms, with a protective and reversal stop under the last swing bottom. She does the opposite for a short position, for example, entering the market on the short side when the market crosses the last swing bottom. This type of trading technique is encouraged when the market has reached an extreme level in terms of price and time.

BASIC TRADING INSTRUCTIONS

Buy and Sell Points

After constructing the trend indicator charts and studying the swing tops, swing bottoms, and stop placement, it is fairly simple for a trader to initiate trades using this trading tool. Following is a generic explanation of how to use the trend indicator to enter the market.

Using the trend indicator only to enter a market allows the trader to be guided in and out of the market by the changes in the trend (Figures 8.4 and 8.5). Following the proper construction of the trend indicator charts, determine the current position of the market relative to its historical range or the range

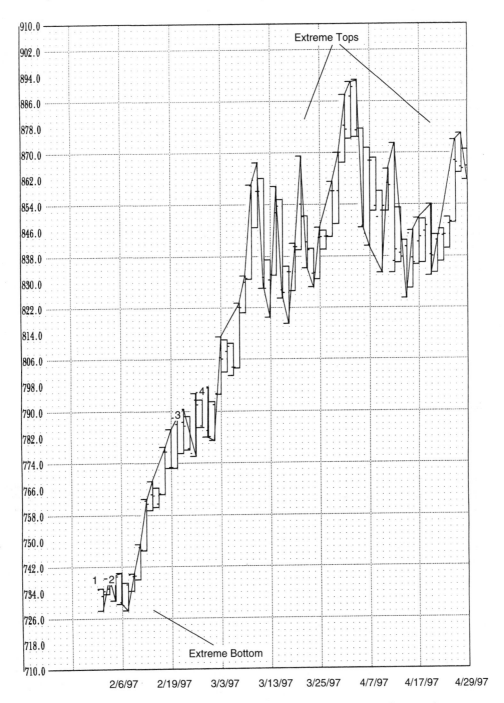

Figure 8.4   Minor trend indicator and buy points. Buying strength near the contract high is not suggested as the frequency of a whipsaw trade increases, while buying from an extreme bottom is suggested when the market crosses the minor tops identified by 1, 2, 3, and 4.

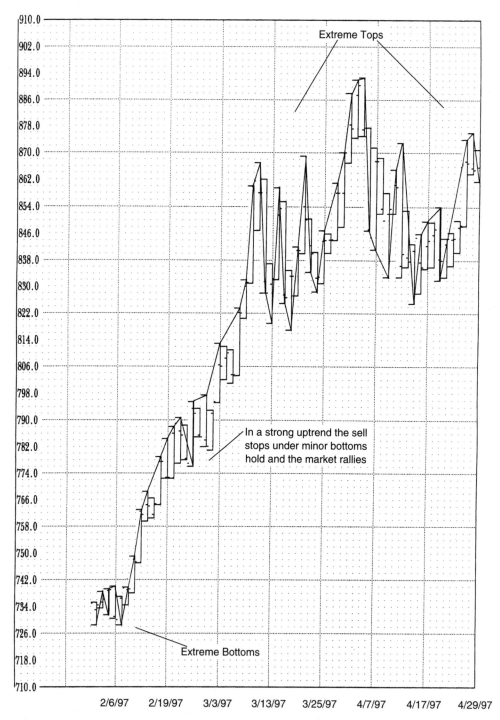

Figure 8.5   Minor trend indicator and sell points. Whipsaw action can occur with this chart. Near the top, the frequency of minor bottoms and sell points increases.

of the current active contract, as this trading tool works best when the market is at a historical high or low or following a prolonged move up or down.

The trend indicator can be initiated at any point on the chart, but certain levels have proved to be more successful than others. Starting the trend indicator from an extreme level will probably be more successful than starting the trend indicator in the middle of a major campaign. The following are explanations of trend indicator trades initiated from four common price levels.

Initiating a Trend Indicator Buy Signal from an Extreme Low. From a flat position and following a prolonged move down in terms of price and time and when the market is at an extremely low price level (Figures 8.6–8.8), place a buy stop for one contract over the last swing top, then wait for the market action to reach the stop and fill the order. After receiving the fill, place a sell stop order under the last swing bottom. If the market continues to rally, then stay in the position as long as the market continues to make higher-highs and higher-lows, with the sell stop maintained under the last swing bottom. Throughout the life of the rally, the market may develop a series of higher-tops. When this happens, continue to follow the market up by moving the sell stop and placing it under each new swing bottom and locking in profits along the way. Once the market forms a swing top and breaks the last swing bottom, the position is stopped out and the trader is flat.

Initiating a Trend Indicator Sell Signal from an Extreme High. From a flat position and following a prolonged move up in terms of price and time and when the market is at an extremely high price level (Figures 8.9–8.11), place a sell stop for one contract under the last swing bottom, then wait for the market action to reach the stop and fill the order. After receiving the fill, place a buy stop order over the last swing top. If the market continues to break, then stay in the position as long as the market continues to make lower-lows and lower-highs with the buy stop maintained over the last swing top. Throughout the life of the break, the market may develop a series of lower-tops. When this happens, continue to follow the market down by moving the buy stop and placing it over each new swing top and locking in profits along the way. Once the market forms a swing bottom and breaks the last main top, the position is stopped out and the trader is flat.

Reversal Stops

Initiating a Buy Signal with a Reversal Stop. As mentioned earlier, the safest time to initiate a buy is following a prolonged move down in terms of

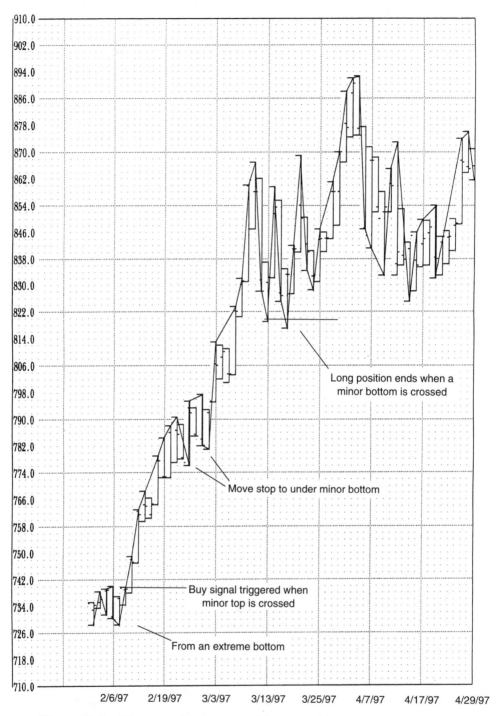

Figure 8.6   Minor trend indicator and buy signal from an extreme low.

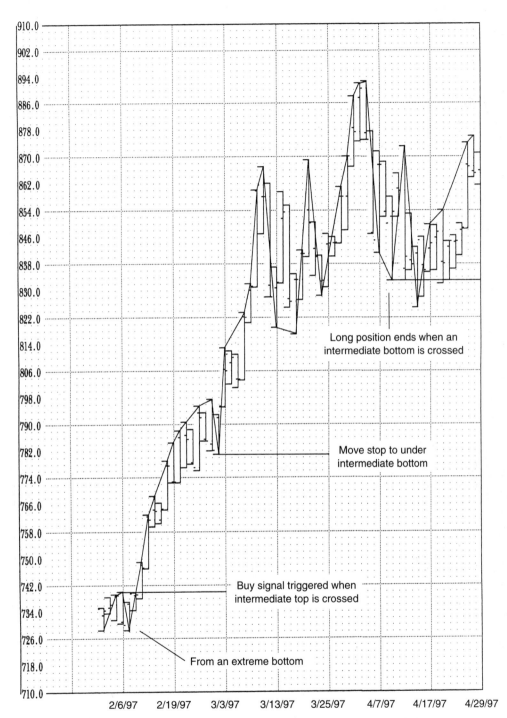

Figure 8.7   Intermediate trend indicator and buy signal from an extreme bottom.

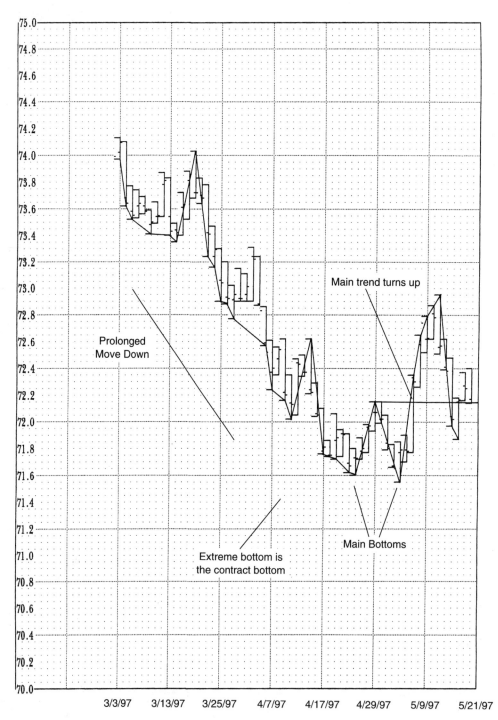

Figure 8.8   Main trend indicator and buy signal from an extreme bottom.

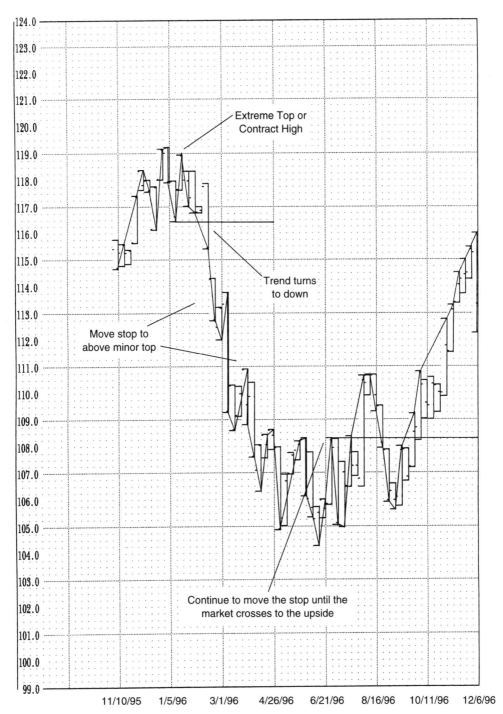

Figure 8.9   Minor trend indicator and sell signal from an extreme high.

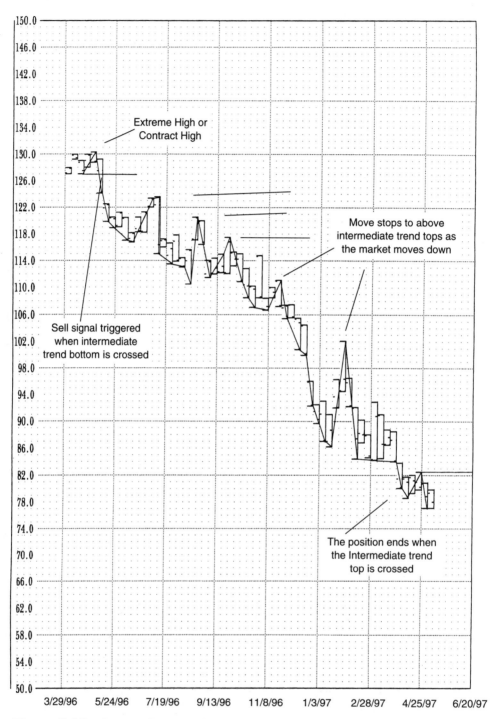

Figure 8.10   Intermediate trend indicator and sell signal from an extreme high.

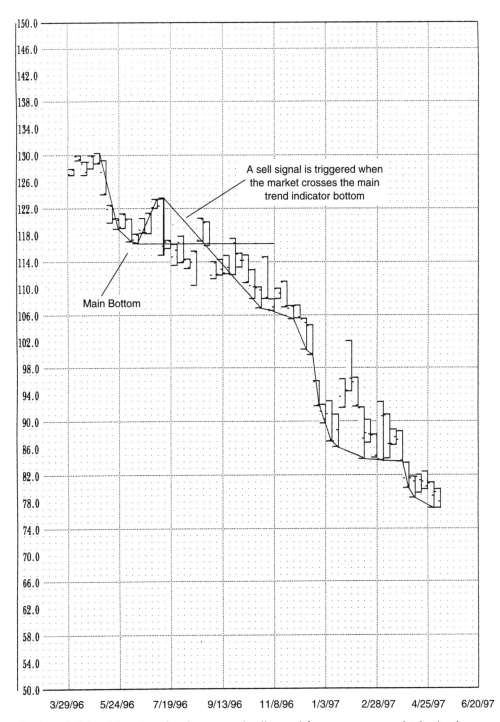

Figure 8.11   Main trend indicator and sell signal from an extreme high. As the market approaches an extreme low, the 7–10 week rule should be executed.

price and time or when the market has reached an extremely low price level. While this is often the most successful pattern to trade, more active traders may choose to buy following the liquidation of a short position. After a buy stop and reversal is reached, the trader simply follows the upward swings of the market and moves the sell and reversal stops up each time a new swing bottom forms. He maintains the same long position as long as the market continues to make higher tops and higher bottoms. The trade is liquidated and the position reversed when the last swing bottom is crossed and the sell stop is hit.

A long position triggered by a buy stop and reversal is often more risky than a buy signal generated following a prolonged move down in terms of price and time or from an extremely low level. This is because the buy is often triggered at a poor price level such as the middle of the contract range. Choppy, two-sided trading may occur at this level, and whipsawlike trading may be common. The frequency of loss therefore increases because of losing trades and high commission costs. It should be noted that the characteristic described is more common with the minor trend indicator than with the intermediate and main trend indicators. Through study and research the trader will determine which trend indicator is best suited for her trading style. This topic was discussed in more detail in previous chapters.

The only time a buy reversal signal is recommended is following a prolonged move down in terms of price and time that has taken the market to a historically low price level while the trader was in a short position and riding the trend indicator down. In this case, the trader will have excess capital to work with, since the original position was a profitable short position. In other words, the trader is risking the market's money.

Initiating a Sell Signal with a Reversal Stop. Just as with the reversal stop buy signal discussed earlier, initiating a sell signal with a reversal stop is more risky than initiating a short position from an extremely high level. This is because the trader has little control over the price level at which the position may be triggered. If the sell is triggered at or near a historical support level or major percentage retracement zone, the trader may find himself trading on both sides of the market for several time periods until the market can break away from the support prices. This type of signal is recommended for aggressive traders who wish to trade more actively and can withstand whipsaw trading activity and increased commission costs.

The only time a sell reversal signal is recommended is following a prolonged move up in terms of price and time that has taken the market to a historically high price level while the trader was in a long position and riding the main trend indicator up. In this case, the trader will have excess capital to work with, since the original position was a profitable long position. In this case, the trader is risking the market's money.

PYRAMIDING: A GENERAL DESCRIPTION

After building a swing chart and watching how the market performs, the trader often begins to think of pyramid trading the swings. Pyramiding is not as popular as it once was because of the perception of higher volatility and shorter swings in today's markets. The fear of getting caught with a large position in a whipsaw market often discourages traders from considering a pyramid. Traders need to study and research the market in order to learn how to pyramid, and a properly constructed swing chart along with market timing can help them plan a strong pyramid campaign.

Pyramiding often fails today because the trader does not give the market enough time to develop the long-term trend. This is because many traders only look at the nearby contract to trade and ignore the deferred contracts because they believe that a market with low open interest cannot be traded. Deciding which market to trade depends on individual trading style. Thus, short-term or day traders have to trade in the market that has the most liquidity, while fear of poor fills keeps many traders out of deferred contracts.

If you want to pyramid trade, then you have to look to the deferred contracts, which means you cannot be afraid of trading a contract six months to one year in the future. As we just said, this confidence is gained through study and research of the market. In other words, for a trader to be successful at pyramiding he must overlook the possibility of a short-term bad fill and focus on the long-term potential of the market.

The action of the market is relative. Short-term traders rely on fast-moving markets because it is their intention to move in and out quickly and need the volatility to accomplish this. A pyramid trader, on the other hand, accepts the fact that the position may take time to develop and is not worried about day-to-day market activity. Thus, if your intention is to trade the long-term, you must buy the data and build the charts to study.

Since chart services do not have the space to cover all the trading markets, they sell the chart of the most active contract. Ideally, however, the trader should use the longer-term charts to plan the pyramid. The monthly and weekly charts usually offer the best indication of which market to pyramid. These charts offer the trader the ability to see which markets are trading at extreme levels and so are most likely to lead to a valid long-term pyramid.

As mentioned earlier, pyramiding today often fails because the trader does not allow enough time for the trend to develop. If you trade the nearby contract, a pyramid will often fail because the rollover occurs too soon in the development process. When trading soybeans, for example, a pyramid started in October with November soybeans is interrupted by the rollover to January soybeans. The process of rolling from one contract to the other often confuses the trader, especially when rolling from old crop contracts to new crop contracts. This constant rollover can force the analyst to concentrate on properly rolling from one contract to the next rather than on the actual trading action.

In summary, if you want to have success in pyramiding the long-term trend of a market, you must trade a deferred contract, accept the possibility of a short-term bad fill due to low liquidity, and research and plan the trading strategy.

THE BUY PYRAMID

When deciding on a long-term buy pyramid, look for a market at a historically low level. Volatility is often low at these extreme levels, especially if the market is completing a prolonged down move. With the volatility low and trading ranges tight, stop-loss orders can be more easily controlled.

Pyramiding with the Minor Trend Indicator

There are two different ways to pyramid when trading with the minor trend indicator:

1. Buying when the minor trend top is crossed.
2. Buying at fixed intervals in the direction of the minor trend.

Pyramid Buying Using the Minor Swings Only. The long pyramid can begin with a simple crossing of a minor top following a prolonged down move in terms of both price and time. Of course, a long pyramid does not just happen by accident, but must be planned. After executing the first trade to begin the pyramid, the trader simply follows the swings of the market by adding to the position as the market continues to move higher and to cross minor tops (Figure 8.12).

This method involves buying strength, so the trader must be aware that there will be normal down swings in the market after buy signals have been triggered. This action can turn a profitable position into break-even or losing positions because of the subsequent purchase of higher-priced units.

Pyramid Buying at Fixed-Price Levels Using the Minor Trend Indicators. A second way to build a buy pyramid is to buy at fixed price levels after the first buy signal has been triggered. The safest way to determine which fixed interval to use is by studying the past history of the contract's

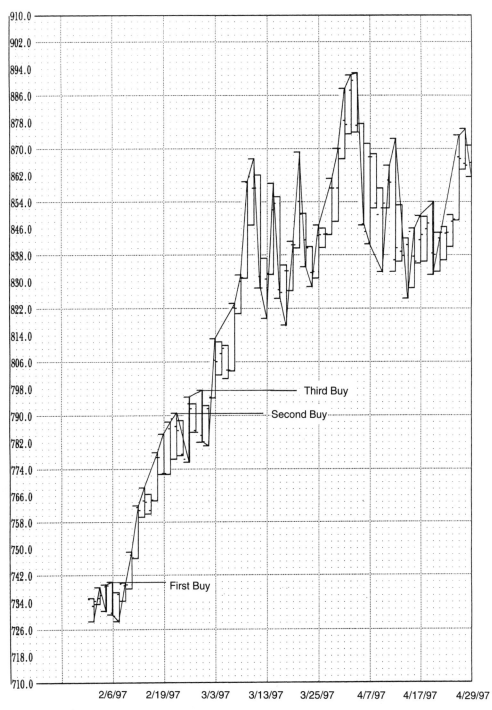

Figure 8.12   Minor trend indicator and a buy pyramid. From an extreme bottom, the trader buys each time the market crosses a minor trend top.

minor swings. Remember, in a pyramid from a bottom the trader is buying strength. If the average upswing in soybeans is 20 cents, then do not start adding to the pyramid after a 20-cent rally. Instead find the mid-point of the average upswing from which the market is likely to accelerate to the upside. The idea is to buy with the trend, but at a better price than buying over a swing top. This better price is a predetermined price increment, such as a percentage retracement point or a Gann angle. (These two concepts are discussed in more detail in later chapters.) The information learned from building and studying the historical swings of a specific market is necessary for building a successful pyramid. Use the historical data to learn the characteristics of the swings.

Using this pyramiding method can also turn profitable positions into break-even or losing positions because of the subsequent purchase of higher-priced units, but to a lesser degree than the first method.

Pyramid Buying at Fixed-Time Intervals Using the Minor Swing Chart. The expression "beating the market" is often used in trading. However, fixed-time-interval trading actually goes with the rhythm of the market rather than trying to beat it. If, as determined by the information gathered from previous swings, the market has tended to correct a certain number of time periods from a top, then buy when the market trades lower for an equal amount of time as the previous break. For example, if the first minor swing is 10 days up and 4 days down and the second minor swing is 15 days up and 4 days down, then look to buy the next 4-day break following a rally.

For this pyramid to work, it is important that the market continue to trade in this manner. If a rally fails to equal a previous rally in terms of time, or the subsequent break is greater than the previous break, then time is indicating a change in trend. Keep in mind that you are attempting to trade with the time movement of the market. When time is up or the pattern changes, then consider the trend changed.

Pyramiding with the Intermediate Trend Indicator

There are three different ways to pyramid when trading with the intermediate trend indicator:

1. Buying when the intermediate trend top is crossed.
2. Buying at fixed intervals in the direction of the intermediate trend.
3. Buying using a combination of the minor and intermediate trends.

Again, this type of trading should begin at an extreme price level. Use historical facts or the data observed from the history of the previous swings to determine this information.

Pyramid Buying Using the Intermediate Swings Only. The first style of pyramiding is buying with the intermediate trend indicator (Figure 8.13). From an extremely low level buy the first time the market crosses an intermediate swing top and place a stop-loss under the last intermediate swing bottom. The second unit is added when the market crosses the next intermediate top. Continue to trade in this manner until the market reaches an extremely high level or until the market crosses the last intermediate swing bottom.

Pyramid Buying at Fixed-Price Levels Using the Intermediate Swing Chart. The second pyramid method is to buy at fixed-price levels (see Figure 8.13). Begin the pyramid the same way as with the first method. As the move develops, add to the position at fixed-price levels. One way to determine a good fixed-price level is to study the size of previous swings. If the market has a strong tendency to rally 10 cents, then try to buy every 5 cents in anticipation of a 10-cent rally.

Also look at the size of previous breaks in the market that do not change the trend. For example, if the market has a tendency to break 5 cents from tops, then buy 5-cent breaks. These breaks can also be at percentage retracement levels or into uptrending Gann angles.

The idea is to buy at fixed-price levels that are at better prices than buying breakouts over the last intermediate swing top. Study and practice is needed to learn this trading technique.

Pyramid Buying at Fixed-Time Intervals Using the Intermediate Swing Chart. The expression "beating the market" is used in trading. However, fixed-time-interval trading actually goes with the rhythm of the market rather than trying to beat it. If, as determined by the information gathered from previous swings, the market has tended to correct a certain number of time periods from a top, then buy when the market trades lower for an equal amount of time as the previous break. For example, if the first swing is 10 days up and 4 days down and the second swing is 15 days up and 4 days down, then look to buy the next 4-day break following a rally.

For this pyramid to work, it is important that the market continue to trade in this manner. If a rally fails to equal a previous rally in terms of time, or the subsequent break is greater than the previous break, then time is indicating a change in trend. Keep in mind that you are attempting to trade with the time

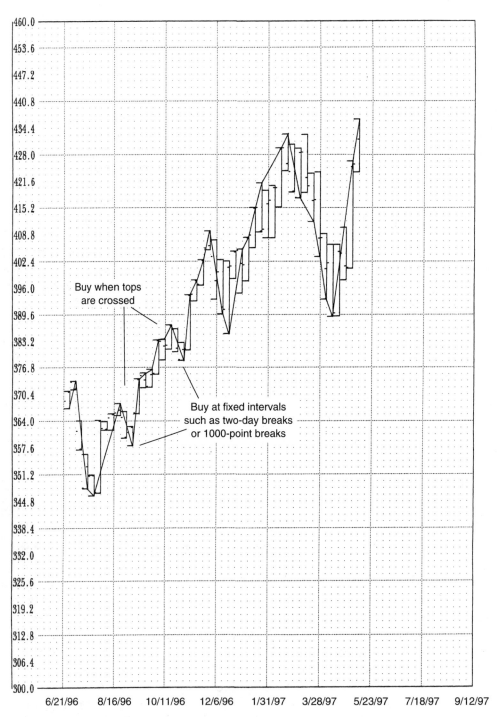

Figure 8.13   Intermediate trend indicator with different ways to pyramid.

movement of the market. When time is up or the pattern changes, then consider the trend changed.

Pyramid Buying Using a Combination of the Minor Trend Indicator and the Intermediate Trend Indicator. The third way to enter the market is to begin the position when the market crosses the last intermediate swing top. Additional positions are added to the long position using the minor or one-day swing chart. All trades triggered by the minor swing chart will be in the direction of the intermediate trend. Protective stops are placed below the intermediate bottoms for the intermediate trend longs and below the minor bottoms for the minor trend longs. A variation of this technique is to place all of the stops under the intermediate bottom.

This is an aggressive trading style and should be initiated at an extremely low or historically low price level. This type of trading resembles a pyramid because it will be large at the bottom and smaller at the top, as the trader has the option of liquidating positions as the market moves higher.

Pyramiding with the Main Trend Indicator

There are four different ways to pyramid when trading with the main trend indicator:

1. Buying when the main top is crossed.
2. Buying at fixed intervals in the direction of the main trend.
3. Buying using a combination of the minor and main trends.
4. Buying using a combination of the intermediate and main trends.

Again, this type of trading should begin at an extreme price level. Use historical facts or the data observed from the history of the previous swings to determine this information.

Pyramid Buying Using the Main Trend Swings Only. The first style of pyramiding is buying with the main trend indicator (Figure 8.14). From an extremely low level buy the first time the market crosses a main swing top and place a stop-loss under the last main swing bottom. The second unit is added when the market crosses the next main top. Continue to trade in this manner until the market reaches an extremely high level or until the market crosses the last main swing bottom.

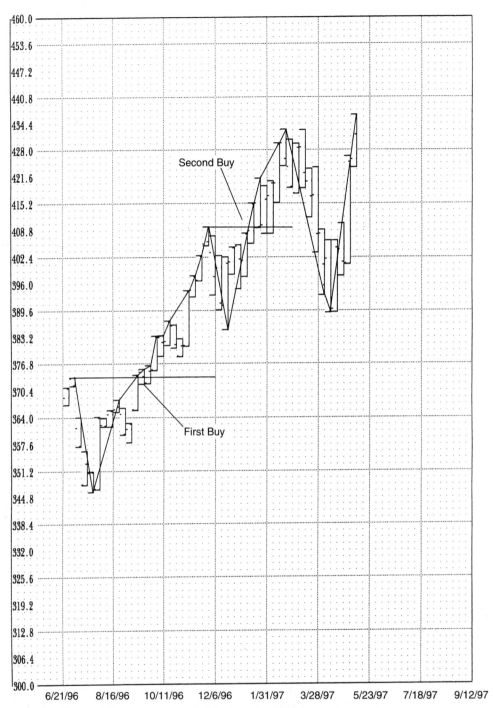

Figure 8.14   Main trend indicator and a buy pyramid. The main trend indicator yields few pyramid signals due to the infrequency of main tops and bottoms. In addition, buy signals may occur well above an extreme bottom or near an extreme top.

Pyramid Buying at Fixed-Price Levels Using the Main Trend Chart.
The second pyramid method is to buy at fixed-price levels. Begin the pyramid the same way as with the first method. As the move develops, add to the position at fixed-price levels. One way to determine a good fixed-price level is to study the size of previous swings. If the market has a strong tendency to rally 30 cents, then try to buy every 15 cents in anticipation of a 30-cent rally.

Also look at the size of previous breaks in the market that do not change the trend. For example, if the market has a tendency to break 20 cents from tops, then buy 20-cent breaks. These breaks can also be at percentage retracement levels or into uptrending Gann angles.

The idea is to buy at fixed-price levels that are at better prices than buying breakouts over the last intermediate swing top. Study and practice is needed to learn this trading technique.

Pyramid Buying at Fixed-Time Intervals Using the Main Trend Chart.
The expression "beating the market" is often used in trading. However, fixed-time-interval trading actually goes with the rhythm of the market rather than trying to beat it. If, as determined by the information gathered from previous main swings, the market has tended to correct a certain number of time periods from a top, then buy when the market trades lower for an equal amount of time as the previous break. For example, if the first main swing is 20 periods up and 7 periods down and the second swing is 25 periods up and 7 periods down, then look to buy the next 7-period break following a rally.

For this pyramid to work, it is important that the market continue to trade in this manner. If a rally fails to equal a previous rally in terms of time, or the subsequent break is greater than the previous break, then time is indicating a change in trend. Keep in mind that you are attempting to trade with the time movement of the market. When time is up or the pattern changes, then consider the trend changed.

Pyramid Buying Using a Combination of the Minor Trend Indicator and the Main Trend Indicator. The third way to enter the market is to begin the position when the market crosses the last main swing top. Additional positions are added to the long position using the minor or one-day swing chart. All trades triggered by the minor swing chart will be in the direction of the main trend. Protective stops are placed below the main bottoms for the main trend longs and below the minor bottoms for the minor trend longs. A variation of this technique is to place all of the stops under the main trend bottom.

This type of trading encourages the trader to stay with the main trend and to take advantage of the minor upswings inside of the main upswings. This technique also keeps the trader in the market as long as the main trend remains up, but directs her to lighten her position if the minor trend indicator shows signs of weakness.

This is an aggressive trading style and should be initiated at an extremely low or historically low price level. This type of trading resembles a pyramid because it will be large at the bottom and smaller at the top, as the trader has the option of liquidating positions as the market moves higher.

Pyramid Buying Using a Combination of the Intermediate Trend Indicator and the Main Trend Indicator. The fourth way to enter the market is to begin the position when the market crosses the last main swing top. Additional positions are added to the long position using the intermediate or two-day swing chart. All trades triggered by the intermediate swing chart will be in the direction of the main trend. Protective stops are placed below the main bottoms for the main trend longs and below the intermediate bottoms for the intermediate trend longs. A variation of this technique is to place all of the stops under the main trend bottom.

This type of trading encourages the trader to stay with the main trend and to take advantage of the intermediate upswings inside of the main upswings. This technique also keeps the trader in the market as long as the main trend remains up, but directs him to lighten his position if the intermediate trend indicator shows signs of weakness.

This is an aggressive trading style and should be initiated at an extremely low or historically low price level. This type of trading resembles a pyramid because it will be large at the bottom and smaller at the top, as the trader has the option of liquidating positions as the market moves higher.

The True Buy Pyramid

Depending on how aggressive the trader is, and how confident she is in her analysis of the market to determine if it is at an extreme level, she can begin her position with what I call a true pyramid.

A true pyramid is triggered by a long signal and is characterized by a large position near the bottom and a smaller position near the top. Traders using this method should be skilled at calculating resistance so they can successfully liquidate positions at appropriate price levels.

These resistance points can be various combinations of former intermediate tops, especially if the rally began after a severe decline. Additional profit objectives are percentage retracement points and Gann angles from previous tops, if determinable. These additional resistance points are discussed in later chapters.

THE SELL PYRAMID

When deciding on a long-term sell pyramid, look for a market at a historically high level. Volatility is often high at these extreme levels, especially if the market is completing a prolonged move up. With the volatility high and trading ranges wide, stop-loss orders should be monitored closely so that risk can be more easily controlled.

Pyramiding with the Minor Trend Indicator

There are two different ways to pyramid when trading with the minor trend indicator:

1. Selling when the minor trend top is crossed.
2. Selling at fixed intervals in the direction of the minor trend.

Pyramid Selling Using the Minor Swings Only. The short pyramid can begin with a simple crossing of a minor bottom following a prolonged down move in terms of both price and time. Of course, a short pyramid does not just happen by accident, but must be planned. After executing the first trade to begin the pyramid, the trader simply follows the swings of the market by adding to the position as the market continues to move lower and to cross minor bottoms (Figure 8.15).

This method involves selling weakness, so the trader must be aware that there will be normal upswings in the market after sell signals have been triggered (Figure 8.16). This action can turn a profitable position into a break-even or losing position because of the sale of lower-priced subsequent units.

Pyramid Selling at Fixed-Price Levels Using the Minor Swing Indicator. A second way to build a sell pyramid is to sell at fixed-price levels after the first sell signal has been triggered (Figure 8.17). The safest way to determine which fixed interval to use is by studying the past history of the contract's minor swings. Remember, in a pyramid from a top the trader is selling weakness. If the average downswing in silver is 20 cents, then do not start adding to the pyramid after a 20-cent break. Instead, find an average point from which the market is likely to accelerate to the downside. This figure could be 5 or 10 cents lower. The idea is to sell with the trend, but at a better price than selling under a swing bottom. This better price is a predetermined price increment. This technique may also involve the calculation of 50% points or

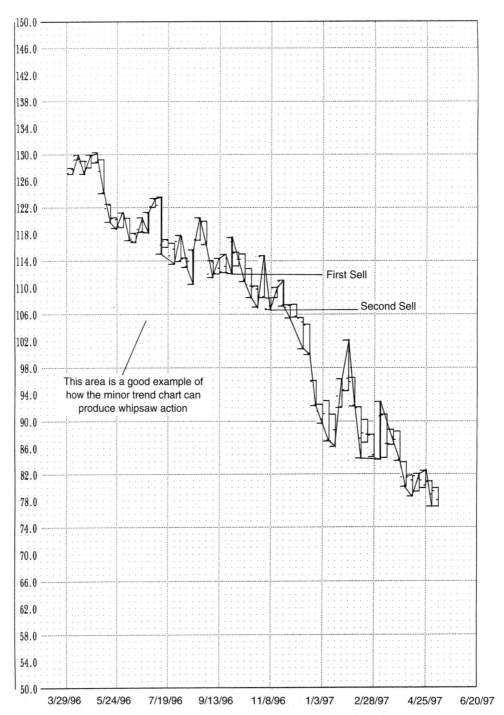

Figure 8.15   Minor trend indicator and pyramid selling with the trend indicator. This method tries to build multiple positions by selling each time the market crosses a minor trend bottom.

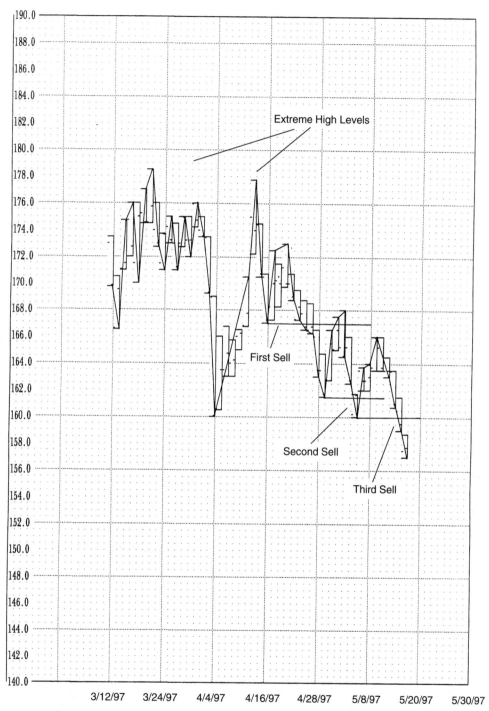

Figure 8.16   Minor trend indicator and pyramid selling with minor swings. From an extreme high level, sell each time the market crosses a minor bottom.

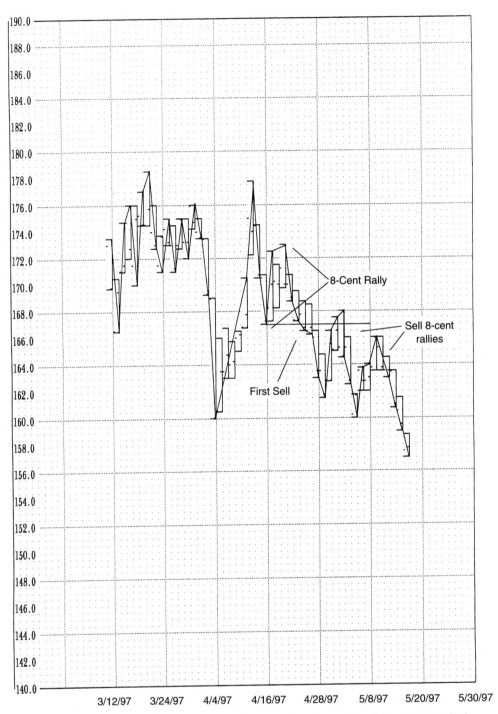

Figure 8.17   Minor trend indicator and pyramid selling at fixed levels. Watch the size of the last rally to determine future sell points. In this case, the last rally was 8 cents. Once the first trade is triggered, sell each 8-cent retracement rally.

uptrending angles. The information learned from building and studying the historical swings of a specific market is necessary for building a successful pyramid. Use the historical data to learn the characteristics of the swings.

Using this pyramiding method can also turn profitable positions into break-even or losing positions because of the subsequent sale of lower-priced units, but to a lesser degree than the first method.

Pyramid Selling at Fixed-Time Intervals Using the Minor Swing Chart. The expression "beating the market" is often used in trading. However, fixed-time-interval trading actually goes with the rhythm of the market rather than trying to beat it. If, as determined by the information gathered from previous swings, the market has tended to correct a certain number of time periods from a bottom, then sell when the market trades higher for an equal amount of time as the previous rally. For example, if the first minor swing is 10 periods down and 4 periods up and the second minor swing is 15 periods down and 4 periods up, then look to sell the next 4-period rally following a break.

For this pyramid to work, it is important that the market continue to trade in this manner. If a break fails to equal a previous break in terms of time, or the subsequent rally is greater than the previous rally, then time is indicating a change in trend. Keep in mind that you are attempting to trade with the time movement of the market. When time is up or the pattern changes, then consider the trend changed.

Pyramiding with the Intermediate Trend Indicator

There are three different ways to pyramid when trading with the intermediate trend indicator:

1. Selling when the intermediate trend top is crossed.
2. Selling at fixed intervals in the direction of the intermediate trend.
3. Selling using a combination of the minor and intermediate trends.

Again, this type of trading should begin at an extreme price level. Use historical facts or the data observed from the history of the previous swings to determine this information.

Pyramid Selling Using the Intermediate Swings Only. The first style of pyramiding is selling with the intermediate trend indicator. From an extremely low level, sell the first time the market crosses an intermediate swing bottom and place a stop-loss under the last intermediate swing top. The second unit is added when the market crosses the next intermediate bottom. Continue to trade in this manner until the market reaches an extremely low level or until the market crosses the last intermediate swing top.

Pyramid Selling at Fixed-Price Levels Using the Intermediate Swing Chart. The second pyramid method is to sell at fixed-price levels. Begin the pyramid the same way as with the first method. As the move develops, add to the position at fixed-price levels. One way to determine a good fixed-price level is to study the size of previous swings. If the market has a strong tendency to break 10 cents, then try to sell every 5 cents in anticipation of a 10-cent break.

Also look at the size of previous rallies in the market that do not change the trend. For example, if the market has a tendency to rally 5 cents from bottoms, then sell 5-cent rallies. These rallies can also be at percentage retracement levels or into uptrending Gann angles.

The idea is to sell at fixed-price levels that are at better prices than selling breakdowns under the last intermediate swing bottom. Study and practice is needed to learn this trading technique.

Pyramid Selling at Fixed-Time Intervals Using the Intermediate Swing Chart. The expression "beating the market" is used in trading. However, fixed-time-interval trading actually goes with the rhythm of the market rather than trying to beat it. If, as determined by the information gathered from previous swings, the market has tended to correct a certain number of time periods from a bottom, then sell when the market trades higher for an equal amount of time as the previous rally. For example, if the first swing is 10 days down and 4 days up and the second swing is 15 days down and 4 days up, then look to sell the next 4-day rally following a break.

For this pyramid to work, it is important that the market continue to trade in this manner. If a break fails to equal a previous break in terms of time, or the subsequent rally is greater than the previous rally, then time is indicating a change in trend. Keep in mind that you are attempting to trade with the time movement of the market. When time is up or the pattern changes, then consider the trend changed.

Pyramid Selling Using a Combination of the Minor Trend Indicator and the Intermediate Trend Indicator. The third way to enter the market is to begin the position when the market crosses the last intermediate swing bottom. Additional positions are added to the short position using the minor or one-day swing chart. All trades triggered by the minor swing chart will be in the direction of the intermediate trend. Protective stops are placed above the intermediate tops for the intermediate trend shorts and above the minor tops for the minor trend shorts. A variation of this technique is to place all of the stops over the intermediate top.

This is an aggressive trading style and should be initiated at an extremely high or historically high price level. This type of trading resembles an inverted pyramid because it will be large at the top and smaller at the bottom, as the trader has the option of liquidating positions as the market moves lower.

Pyramiding with the Main Trend Indicator

There are four different ways to pyramid when trading with the main trend indicator:

1. Selling when the main top is crossed.
2. Selling at fixed intervals in the direction of the main trend.
3. Selling using a combination of the minor and main trends.
4. Selling using a combination of the intermediate and main trends.

Pyramid Selling Using the Main Trend Swings Only. The first style of pyramiding is selling with the main trend indicator. From an extremely high level sell the first time the market crosses a main swing bottom and place a stop-loss over the last main swing top. The second unit is added when the market crosses the next main swing bottom. Continue to trade in this manner until the market reaches an extremely low level or until the market crosses the last main swing top.

Pyramid Selling at Fixed-Price Levels Using the Main Trend Chart. The second pyramid method is to sell at fixed-price levels. Begin the pyramid the same way as with the first method. As the move develops, add to the position at fixed-price levels. One way to determine a good fixed-price level is to study the size of previous swings. If the market has a strong tendency to break 40 cents, then try to sell every 5 cents in anticipation of a 40-cent break.

Also look at the size of previous rallies in the market that do not change the trend. For example, if the market has a tendency to rally 15 cents from bottoms, then sell 15-cent rallies. These rallies can also be at percentage retracements levels or into downtrending Gann angles.

The idea is to sell at fixed-price levels that are at better prices than selling breakouts under the last intermediate swing bottom. Study and practice is needed to learn this trading technique.

Pyramid Selling at Fixed-Time Intervals Using the Main Trend Chart.

The expression "beating the market" is often used in trading. However, fixed-time-interval trading actually goes with the rhythm of the market rather than trying to beat it. If, as determined by the information gathered from previous swings, the market has tended to correct a certain number of time periods from a bottom, then sell when the market trades higher for an equal amount of time as the previous rally. For example, if the first swing is 10 periods down and 4 periods up and the second swing is 15 periods down and 4 periods up, then look to sell the next 4-period rally following a break.

For this pyramid to work, it is important that the market continue to trade in this manner. If a break fails to equal a previous break in terms of time, or the subsequent rally is greater than the previous rally, then time is indicating a change in trend. Keep in mind that you are attempting to trade with the time movement of the market. When time is up or the pattern changes, then consider the trend changed.

Pyramid Selling Using a Combination of the Minor Trend Indicator and the Main Trend Indicator.

The third way to enter the market is to begin the position when the market crosses the last main swing bottom. Additional positions are added to the short position using the minor or one-day swing chart. All trades triggered by the minor swing chart will be in the direction of the main trend. Protective stops are placed over the main tops for the main trend shorts and over the minor tops for the minor trend shorts. A variation of this technique is to place all of the stops over the main trend top.

This is an aggressive trading style and should be initiated at an extremely high or historically high price level. This type of trading resembles an inverted pyramid because it will be large at the top and smaller at the bottom, as the trader has the option of liquidating positions as the market is moving lower.

Pyramid Selling Using a Combination of the Intermediate Trend Indicator and the Main Trend Indicator.

The fourth way to enter the market is to begin the position when the market crosses the last main swing bottom. Additional positions are added to the short position using the intermediate or two-day swing chart. All trades triggered by the intermediate swing chart will be in the direction of the main trend. Protective stops are placed over the main tops for the main trend shorts and over the intermediate tops for the intermediate trend shorts. A variation of this technique is to place all of the stops over the main top.

This is an aggressive trading style and should be initiated at an extremely high or historically high price level. This type of trading resembles an inverted pyramid because it will be large at the top and smaller at the bottom, as the trader has the option of liquidating positions as the market moves lower.

The Inverted Sell Pyramid

Depending on how aggressive the trader is, and how confident he is in his analysis of the market to determine if it is at an extreme level, he can begin his position with what is known as an inverted pyramid.

A true pyramid is triggered by a long signal and is characterized by a large position near the bottom and a smaller position near the top. An inverted pyramid is triggered by a short signal and is characterized by a large position near the top and a smaller position near the bottom. Traders using this method should be skilled at calculating support so they can successfully liquidate positions at appropriate price levels.

These support points can be various combinations of former intermediate bottoms, especially if the rally began after a sharp rally. Additional profit objectives are percentage retracement points and Gann angles from previous bottoms, if determinable. These additional support points are discussed in later chapters.

SWING CHART NEGATIVES

The Whipsaw Market

The biggest negative factor affecting the swing chart trader is the whipsaw market. A *whipsaw* is a series of false changes in trend characterized by rallies and breaks that do not follow through to the upside or downside and change direction after one or two bars following the last change in trend.

In order to prevent this from happening filters can be built. Such a filter can be as simple as increasing the size of the stop placement above a top or below a bottom. This would require that the market make a minimum price move before you shift the trend line indicator or change the minor trend indicator from one day to two or three days.

Filters have to consider the price level at which the market is currently trading. High price levels, for example, need wider stops above swing tops because of greater volatility and wider ranges. At low price levels, ranges tend to be more narrow and volatility is not as great.

Lost Motion

When researching filters to use with swing charts, the trader will encounter a concept Gann referred to as "lost motion." *Lost motion* (Figure 8.18) can best be defined as the amount of penetration a market allows above a swing top without changing the trend to up, or below a swing bottom without changing the trend to down.

As we said in the generic examples of how the swing chart operates, you should buy when the market crosses a swing top and sell when the market crosses a swing bottom. The word "crosses," however, was not defined. This is because each market has its own lost-motion figure (Figure 8.19).

In the soybean market, for example, a swing top is often crossed by between 3 and 5 cents before the market turns down and resumes the downtrend. This means that stops placed 1–3 cents over a swing top can get caught without continuing higher (Figure 8-20).

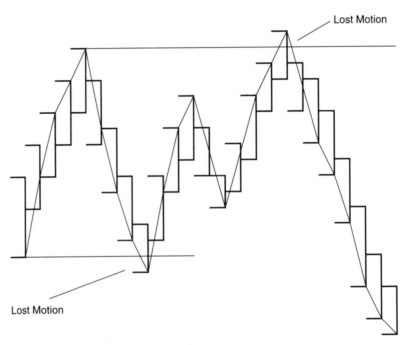

Figure 8.18   Lost motion on a swing chart.

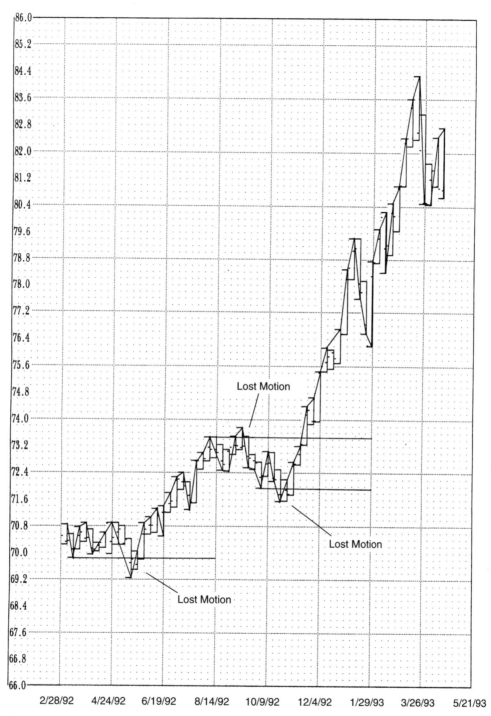

Figure 8.19   Lost motion minor swing chart. Lost motion occurs more often on a minor swing chart because of the frequency of the swings.

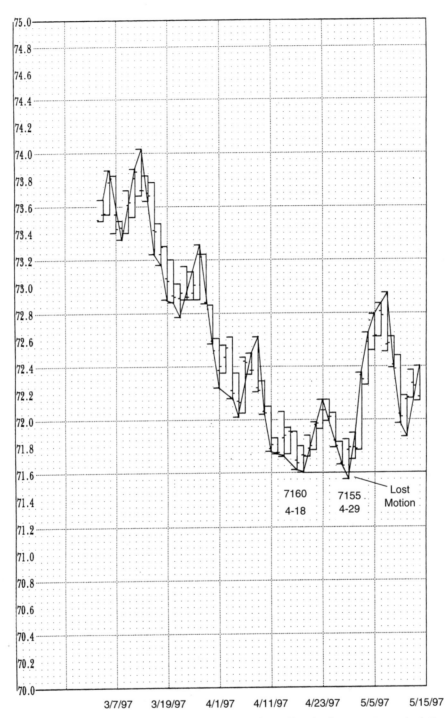

Figure 8.20   Lost motion intermediate swing chart. For the lost motion calculation, subtract the second bottom from the first bottom: 7160 − 7155 = 5 points.

The same is true for a stop placed under swing bottoms. At times the market will take out a swing bottom by as much as 5 cents before turning around and resuming the main uptrend.

It is important that the trader record the occurrences of lost motion so that she can strategically place stops that when hit will change the trend to up or down. This can be accomplished by keeping accurate charts of this "false breakout." Mark on the chart when failed breakouts occurred. They are most likely to show up near extreme tops and extreme bottoms. The analyst should note that these figures can be kept historically so that a large database of these phenomena can be developed and kept for reference. From these data, the analyst should be able to determine the maximum, minimum, and average of lost motion for each market.

In addition to the historical perspective, the chartist should keep a record of the lost motion unique to the current active chart. By charting the swings of a market from the first day of trading, the trader will have an accurate record of its lost motion before it becomes the actively traded contract.

Traders should also note the lost motion of a market at particular price levels. For example, the lost motion of a soybean market is much higher when a market is trading between $8.00 and $9.00 per bushel than it is when trading between $6.00 and $5.00 per bushel.

The concept of lost motion is very important because it occurs when using percentage retracements and Gann angles to find support and resistance. For instance, a market will often penetrate a 50% price or Gann angle, then recover and resume the trend. The lost motion discovered by studying the swing charts can often be used as a starting point when researching this phenomenon on a percentage retracement or Gann angle chart.

SUMMARY

This concludes our discussion of swing charts and how to use them to trade. The swing chart technique is a very important part of Gann analysis, as all of the other charts begin with the construction of the swing chart. In order to draw Gann angles properly you must have properly identified tops and bottoms. To find percentage retracement levels you must have identified tops and bottoms. Finally, in order to count time periods for cycles, you must have the proper starting points in the form of swing tops and swing bottoms.

9　Price

HORIZONTAL SUPPORT AND RESISTANCE

Gann used a number of methods to determine support and resistance. Using his methodology, he determined that support and resistance exist horizontally and diagonally. The horizontal support consists of swing tops, swing bottoms, and percentage retracement points. They are known as *horizontal* support and resistance points because when drawn on a chart, they extend far to the right. The swing chart support and resistance move on into infinity while the percentage levels remain intact as long as the market remains inside of the range that created them. Diagonal support and resistance, on the other hand, are created by Gann angles. The intersection of the two methods becomes a strong support or resistance level.

THE SWING CHARTS

In the chapters on the trend indicators, we learned how to build swing charts using the minor trend, the intermediate trend, and the main trend. On each of these charts, we identified tops and bottoms. As we move toward more advanced price and time studies, we will learn that these prices are not only important in the short term, but also extend out into infinity (Figure 9.1).

Swing Tops

After a market has posted a top, this top should be extended to the right on the chart. This is done by drawing a red line from the top out to the right. This line represents the top extended over time. As the market continues to trade, it may trade up to or over this line several times. The first time the market reaches this top, selling pressure should be expected. Watch for topping action in the form of a double-top formation or a signal top.

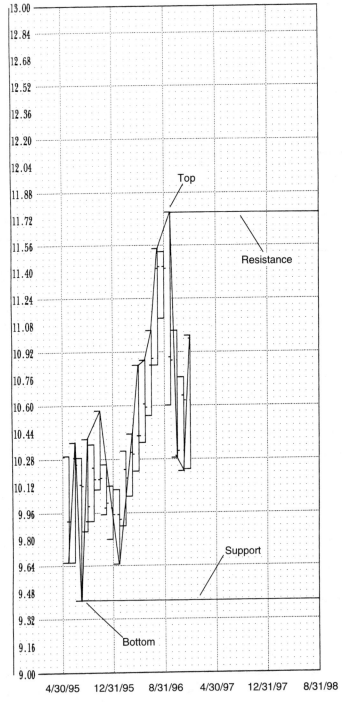

Figure 9.1   Swing charts identify support and resistance.

When the market crosses the top, the trend changes to up or continues the current trend. The top that is crossed now becomes a level to watch for bottoms. One of Gann's favorite rules was "old tops become new bottoms." This action is important to watch because often a market will cross a top, take out the stops, then return to the top. If it is a valid top formation, this old top should hold as a new bottom.

Each top is important to track because each is related to future tops. This is why tops should be extended into infinity (i.e., the future). Although it may be difficult to keep track of the minor tops, the intermediate and especially the main tops should be extended.

Swing Bottoms

After a market has posted a bottom, this bottom should be extended to the right on the chart. This is done by drawing a red line from the bottom out to the right. This line represents the bottom extended over time. As the market continues to trade, it may trade down to or under this line several times. The first time the market reaches this bottom, buying pressure should be expected. Watch for bottoming action in the form of a double-bottom formation or a signal bottom.

When the market crosses the bottom, the trend changes to down or continues the current trend. The bottom that is crossed now becomes a level to watch for tops. Another of Gann's favorite rules was "old bottoms become new tops." This action is important to watch because often a market will cross a bottom, take out the stops, then return to the bottom. If it is a valid bottom formation, this old bottom should hold as a new top.

Each bottom is important to track because each is related to future bottoms. This is why bottoms should be extended into infinity. Although it may be difficult to keep track of the minor bottoms, the intermediate and especially the main bottoms should be extended into the future.

Besides determining future tops and bottoms, the swing charts are used to forecast future price action by following the swings of the market. In order to determine possible future price direction, keep a record of the size of the rallies. It is important to study the past upswings so that future upswings can be forecast. Conversely, keep a record of the previous downswings to forecast future downswings.

Constructing the swing chart is the first step to price and time analysis, because it sets in motion all of the other technical analysis tools. Together a swing bottom and a swing top form a trading range. This range contains key support and resistance points that must be determined for successful trading. In the next two sections of this chapter, we look at those important support and resistance points. The first section describes how to draw and interpret the Gann angles, while the second section describes how to calculate and interpret the percentage retracement levels.

GANN ANGLES

This section of Gann theory is probably the most popular, as many traders use Gann angles in their personal trading and forecasting. These angles are often compared to trend lines when in fact they are not. A Gann angle is a diagonal line that moves at a uniform rate of speed. A trend line is created by connecting bottoms to bottoms in the case of an uptrend and tops to tops in the case of a downtrend (Figure 9.2).

When creating Gann angle charts, the swing charts once again become significant, as the swing top is the origin of the downtrending angles and the swing bottom is the origin of the uptrending angles. All three trend indicator charts can be used to determine the placement of the angles, but as in swing-chart trading, too many angles can confuse the trader. Because of this, Gann angles originating from minor tops and minor bottoms are discouraged, as the frequency of the angles creates an almost spiderweb-like appearance. This can lead to a condition called *analysis paralysis*, wherein the analyst is literally kept from making a move in the market because the enormous number of angles masks the support and resistance prices.

The best charts from which to place Gann angles are the intermediate trend chart and the main trend chart, the optimal one being the intermediate chart, as it provides just the right number of angles from which to determine and forecast support and resistance. Angles drawn from the main trend indicator chart are also important, but occur less often. They are strong because they are an extension of the strong bottoms and tops, but their infrequency on this chart often forces the trader to take unnecessary risks.

Importance of Gann Angles

There are basically 18 geometric forms to explain the angle theory (see Figures 9.3–9.21). These forms tend to repeat more often than others, and are considered important because they have withstood the test of time.

1. Square of the range from a low price
2. Square of the range from a high price
3. Strong-position bull market above a 1×1 angle
4. Weak-position bull market below a 1×1 angle
5. Strong-position bear market below a 1×1 angle

Figure 9.2   Uptrending Gann angle chart of 1997 weekly July sugar.

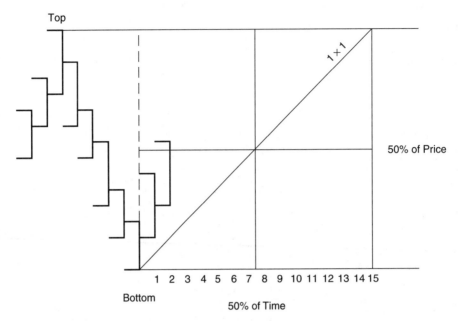

Figure 9.3 Square of the range from a low price. The intersection of the Gann angle and 50% of price forms a major support.

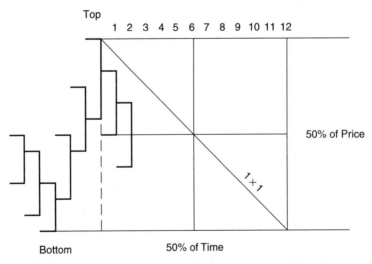

Figure 9.4 Square of the range from a high price. The intersection of the Gann angle and 50% of price forms a major resistance.

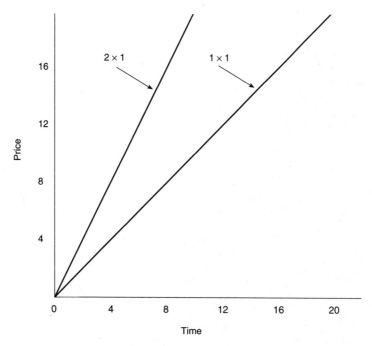

Figure 9.5   Strong-position bull market above a 1×1 angle.

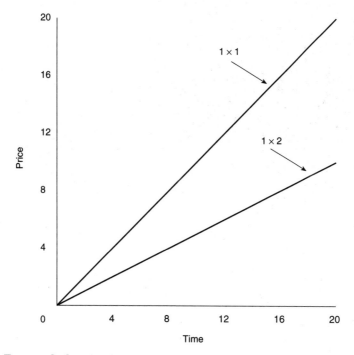

Figure 9.6   Weak-position bull market below a 1×1 angle.

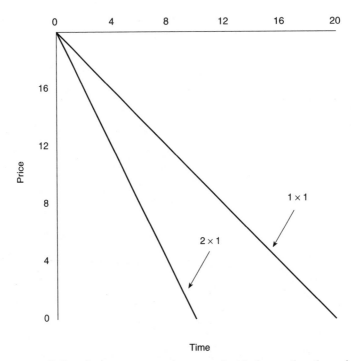

Figure 9.7   Strong-position bear market below a 1 × 1 angle.

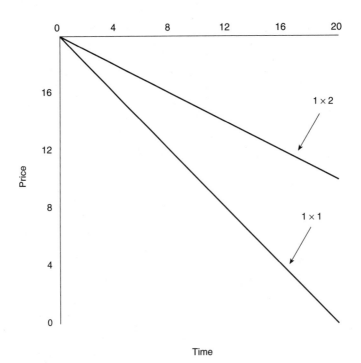

Figure 9.8   Weak-position bear market above a 1 × 1 angle.

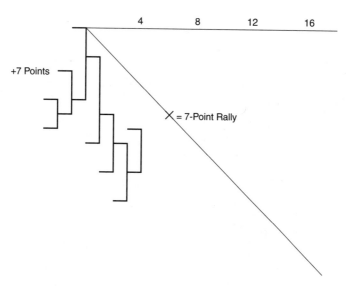

Figure 9.9   Swing chart and angles from a top. Use swing charts and angles to forecast price action. Note that here a combination of the swing-chart target and the Gann angle forms support.

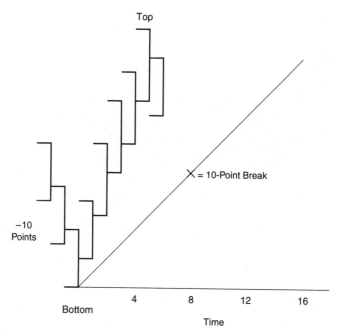

Figure 9.10   Swing chart and angles from a bottom. Look for a swing-chart target to balance on a Gann angle. Note here the combination of the swing-chart target and Gann angle.

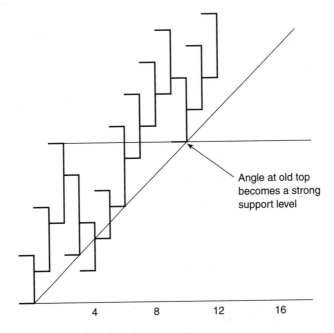

Figure 9.11   Angle at old top, new support.

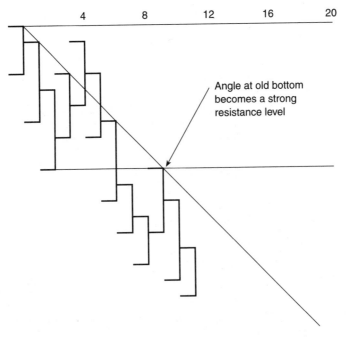

Figure 9.12   Angle at old bottom, new resistance.

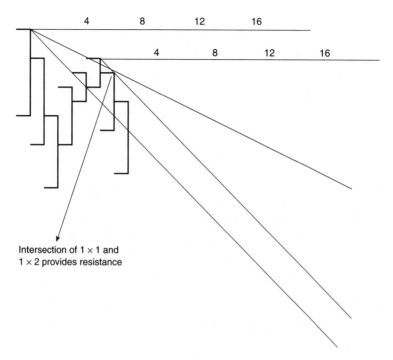

Figure 9.13   Angles from double tops.

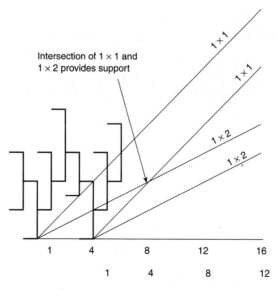

Figure 9.14   Angles from double bottoms.

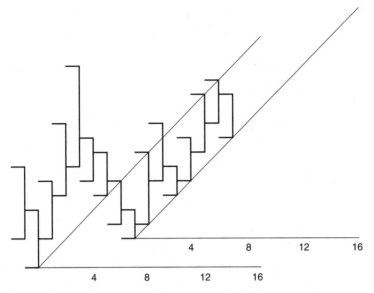

Figure 9.15   Uptrending channel from a double bottom. Double bottoms form uptrending channels that guide the markets higher.

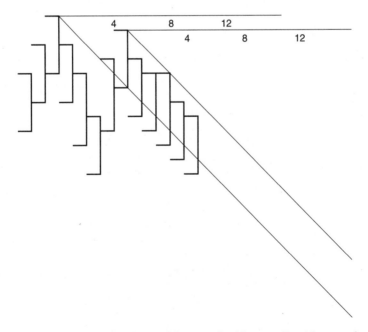

Figure 9.16   Downtrending channel from a double top. Double tops form downtrending channels that guide the market lower.

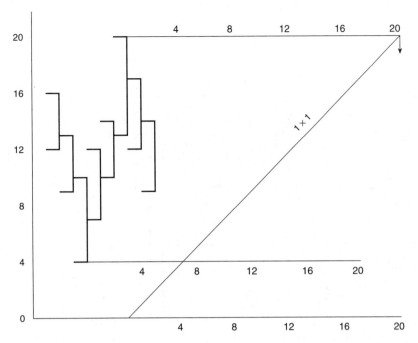

Figure 9.17   Zero angle from a high price. The high price squares time when the angle from 0 reaches the high price.

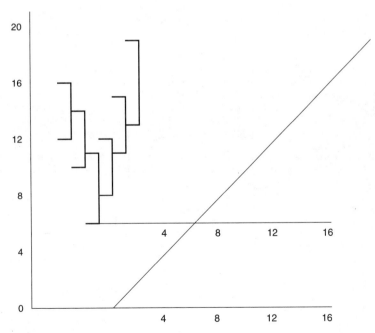

Figure 9.18   Zero angle from a low price. The low price squares time when the angle from 0 reaches the low price.

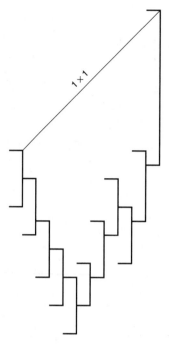

Figure 9.19 Angle from a top forecasts a future top. A 1 × 1 angle drawn up from a top can forecast a future top.

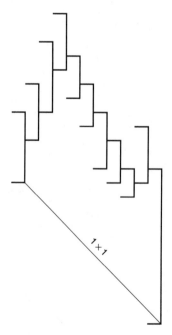

Figure 9.20 Angle from a bottom forecasts a future bottom. A 1 × 1 angle drawn down from a bottom can forecast a future bottom.

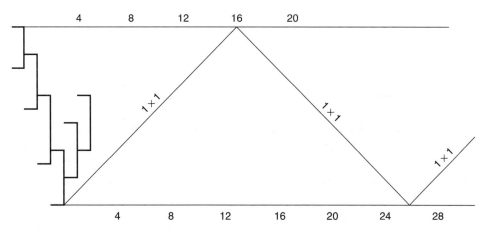

Figure 9.21 Angles repeat as long as the market remains inside the range.

   6. Weak-position bear market above a 1×1 angle
   7. Swing chart and angles from a top
   8. Swing chart and angles from a bottom
   9. Angle at old top, new support
  10. Angle at old bottom, new resistance
  11. Angles from double tops
  12. Angles from double bottoms
  13. Uptrending channel from a double bottom
  14. Downtrending channel from a double top
  15. Zero angle from a high price
  16. Zero angle from a low price
  17. Angle from a top forecasts a future top
  18. Angle from a bottom forecasts a future bottom
  19. Angles repeat as long as the market remains inside the range

The basic premise behind Gann angles is as follows: If you know the angles that are likely to forecast tops and bottoms many weeks and months ahead of the actual event, you will then be able to trade more successfully. This is because the geometric angles accurately forecast tops and bottoms. The important items to remember before you try this method are:

- Each commodity is unique. You will be required to study and practice using the angles for each market you are going to trade in order to determine its characteristics. Learn to select the scale that is applicable to each commodity. Arbitrarily selecting any scale will throw the whole chart off.
- The markets are geometric in their design and function. Every point on the chart is geometrically aligned to some other point on the chart. Therefore, the market will obey geometric laws measured by geometric angles.

- Weekly charts are by far the most useful for forecasting, then monthly charts, while the daily charts are best for volatile, active markets.

How to Construct Gann Angle Charts

As mentioned earlier, in order to build a Gann angle chart, the trader must have already built a trend indicator chart. In this section, we will primarily use the intermediate trend indicator chart. This is because the best Gann angle charts are built when following the two-period swings in the market.

Scale

Gann angles move at uniform rates of speed, which makes Gann angle charts sensitive to price scale. A properly constructed chart must be made with the proper scale in order to have any value. As we said earlier, each market has its own unique price scale, and the markets are geometric in design and function. Thus, they will follow geometric laws when charted.

A study of the charts and manuscripts of W. D. Gann shows that he chose a price scale that agreed with a geometric design or formula. When the markets were trading at lower levels, a smaller unit of price was used. When trading at higher levels, a larger unit of price was used.

One rule to remember is, choose a price scale that follows a geometric progression and is in direct relation to the level of the price. If this is practiced, geometric angles will measure price and time in an accurate manner. Price units for daily, weekly, or monthly charts that follow a geometric design can be one of the following:

1–2–4
1–4–8
2–4–8
4–8–16
1/8–1/4–1/2
0.10–0.20–0.40
0.20–0.40–0.80
0.125–0.25–0.50
0.25–0.50–1
4/32–8/32–16/32

It must be remembered that Gann used an eight-squares-to-the-inch paper with each fourth line accented as his only charting medium from 1904 until his death in 1955. He chose this chart paper because of its geometric design.

Other papers based on 5 and 10 lines are not acceptable. The Ganntrader 2 software program is also programmed around this specific geometric law.

Gann angles are a function of price and time, which is why the price scale is so important. Since the angles move at a uniform rate of speed, they have predictive value. This is another reason why the proper scale has to be used—if the scale is off, then the prediction will be off.

Table 9.1 lists the price scales that are the best for each futures market. These price scales should be used when building Gann-style charts. They have been tested and have yielded accurate results. Study and practice with these scales to see if they suit your trading style. If you want to develop your own scales, then study the two following subsections.

How to Determine the Scale for Markets Not Listed. The easiest way to determine the scale of a market is by taking the difference between top-to-top and bottom-to-bottom and dividing it by the time it took the market to

Table 9.1 Optimum Price Scales

Market	Day	Week	Month
Corn	1 cent	2 cents	4 cents
Soybeans	2 cents	4 cents	8 cents
Wheat	1 cent	2 cents	4 cents
Oats	1 cent	2 cents	4 cents
Bean oil	10 points	20 points	40 points
Soy meal	50 points	100 points	200 points
Live cattle	10 points	20 points	40 points
Live hogs	10 points	20 points	40 points
Pork bellies	50 points	100 points	200 points
Cocoa	5 points	10 points	20 points
Sugar	4 points	8 points	16 points
Coffee	50 points	100 points	200 points
Orange juice	50 points	100 points	200 points
Cotton	25 points	50 points	100 points
Crude oil	10 points	20 points	40 points
Heating oil	25 points	50 points	100 points
Unleaded gas	25 points	50 points	100 points
Gold	1 dollar	2 dollars	4 dollars
Silver	1 cent	2 cents	4 cents
Platinum	1 dollar	2 dollars	4 dollars
Copper	25 points	50 points	100 points
Treasury bonds	$4/32$nds	$8/32$nds	$16/32$nds
S&P 500	80 points	160 points	320 points
Eurodollars	2 points	4 points	8 points

move from top-to-top and bottom-to-bottom. This equation yields the speed of the uptrend and downtrend lines. For example, if the difference between top-to-top and bottom-to-bottom is 50 and the time is 27 days, then the speed of the trend line connecting these two points is 1.85. The average speed of the trend line can be determined by making this calculation several times. After determining the average speed of the trend line, round it to the next whole number. In this example, if the average uptrend line moves 1.95 per day, then assume the Gann scale is 2. This approach should only be used for markets not on the scale list in Table 9.1.

Equation to Determine the Proper Scale of a Market. The distance between two main bottoms divided by the time between the main bottoms equals the speed or scale of the angle. This same formula can be applied to the distance between two main tops. Once a series of scales has been determined, the trader can determine the average scale and round off to the nearest whole number.

$$\text{Uptrending Scale} = \frac{\text{Main Bottom 2} - \text{Main Bottom 1}}{\text{Difference in Time Between Bottoms}}$$

$$\text{Downtrending Scale} = \frac{\text{Main Top 1} - \text{Main Top 2}}{\text{Difference in Time Between Tops}}$$

Example 1: 1997 Daily July Soybeans
    Main bottom February 7, 1997 at 7.28½. Main bottom April 15, 1997 at 8.25. The difference in time is 45 market days.

$$\frac{8.25 - 7.28\frac{1}{2}}{45 \text{ days}} = \frac{96\frac{1}{2} \text{ cents}}{45 \text{ days}} = 2.14 \text{ cents/day}$$

This is close to the suggested daily scale of 2 cents per day.

Example 2: 1997 Daily June Canadian Dollar
    Main top January 22, 1997 at 7568. Main top March 13, 1997 at 7403. The difference in time is 36 market days.

$$\frac{7568 - 7403}{36 \text{ days}} = \frac{165 \text{ points}}{36 \text{ days}} = 4.58 \text{ points/day}$$

This is close to the suggested daily scale of 5 points per day (Figure 9.22).

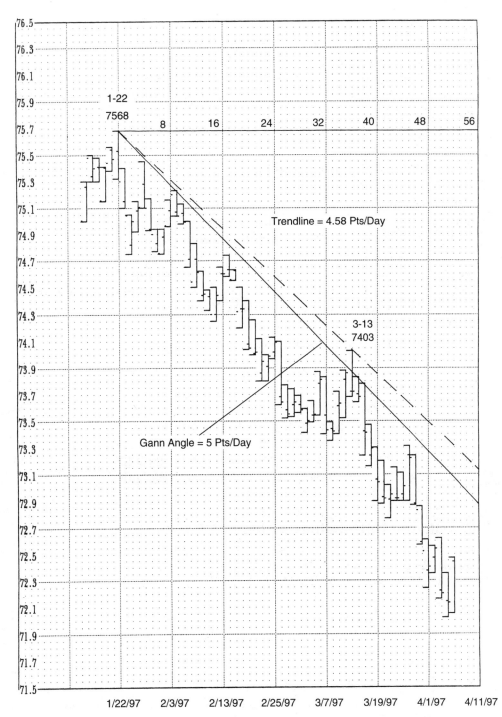

Figure 9.22   Example: 1997 daily June Canadian dollar chart.

If the bottom-to-bottom and top-to-top data suggested in the chapters on the trend indicator has been maintained, then sufficient information is available to research and analyze the scale of a market properly.

To experiment with the scale, it is necessary to be willing to build a number of charts. The easiest way to determine the proper scale of a market is to use mathematics.

Calculating the Gann Angles

Gann angles are very easy to construct. Since they are a function of price and time, all that is needed to draw them properly are a properly constructed chart, a green pen, a red pen, a calculator, and a ruler.

A properly constructed chart is one that was charted to scale by market day only. Holidays and weekends cannot be included on this chart because there is no price activity during these periods. Each grid has a point value, so using blank grids will throw off the angle, that is, an angle may be higher or lower than expected.

The basic equation for calculating Gann angles is

$$Price \times Time$$

Knowing basic algebra helps us calculate either price or time when given two variables. If we know the correct scale and are given a base price and a future price, we can predict when the market will most likely trade this price. If we know the scale to use and are given a base price and a future date, we can predict where the angle will be during that given time period.

Calculating Uptrending Angles

Gann Angles from an Intermediate Bottom
Strong Market on the Bull Side of the 1 × 1 Angle

First Important Angle: 1 × 1

The first and most important angle to draw is the 1 × 1 angle, which consists of one unit of price for one unit of time.

> Step 1: On a properly constructed chart use your red pen to draw a line from the main bottom across to the right. This line can be extended to the end of the chart. Count and number the bars from the main bottom to the end of the chart. It is easiest to count by 4.

Step 2: From the intermediate bottom, prepare to draw the 1 × 1 angle.

The basic formula is scale multiplied by time plus the main bottom.

Example: 1997 Daily June Live Cattle market. Scale is 10 points per day. Intermediate bottom is 6300 on April 8, 1997.

From the 6300 intermediate bottom on April 8, 1997, draw a line with the red pen to the right. Extend the line until the contract expiration.

Count the number of market days from April 8, 1997. Identify every fourth or eighth day on the chart (Figure 9.23).

Since the contract expires on June 20, 1997, the distance in time from the bottom on April 8, 1997 is 52 market days.

Since the scale is 10 points per market day, 52 market days times 10 points per market day equals 520 points.

Add this figure to the intermediate bottom. In this case, 6300 plus 520 points places the 1 × 1 Gann angle at 6820. Take the green pen and draw a 1 × 1 angle from the bottom at 6300 to 6820.

Each day this angle is at an exact point on the chart. For example, May 9, 1997 is 23 market days from the intermediate bottom at 6300. The 1 × 1 angle from the 6300 bottom on May 9, 1997 is at 6530 (Figure 9.24).

Alternative Method of Calculating the 1 × 1 Angle or Determining Price

If the intermediate bottom and scale are known, it is possible to estimate the date on which the market is likely to trade a specific price. Using the 1997 June Live Cattle market, we know the intermediate bottom is at 6300. The question is, "Based on the current scale and using the 1 × 1 angle, when is the market most likely to trade 6582?" (Figure 9.25).

The question is *easy* to answer. Simply subtract the intermediate bottom from the target price and divide by the scale. This will give you the market day on which the 1 × 1 angle will cross this price. Look for the market day on the chart and find the date associated with it. This does not mean the market will be trading at this price on this date. It just means that if the market follows the 1 × 1 angle, then at a minimum it will be at that price.

Solution

$$6582 - 6300 = 282$$
$$282 \div 10 \text{ points} = 28.2$$

The answer, 28.2 market days, is associated with May 16, 1997.

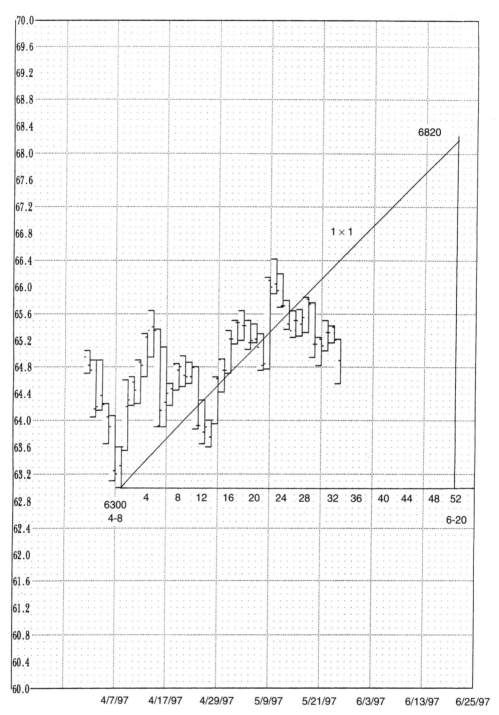

Figure 9.23   Calculating uptrending angles: preparing to draw the 1×1 angle by identifying every fourth or eighth day on the chart.

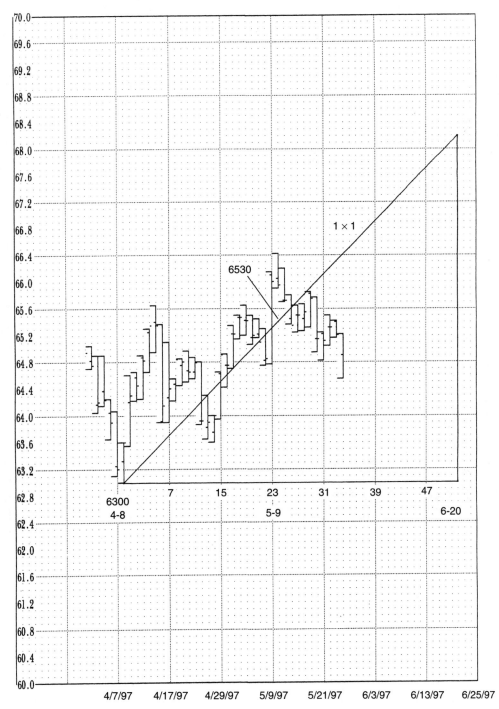

Figure 9.24   Calculating uptrending angles: marking the 1 × 1 angle for a specific date.

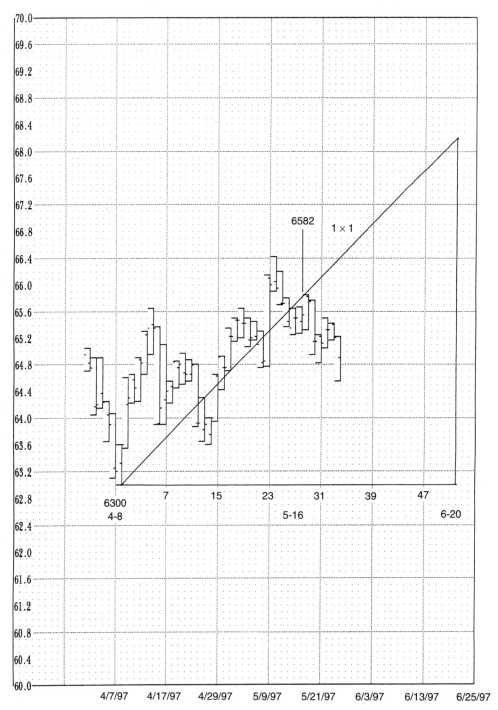

Figure 9.25 Alternative method of calculating the 1 × 1 angle.

Gann Angles from an Intermediate Bottom
Strong Market on the Bull Side of the 1 × 1 Angle

Second Important Angle: 2 × 1

The second angle to draw is the 2 × 1 angle, which consists of two units of price for one unit of time.

> Step 1: Having placed the 1 × 1 angle on the chart, add the 2 × 1 angle to the chart.
> Step 2: From the intermediate bottom, prepare to draw the 2 × 1 angle.

The basic formula is scale multiplied by time plus the intermediate bottom.

Example: 1997 Daily June Live Cattle market. Scale is 10 points per day. Intermediate bottom is 6300 on April 8, 1997.

> From the 6300 intermediate bottom on April 8, 1997, count the number of market days from April 8, 1997. Identify every fourth or eighth day on the chart (Figure 9.26).
> In this example, the 15th market day from the top has been chosen as a reference point.
> Since the scale is 10 points per market day, 15 market days times 10 points per market day equals 150 points. (Up to this point, this is the same calculation as for the 1 × 1 angle.) Multiply 150 by 2 because you are looking for an angle moving twice as fast as the 1 × 1. This yields a figure of 300 points.
> Add this figure to the intermediate bottom. In this case, 6300 plus 300 points places the 2 × 1 Gann angle at 6600. Take the red pen and draw a 2 × 1 angle from the bottom at 6300 to 6600.
> Each day this angle is at an exact point on the chart. For example, May 9, 1997 is 23 market days from the intermediate bottom at 6300. The 2 × 1 angle from the 6300 bottom on May 9, 1997 is at 6760 (Figure 9.27).

Alternative Method of Calculating the 2 × 1 Angle
or Determining Price

If the intermediate bottom and scale are known, it is possible to estimate the date on which the market is likely to trade a specific price. Using the 1997 June Live Cattle market, we know the intermediate bottom is at 6300. The question is, "Based on the current scale and using the 2 × 1 angle, when is the market most likely to trade 6582?"

The question is easy to answer. Simply subtract the intermediate bottom from the target price and divide by the scale. Take this figure and divide by 2

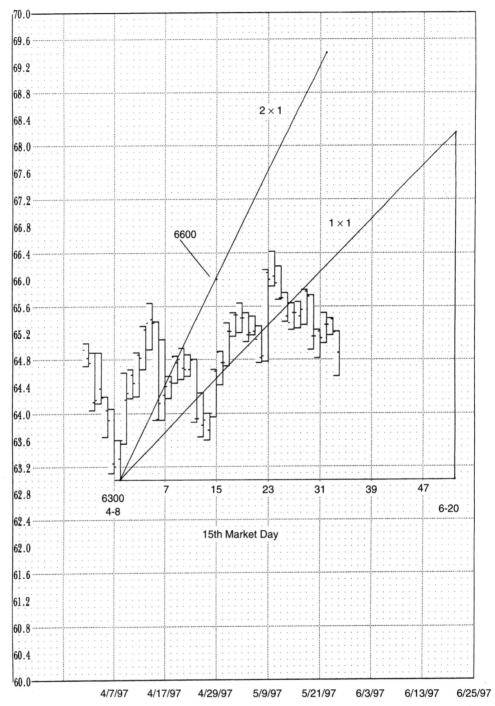

Figure 9.26 Calculating Gann angles from an intermediate bottom: 2 × 1.

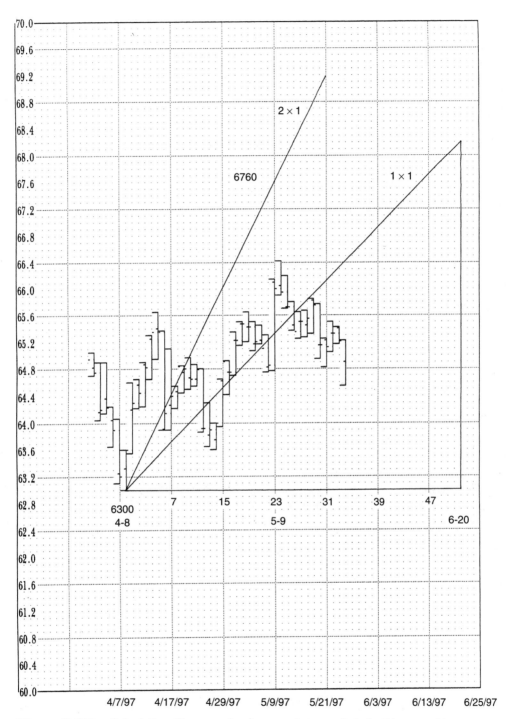

Figure 9.27   Calculating Gann angles from an intermediate bottom: marking the 2 × 1 angle for a specific date.

to get the 2×1 angle. This will give you the market day on which the 2×1 angle will cross this price. Look for the market day on the chart and find the date associated with it (Figure 9.28). This does not mean the market will be trading at this price on this date. It just means that if the market follows the 2×1 angle, then at a minimum it will be at that price.

Solution

$$6582 - 6300 = 282$$
$$282 \div 10 \text{ points} = 28.2$$
$$28.2 \div 2 = 14.1$$

The answer, 14.1 market days, is associated with April 28, 1997.

Gann Angles from an Intermediate Bottom
Strong Market on the Bull Side of the 1×1 Angle

Third Important Angle: 1×2

The third angle to draw is the 1×2 angle, which consists of one unit of price for two units of time.

Step 1: Having placed the 1×1 angle on the chart, add the 1×2 angle to the chart.
Step 2: From the intermediate bottom, prepare to draw the 1×2 angle.

The basic formula is scale multiplied by time plus the intermediate bottom.

Example: 1997 Daily June Live Cattle market. Scale is 10 points per day. Main bottom is 6300 on April 8, 1997.

From the 6300 intermediate bottom on April 8, 1997, count the number of market days from April 8, 1997. Identify every fourth or eighth day on the chart (Figure 9.29).
Since the contract expires on June 20, 1997, the distance in time from the bottom on April 8, 1997 is 52 market days.
Since the scale is 10 points per market day, 52 market days times 10 points per market day equals 520 points. (Up to this point, this is the same calculation as for the 1×1 angle.) Divide 520 by 2 because you are looking for an angle moving half as fast as the 1×1. This yields a figure of 260 points.
Add this figure to the intermediate bottom. In this case, 6300 plus 260 points places the 1×2 Gann angle at 6560. Take the red pen and draw a 1×2 angle from the bottom at 6300 to 6560.

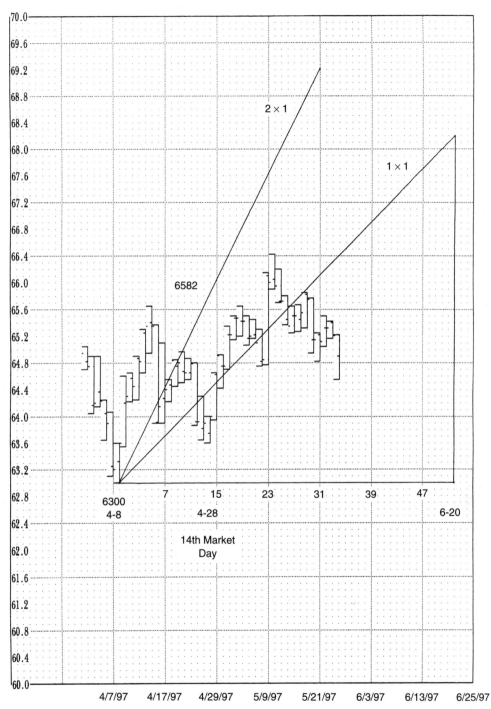

Figure 9.28   Alternative method of calculating the 2 × 1 angle.

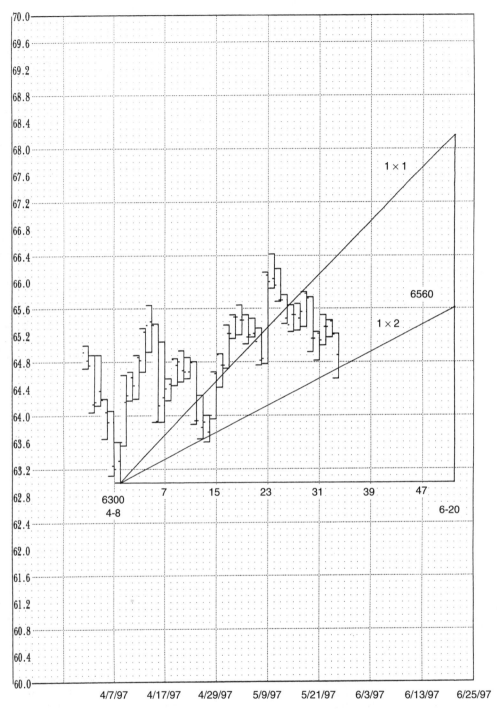

Figure 9.29   Calculating Gann angles from an intermediate bottom: 1 × 2.

Each day this angle is at an exact point on the chart. For example, May 9, 1997 is 23 market days from the intermediate bottom at 6300. The 1 × 2 angle from the 6300 bottom on May 9, 1997 is at 6415.

Alternative Method of Calculating the 1 × 2 Angle or Determining Price

If the intermediate bottom and scale are known, it is possible to estimate the date on which the market is likely to trade a specific price. Using the 1997 June Live Cattle market, we know the intermediate bottom is at 6300. The question is, "Based on the current scale and using the 1 × 2 angle, when is the market most likely to trade 6440?" (Figure 9.30).

The question is easy to answer. Simply subtract the intermediate bottom from the target price and divide by the scale. Take this figure and multiply by 2 to get the 1 × 2 angle. This will give you the market day on which the 1 × 2 angle will cross this price. Look for the market day on the chart and find the date associated with it. This does not mean the market will be trading at this price on this date. It just means that if the market follows the 1 × 2 angle, then at a minimum it will be at that price.

Solution

$$6440 - 6300 = 140$$
$$140 \div 10 \text{ points} = 14.$$
$$14 \times 2 = 28$$

The answer, 28 market days, is associated with May 16, 1997.

Calculating Downtrending Angles

Gann Angles form an Intermediate Top
Strong Market on the Bear Side of the 1 × 1 Angle

First Important Angle: 1 × 1

The first and most important angle to draw is the 1 × 1 angle, which consists of one unit of price for one unit of time.

Step 1: On a properly constructed chart use your red pen to draw a line from the intermediate top across to the right. This line can be extended to the end of the chart. Count and number the bars from the intermediate bottom to the end of the chart. It is easiest to count by 4.

Step 2: From the intermediate top, prepare to draw the 1 × 1 angle.

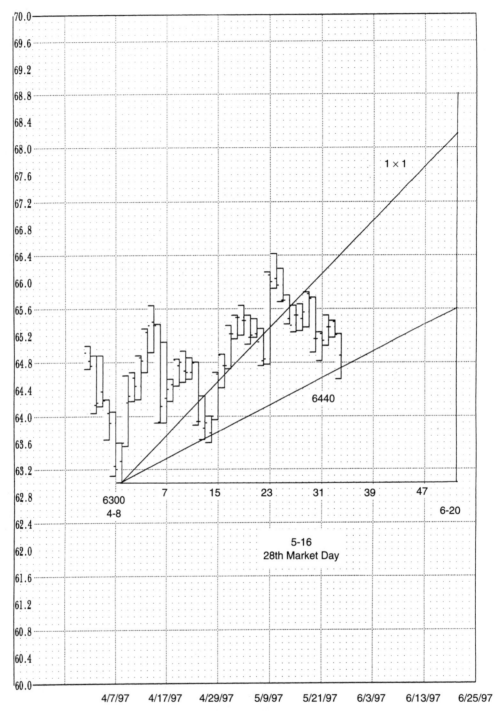

Figure 9.30   Alternative method of calculating the 1 × 2 angle.

The basic formula is the intermediate top minus the time multiplied by the scale.

Example: 1997 Daily July Silver market. Scale is 1 point per day. Intermediate top is 493 on May 12, 1997.

From the 493 intermediate top on May 12, 1997, draw a line with the red pen to the right. Extend the line until, for example, the first delivery day.

Count the number of market days from May 12, 1997. Identify every fourth or eighth day on the chart.

Since the first delivery day is July 1, 1997, the distance in time from the top on May 12, 1997 is 35 market days (Figure 9.31).

Since the scale is 1 cent per market day, 35 market days times 1 cent per market day equals 35 cents.

Subtract this figure from the main top. In this case, 493 minus 35 cents places the 1×1 Gann angle at 458. Take the green pen and draw a 1×1 angle from the top down to 458.

Each day this angle is at an exact point on the chart. For example, June 10 is 20 market days from the intermediate top at 493. The 1×1 angle from the 493 top on May 12, 1997 is at 473 (Figure 9.32).

Alternative Method of Calculating the 1×1 Angle or Determining Price

If the intermediate top and scale are known, it is possible to estimate the date on which the market is likely to trade a specific price. Using the 1997 July Silver market, we know the intermediate top is at 463. The question is, "Based on the current scale and using the 1×1 angle, when is the market most likely to trade 463?" (Figure 9.33).

The question is easy to answer. Simply subtract the target price from the intermediate top and divide by the scale. This will give you the market day on which the 1×1 angle will cross this price. Look for the market day on the chart and find the date associated with it. This does not mean the market will be trading at this price on this date. It just means that if the market follows the 1×1 angle, then at a minimum it will be at that price.

Solution

$$493 - 463 = 30$$
$$30 \div 1 \text{ cent} = 30$$

The answer, 30 market days, is associated with June 24, 1997.

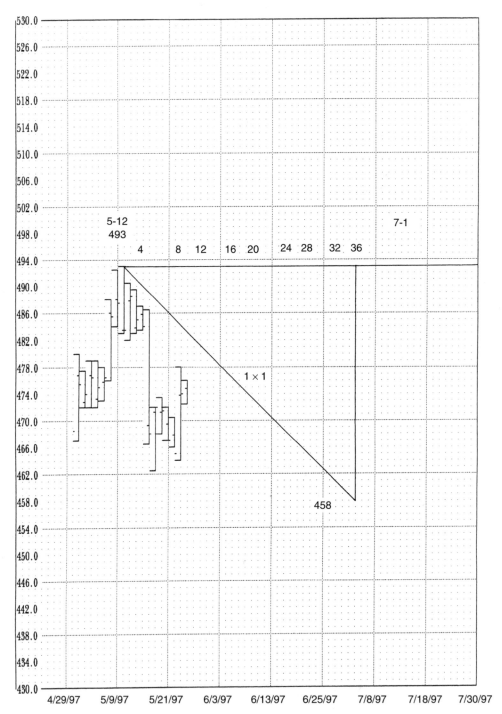

Figure 9.31   Calculating downtrending angles: preparing to draw the 1 × 1 angle by identifying every fourth or eighth day on the chart.

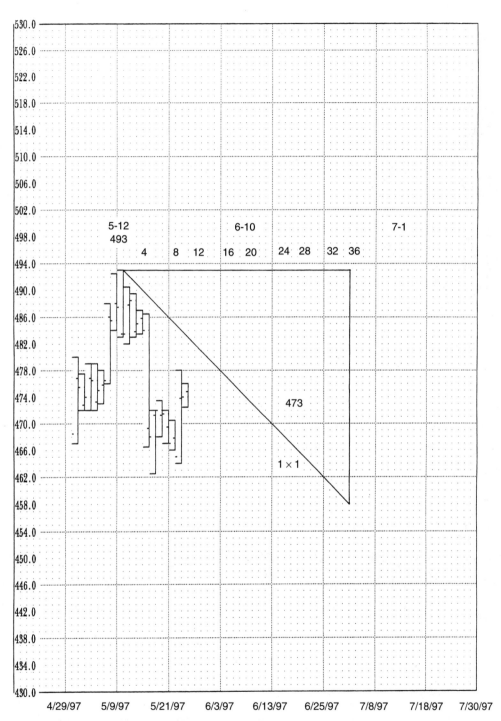

Figure 9.32 Calculating downtrending angles: marking the 1 × 1 angle for a specific date.

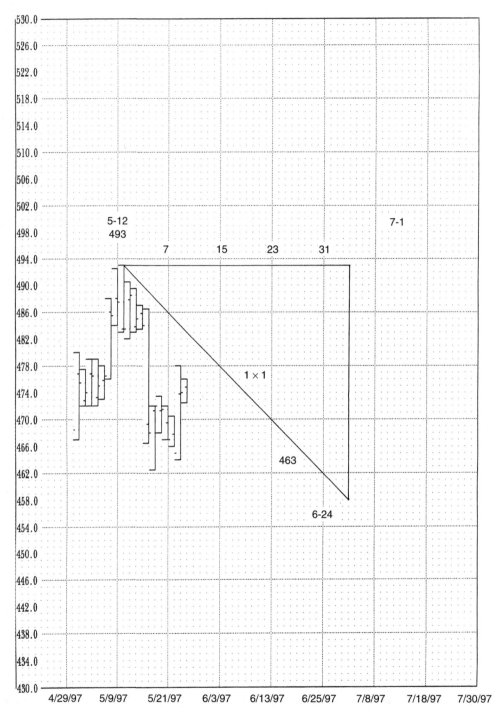

Figure 9.33   Alternative method of calculating the 1 × 1 angle.

Gann Angles from an Intermediate Top
Strong Market on the Bear Side of the 1 × 1 Angle

Second Important Angle: 2 × 1

The second angle to draw is the 2 × 1 angle, which consists of two units of price for one unit of time.

> Step 1: Having placed the 1 × 1 angle on the chart, add the 2 × 1 angle to the chart.
> Step 2: From the intermediate top, prepare to draw the 2 × 1 angle.

The basic formula is the main top minus scale multiplied by time.

Example: 1997 Daily July Silver market. Scale is 1 cent per day. Intermediate top is 493 on May 12, 1997.

> From the 493 intermediate top on May 12, 1997, count the number of market days from May 12, 1997. Identify every fourth or eighth day on the chart.
> Since the first delivery day is July 1, 1997, the distance in time from the top on June 6, 1997 is 15 market days (Figure 9.34).
> Since the scale is 1 cent per market day, 15 market days times 1 cent per market day equals 15 cents. (Up to this point, this is the same calculation as for the 1 × 1 angle.) Multiply 15 by 2 because you are looking for an angle moving twice as fast as the 1 × 1. This yields a figure of 30 cents.
> Subtract this figure from the intermediate top. In this case, 493 minus 30 cents places the 2 × 1 Gann angle at 463. Take the red pen and draw a 2 × 1 angle from the top at 493 to 463.
> Each day this angle is at an exact point on the chart. For example, May 21, 1997 is seven market days from the intermediate top at 493. The 2 × 1 angle from the 493 top on May 12, 1997 is at 479.

Alternative Method of Calculating the 2 × 1 Angle
or Determining Price

If the intermediate top and scale are known, it is possible to estimate the date on which the market is likely to trade a specific price. Using the 1997 July Silver market, we know the intermediate top is at 493. The question is, "Based on the current scale and using the 2 × 1 angle, when is the market most likely to trade 463?" (Figure 9.35).

The question is easy to answer. Simply subtract the target price from the intermediate top and divide by the scale. Take this figure and divide by 2 to get the 2 × 1 angle. This will give you the market day on which the 2 × 1 angle

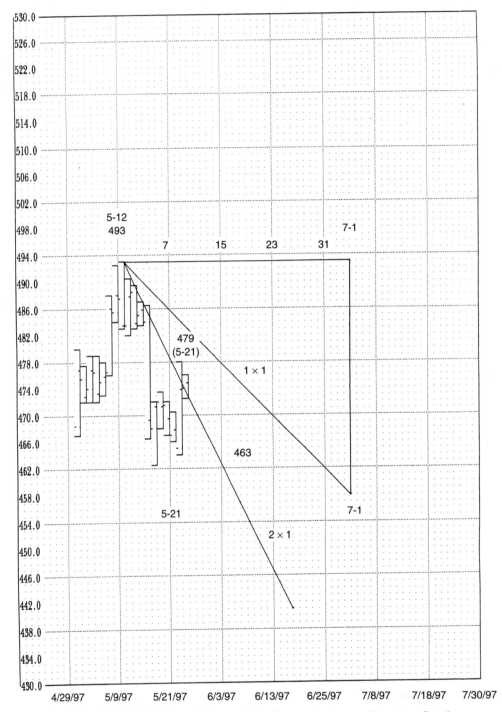

Figure 9.34   Calculating Gann angles from an intermediate top: 2×1.

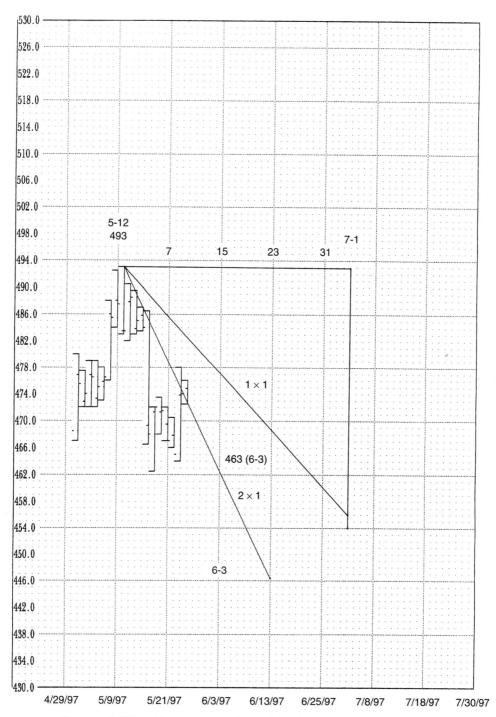

Figure 9.35   Alternative method of calculating the 2 × 1 angle.

will cross this price. Look for the market day on the chart and find the date associated with it. This does not mean the market will be trading at this price on this date. It just means that if the market follows the 2×1 angle, then at a minimum it will be at that price.

Solution

$$493 - 463 = 30$$
$$30 \div 1 \text{ point} = 30$$
$$30 \div 2 = 15$$

The answer, 15 market days, is associated with June 3, 1997.

Gann Angles from an Intermediate Top
Strong Market on the Bear Side of the 1×1 Angle

Third Important Angle: 1×2

The third angle to draw is the 1×2 angle, which consists of one unit of price for two units of time.

Step 1: Having placed the 1×1 angle on the chart, add the 1×2 angle on the chart.
Step 2: From the intermediate top, prepare to draw the 1×2 angle.

The basic formula is the intermediate top minus the scale multiplied by time.

Example: 1997 Daily July Silver market. Scale is 1 cent per day. Intermediate top is 493 on May 12, 1997.

From the 493 intermediate top on May 12, 1997, count the number of market days from May 12, 1997. Identify every fourth or eighth day on the chart.
Since the first delivery day is July 1, 1997, the distance in time from the top on July 1, 1997 is 35 market days (Figure 9.36).
Since the scale is 1 cent per market day, 35 market days times 1 cent per market day equals 35 cents. (Up to this point, this is the same calculation as for the 1×1 angle.) Divide 35 by 2 because you are looking for an angle moving half as fast as the 1×1. This yields a figure of 17.5 cents.
Subtract this figure from the intermediate bottom. In this case, 493 minus 17.5 cents places the 1×2 Gann angle at 475.5. Take the red pen and draw a 1×2 angle from the top at 493 to 475.5.
Each day this angle is at an exact point on the chart. For example, June 10, 1997 is 20 market days from the intermediate top at 493. The 1×2 angle from the 493 top on May 12, 1997 is at 483.

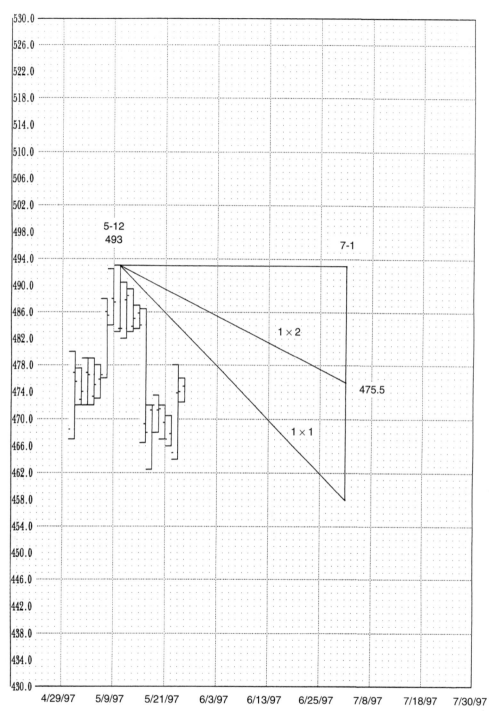

Figure 9.36   Calculating Gann angles from an intermediate top: 1 × 2.

Alternative Method of Calculating the 1 × 2 Angle or Determining Price

If the intermediate top and scale are known, it is possible to estimate the date on which the market is likely to trade a specific price. Using the 1997 July Silver market, we know the intermediate top is at 493. The question is, "Based on the current scale and using the 1 × 2 angle, when is the market most likely to trade 480?" (Figure 9.37).

The question is easy to answer. Simply subtract the target price from the intermediate top and divide by the scale. Take this figure and multiply by 2 to get the 1 × 2 angle. This will give you the market day on which the 1 × 2 angle will cross this price. Look for the market day on the chart and find the date associated with it. This does not mean the market will be trading at this price on this date. It just means that if the market follows the 1 × 2 angle, then at a minimum it will be at that price.

Solution

$$493 - 480 = 13$$
$$13 \div 1 \text{ cent} = 13$$
$$13 \times 2 = 26$$

The answer, 26 market days, is associated with June 18, 1997.

Using the same equations, you should also calculate the 8 × 1, 4 × 1, 1 × 4 and 1 × 8 angles if necessary.

Zero Angles

Angles coming up from price 0 are very important and can be easily utilized on the chart you are keeping. This works better with monthly and weekly charts than with daily charts because the time periods are longer. Unless you are working with a daily chart with two or three years worth of data, the 0 angle may never have enough time to become effective.

Example: If you have an important low at 100 and want to bring all of your important angles up from 0 at the time the 100 was made, simply count over to the right 100 squares of time from the actual 100 bottom and start a 1 × 1 angle upward from 0. You can also count 50 squares for your 2 × 1 angle and 200 for your 1 × 2 angle. Of course, this is if your scale is on the basis of one point. If the scale is something else, you must count accordingly.

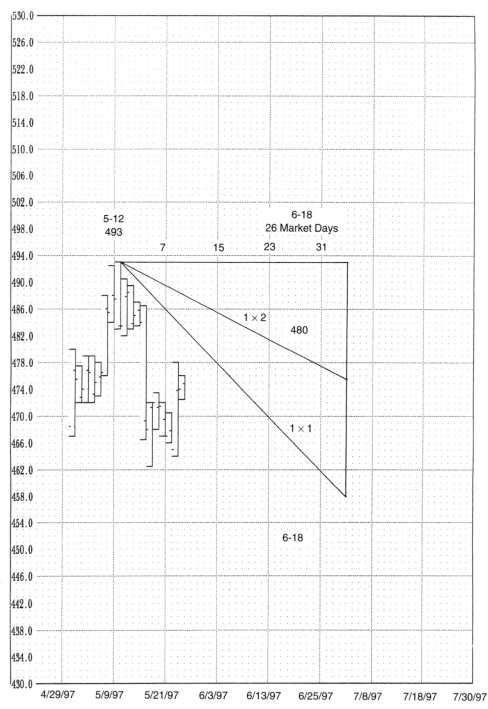

Figure 9.37   Alternative method of calculating the 1 × 2 angle.

The main purpose of this type of charting is to see where price and time equal or square out. This is known as *squaring a low*, and is covered in more detail in Chapter 10.

Example: If you have an important high at 500, and want to bring all of your important angles up from 0 at the time the 500 was made, and your scale was 5, simply count over to the right 100 squares of time from the actual 500 top and start a 1 × 1 angle upward from 0. You can also count 50 squares for your 2 × 1 angle and 250 for your 1 × 2 angle.

The main purpose of this type of charting is to discover where price and time equal or square out. This is known as *squaring a high*, and is covered in more detail in Chapter 10.

How to Use Gann Angles

Putting Gann Angles into Your Trading System. When analysts are speaking Gann, you may hear them say things like, "Stay long until the 1 × 1 angle is broken" or "If it doesn't hold at 50%, watch for a change in trend."

At first you may have trouble interpreting such phrases. For example, What do traders mean by "breaking the 1 × 1" and "doesn't hold"? Or, since so much of Gann involves moving from one angle to the next, how far through an angle must the market travel for it to be a significant break?

Identifying a change in trend using geometric angles is a difficult task. Gann never intended his geometric angle rules to stay fixed, since he considered research, testing, and applying them to the markets to be the key to understanding angles. His books and courses are intended as guidelines; he encouraged experimentation.

Constructing geometric angles is easy; interpreting them is a little harder but not impossible. This section should answer any questions about angles and how to construct a trading system.

Developing any trading system is a three-step process:

1. Decide the type of system: trend-following or support–resistance.

Most trend-following systems are designed to catch larger moves. The biggest fear traders have when using them is that they'll miss "the big one." Gann's combination trend-following and support–resistance system suggests that it is virtually never too late to enter the market after a definite signal—even if you miss the bottom or top, the geometric angle will guide you into position.

The geometric angles also provide valid support and resistance points continually as the market moves up or down away from that bottom or top.

This is because the geometric angles drawn from a bottom or top are actually an extension of the bottom or top and move at a uniform rate of speed. This touches on the core concept of Gann's theory: Tops and bottoms can forecast future tops and bottoms.

2. Establish entry rules.

Developing your entry mechanism centers on one of the Gann rules discussed most often: Buying or selling when the market touches on an angle.

The most important angle is the 1 × 1. Gann said this angle determines the strength and direction of the market, and that you could trade off this angle alone, buying every time price rested on the 45-degree line.

A contract is always strong when it holds above the 1 x 1 angle from a bottom and weak when it is just below the 1 × 1 line from a top.

When the market is weak, the best selling opportunity comes when it rallies up to, but not over, the 1 × 1 line coming down from a two-day top; the best buy exists when the market rests on the 1 × 1 from a bottom. This can occur a number of times during a prolonged move.

Remember, angles merely serve as extensions of bottoms or tops. Each time you buy a market resting on the angle, you are, in effect, buying the bottom from which the angles are drawn. As we said earlier, even if you miss the top or the bottom, it is virtually never too late to get in.

The more important the bottom, the more important the angle drawn from it. It is best to buy at angles from intermediate and main bottoms rather than from one-day bottoms, because the stronger bottom means stronger future angles.

The Rule of All Angles. Another important guideline is what Gann called the Rule of All Angles: When a market breaks an angle, it will move toward the next angle. This is because, as time passes, an angle's importance weakens and the market eventually breaks through. Therefore a market breaking the 2 × 1 angle will begin to move toward the 1 × 1 angle, just as a market breaking the 1 × 1 angle will eventually reach the 1 × 2 angle. Conversely, in an upmove, an angle that holds the 1 × 2 angle is likely to rally to the 1 × 1, just as overtaking the 1 × 1 is likely to lead to a rally to the 2 × 1.

As the market forms the bottom, always remember that when the market is above the 1 × 1 angle line, price is ahead of time; when the market is below the 1 × 1, time is ahead of price; and when the market rests on the 1 × 1, time and price are balanced (Figure 9.38).

On a daily chart, when price crosses the 1 × 1 from a bottom, it may not be strong enough to overcome time. This usually causes the market to rest on

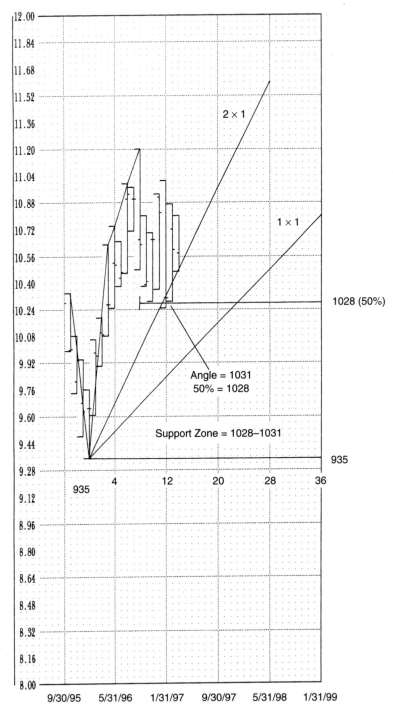

Figure 9.38   Main trend angles and three-month swings of the 1997 monthly July sugar.

the 1×1 or break under it, only to find support at the 1×2. When the time is right and the cycle has run out, the market will usually establish itself on either the 1×2, 1×1, or 2×1 angle. Ideally, the market will follow the 1×1.

Early in a bull market you often see prices edge up slowly with small reactions. As well as time working against the market, angles down from one-period and two-period tops offer resistance.

If you trace imaginary lines from these tops, you will notice that they often hold back prices that are creeping up from intermediate and main bottoms. The strongest moves occur when the market crosses angles from both an intermediate top and an intermediate bottom—it takes more strength to break a trend line based on two periods rather than on one period.

When working the geometric angles, it is no surprise to see that the higher the market moves, the wider apart the angles (Figure 9.39). But this also means the higher the market travels, the farther it is from its base and, therefore, more vulnerable to correction.

When you combine this with the Rule of All Angles, it is little wonder that the market sells off so sharply after breaking a 2×1 angle, only to rally quickly when it reaches the 1×1 angle. The converse is true for rallies.

3. Determine placement of stops.

You want to be stopped out only when the trend changes. The key is knowing the extent to which an angle must be penetrated to effect a trend change. Gann provided several ways to determine this.

The rule determining a change in trend from a top involves waiting for a decline exceeding the previous reaction. The rule for a trend change from a bottom involves waiting for a rise that exceeds the greatest rise of a previous rally. When price penetrates an angle by an amount that exceeds a previous penetration, it shows a probable change in trend (Figure 9.40).

This tells you where to place the stop-loss order. By studying past movement, you can determine what the "average" move through an angle should be. This is known as *lost motion*, which is discussed in the following section. It was also discussed in Chapter 8. The concept of lost motion is exactly the same when applied to angles.

Lost Motion

When applied to angles lost motion occurs when a price penetrates an important support or resistance angle before it regains the angle and resumes the trend. Throughout the course of an uptrend, the market will follow an uptrending angle moving at a uniform rate of speed. At times the market will break to the downside through an angle, only to recover it within one or two

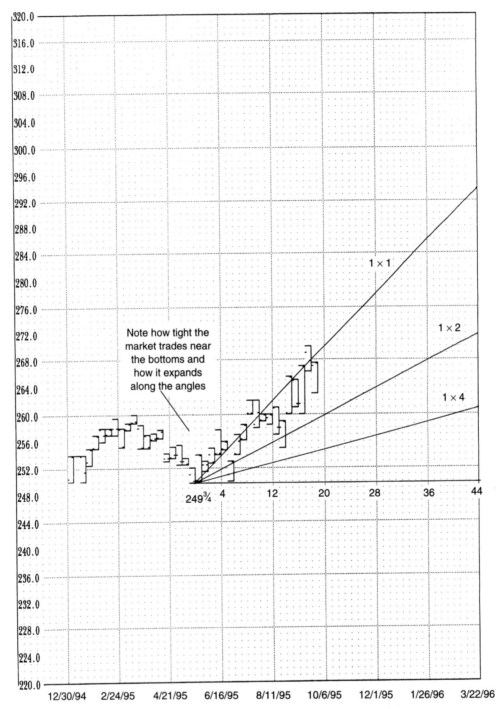

Note how tight the
market trades near
the bottoms and
how it expands
along the angles

Figure 9.39 The higher the market moves, the wider apart the angles.

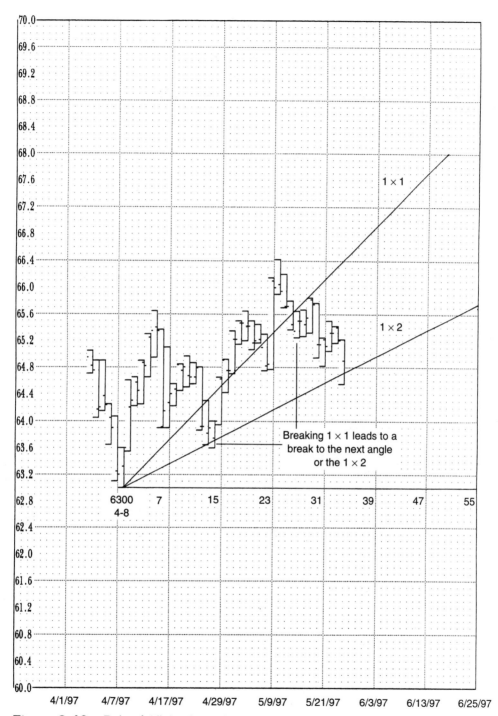

Figure 9.40 Rule of All Angles: When a market breaks an angle, it will move toward the next angle.

days. The idea is to record the amount the market penetrates the angle before recovering it. This helps determine where to place stop-loss orders when
buying off of an uptrending angle. The analysis can be done in two parts: the
historical tendencies of the lost motion through a specific angle, and the immediate tendencies of the lost motion through a specific angle on the current
active start (Figure 9.41).

Determining the historical tendencies of the lost motion through a specific angle requires that a database of these penetrations be maintained. This
database is used by the trader to find an average of the minimum penetration,
after which he places a stop at this amount plus or minus at least one price
unit under the angle. In the case of an uptrending market, the stop is placed
at the lost motion figure minus one unit of price under the uptrending angle,
while for downtrending markets, the stop is placed at the lost motion figure
plus one unit of price over the downtrending angle (Figure 9.42).

Example: Uptrending market with Gann angle at $8.00. Average histori-
cal lost motion is 5 cents. Place the stop at least 6 cents under the uptrending angle (Figure 9.43).

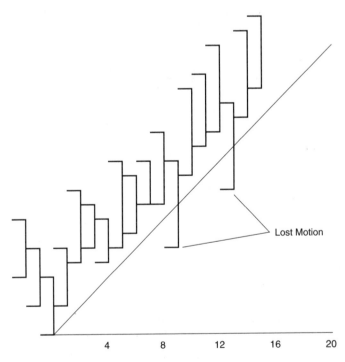

Figure 9.41   Lost motion applied to angles. Determine the amount of the lost
motion, and then use it to help determine stop placement.

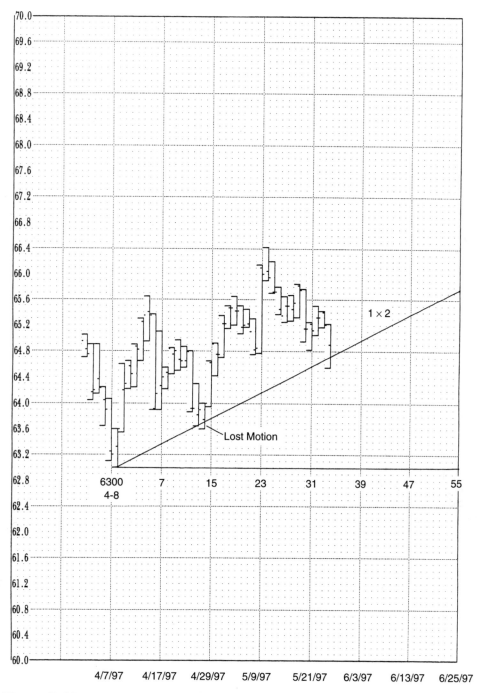

Figure 9.42   Determining the historical tendencies of lost motion through a specific angle. Sometimes the market will break an angle, then regain it and rally. Breaking the angle and regaining it establishes the lost motion. Lost motion helps the trader establish a stop-loss position.

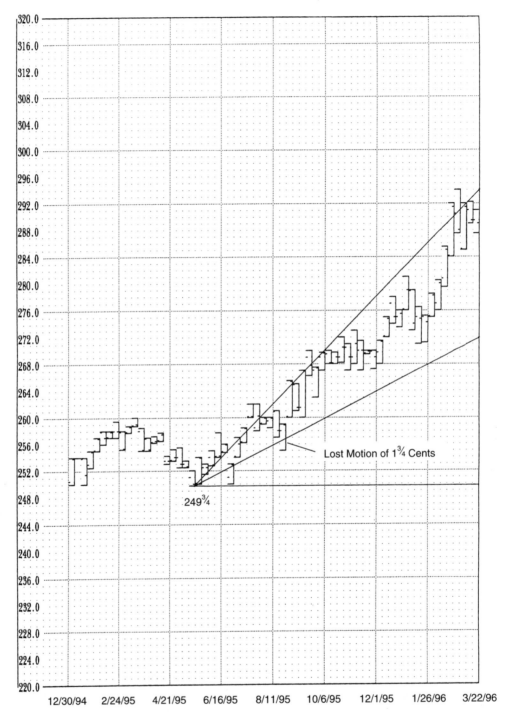

Figure 9.43 Lost motion and a 1×2 angle.

Example: Downtrending market with Gann angle at 108-15. Average historical lost motion is 7 tics. Place the stop at least 8 tics over the downtrending angle.

Lost motion applied to a current market is slightly different. Because Gann Theory is an adaptive theory, the stops often have to be adjusted to the current market conditions. In other words, dollar stops are not used, but stops related to main bottoms, main tops, percentage retracement points, and Gann angles are place. When placing a stop using a Gann angle relating to current market conditions, the trader must record the previous penetrations of the angle from which she is attempting to buy or sell. Once this figure is known, she places a stop at this figure plus or minus at least one unit of price. For example, in an uptrending market, if the previous penetration of the angle is 5 cents, then the stop is placed at least 6 cents under the downtrending angle. In a downtrending market, if the previous penetration is 20 tics, then the stop is placed at least 21 tics over the downtrending angle.

Example: Uptrending market with Gann angle at $6.80. Previous penetration was 5 cents. Place the stop at least 6 cents under the uptrending angle.

Example: Downtrending market with Gann angle at 800.25. Previous penetration was 100 points. Place the stop at least 105 points over the downtrending angle.

The basic idea behind lost motion and Gann angles is to stay with the angle until the market breaks the historical pattern or the immediate pattern. When the angle is penetrated by an amount greater than a previous penetration, the stop-loss order protects the trader from a greater loss. Remember that according to the Rule of All Angles once an angle is penetrated, it is likely to continue to the next angle.

Lost motion will vary according to the angle it is applied to and according to the position of the market. For example, lost motion will be different for 4×1, 2×1, 1×1, 1×2, and 1×4 angles. In addition, it will vary according to the price level of the market. At low prices, the lost motion will be tighter than at high prices.

After studying lost motion as it is applied to main tops, main bottoms, percentage retracements, and angles, the analyst will most likely come to the conclusion that the average lost motion is the same. This is important to know because it indicates that the combinations of these different price levels with properly placed stops according to the lost motion will yield more successful trading results.

Finally, recall that of the reactions under Gann angles that are not changes in trend, most fall under the Gann label of lost motion. Lost motion describes slight breaks through an angle caused by market momentum. In Gann's day, the average lost motion for grains, for example, was 1¾ cents. This is why he suggested a 3-cent stop-loss order so many times in his books and courses. Traders should study and research the lost motion of each market they choose to trade according to the price level the market is trading. Traders should choose the lost motion increment that seems to mistakenly trigger stops least often.

Through study and practice, you can determine lost motion. They are found in penetrations of tops, bottoms, 50% retracement areas, and geometric angles. Any system, including geometric angles, must have rules governing lost motion to place stops accordingly.

This concludes the section on Gann angles. You should now have the basic knowledge necessary to properly calculate the major Gann angles needed to analyze and trade a market. While Gann angles are an important part of determining the strength of the trend, and support and resistance prices, and can be used alone to build trading strategies, they work best when combined with swing tops and bottoms and percentage retracement levels. In the next section, the important percentage levels will be discussed, and you will learn how to draw and calculate accurate retracement levels.

PERCENTAGE RETRACEMENT PRICE LEVELS

The most important percentage retracement point is 50% of the range. This is the price most often traded while a market is inside a range. When a market is in an uptrend, this price is support when the market is trading over this price. If the market breaks under this level, it indicates weakness and a further decline, but does not change the trend to down such as when it crosses a swing bottom.

When a market is in a downtrend, the 50% price is resistance when trading under this price. If the market breaks over this level, it indicates strength and a further rally, but does not change the trend to up such as when it crosses a swing top.

In addition, a market can trade both sides of a 50% price for several time periods while trading inside the range. This particular action should be closely watched, as these swings often demonstrate the lost motion or momentum of a market (Figure 9.44).

Lost motion was defined earlier in relation to swing-chart trading and stop placement. Here we define it as the average penetration of a price through a percentage retracement price that the market can tolerate prior to regaining the percentage retracement price. In other words, it represents the average

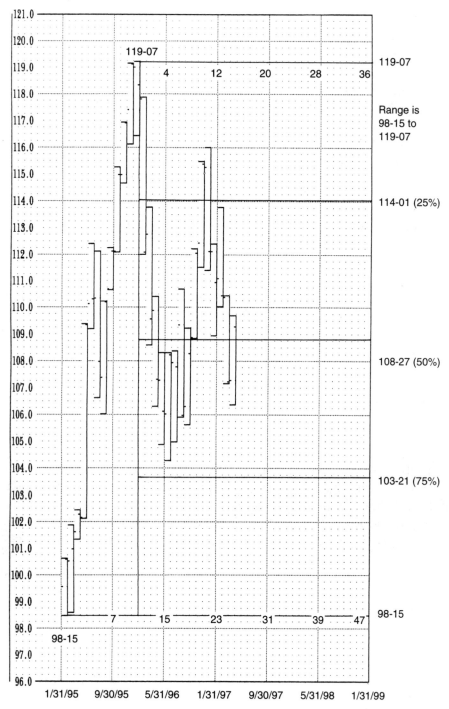

Figure 9.44   Major Gann retracement levels of contract range.

amount measured in price in which the market can break through a percentage retracement point prior to recovering the percentage retracement point.

For example, assume the market is in an uptrend and the swing chart creates a main range with a 50% point at $10.00. During the first day of the week the market breaks to a low price of $9.90. The second day of the week the market rallies back to post a high of $10.12 and a low of $10.01. This action creates a minor bottom at $9.90. The lost motion of this range is the difference between the percentage retracement point and the low price prior to the formation of the minor bottom and the regaining of the percentage price:

$$\$10.00 - \$9.90 = 10 \text{ cents}$$

This lost motion number is important to know because it aids in stop placement when buying against the 50% price during an uptrending market. A stop placed under the price determined by the lost motion is least likely to get hit, and if it does, the market is most likely to continue lower.

The preceding is a simplified example of how to determine the lost motion figure in a market. More sophisticated methods can be developed by taking the average of a series of lost motion points linked with the same 50% price, or all 50% prices in general. It should be noted that the lost motion figure changes according to the price level of a market. For example, at low prices, volatility tends to be low, so the lost motion figure may be relatively lower than the lost motion figure at a high price level, where volatility tends to be high.

It is very important to maintain accurate records of the lost motion amount for each commodity traded at various price levels. Over time the analyst should be able to develop a solid understanding of how a market behaves when trading through a 50% price. This research can prove to be invaluable when developing a trading system and when placing stops to cut losses.

As we said at the beginning of the section, the most important percentage retracement point is 50% of a major range. This major range can be the all-time range or the next two or three all-time ranges. In addition, the 50% price of a contract range along with 50% prices of a main range on the monthly chart, the weekly chart, or the daily chart can provide invaluable support or resistance. Like other price and time concepts discussed in this book, combinations or clusters of 50% prices can provide direction as well as solid support and resistance.

The bigger the range, the better the 50% price, as the market is expected to remain inside the larger ranges for a lengthy period of time. The longer the market spends inside a range, the more the trader can learn about the 50% price. This is especially beneficial when building a database of lost motion. Price clusters created by "ranges within ranges" are very important, as the 50% points of each range are often very close in price and form very solid support or resistance points from which to buy or sell.

While the 50% retracement point is the most important support level inside a range, other important percentage retracement levels include the 25% or ¼ retracement level and the 75% or ¾ retracement level. If these points do not provide enough information to properly determine support or resistance, the ⅓ and ⅔ retracement levels may suit the trader's needs (see Figure 9.45).

The key to working with percentage retracements is to work with the major ranges down to the minor ranges. Use historical major ranges first to determine the historically significant major percentage retracement points. This helps to determine the market's major position relative to time. A market trading under the all-time 50% level may be bottoming, while a market trading over the all-time 50% level may be topping. When looking to forecast the start of major moves, use the all-time ranges. When looking to enter the market for a trade, concentrate your effort on the current major ranges as determined by the monthly, weekly, and daily charts. It is very important to look for clusters of support and resistance, as these points will be most significant when you want to enter into a long or short position.

When trading using the 50% price, always trade in the direction of the main trend. If the main trend is up, then look to buy breaks into the 50% price. If the main trend is down, then look to sell rallies into the 50% price. Finally, it is most important to determine the minimum level of lost motion

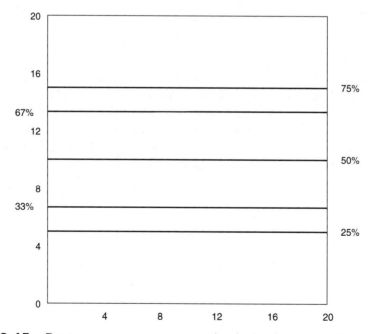

Figure 9.45   Percentage retracement price levels. Inside a range, these are the most important percentage retracement levels.

for each market traded at various price levels. This is the most important analysis tool available for placing protective stops.

The percentage retracement levels are horizontal support and resistance price levels. This is because once identified, these prices remain fixed as long as the market remains inside the range that created it. This is why it is important to work with all-time price ranges and the top-down approach on the current charts. These prices, once formed, are unlikely to get broken; therefore, the percentage retracement levels are likely to last longer. The longer they last, the more valuable information about lost motion and stop placement is learned. This information can help in building a successful trading system.

In addition to the percentage retracement price levels, the swing tops and swing bottoms are important support and resistance points that can be extended into the future on the charts. Once a market passes a top or a bottom, it still remains important. This is because there is a strong tendency for old tops to become new bottoms during uptrends and old bottoms to become new tops during downtrends. It is for this reason that old tops and bottoms should be extended out into the future (Figure 9.46).

The lost motion rule can also be applied to the old support/new resistance and old resistance/new support trading scenario. Research and analyze how far a market is allowed to penetrate an old top to the downside before regaining it and reestablishing support. In addition, study and record how far a market is allowed to penetrate an old bottom to the upside before regaining it and reestablishing resistance. Accurate determination of lost motion is the key to determining a safe stop.

The strongest horizontal support and resistance points occur when the old top or the old bottom is also a percentage retracement price. This combination makes for solid support or resistance. The simplest rule to follow during an uptrend is to buy a break back to a combination of an old top and a 50% price. Conversely, the simplest rule to follow on a break is to sell a rally back to a combination of an old bottom and a 50% price. Compare and combine, when possible, the stop selection chosen when trading this combination and be sure to allow the market plenty of room to work, without exposing yourself to unnecessary risk.

COMBINING THE HORIZONTAL AND DIAGONAL PRICE INDICATORS

While each of these price indicators can be used by itself, they are best when used in combination with another. Some examples of combinations becoming support are:

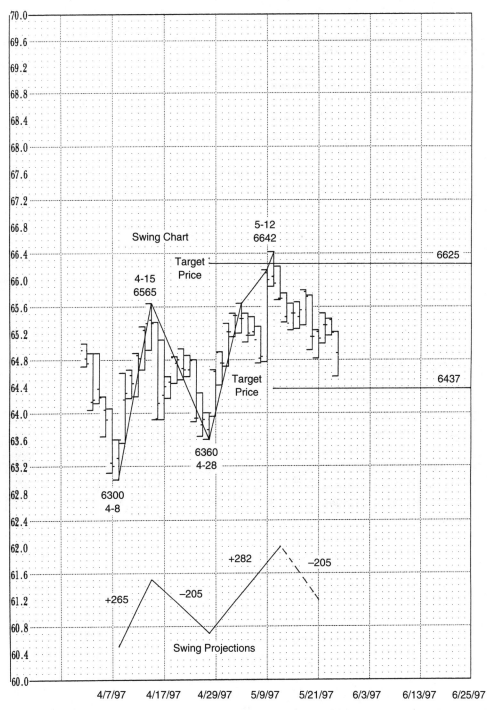

Figure 9.46 Use the swing chart to forecast future price action.

- An uptrending Gann angle and a percentage retracement price. This is an especially strong support level when it is the 50% price and the uptrending 1 × 1 angle (Figures 9.47 and 9.48).
- An uptrending Gann angle and an old top. This is especially strong support when it is the uptrending 1 × 1 angle.
- An uptrending Gann angle and an old bottom (Figure 9.49).
- A swing chart support price and an uptrending Gann angle. This is especially strong support when the angle is the 1 × 1 angle.
- A percentage retracement price and an old top.
- A percentage retracement price and a swing-chart target.
- An old top and a swing-chart target.

Some examples of combinations becoming resistance are:

- A downtrending Gann angle and a percentage retracement price. This is an especially strong resistance level when it is the 50% price and the downtrending 1 × 1 angle.
- A downtrending Gann angle and an old bottom. This is especially strong resistance when it is the downtrending 1 × 1 angle.
- A downtrending Gann angle and an old top.
- A swing chart resistance price and an uptrending Gann angle. This is especially strong support when the angle is the 1 × 1 angle.
- A percentage retracement price and an old bottom.
- A percentage retracement price and a swing-chart target.
- An old bottom and a swing-chart target.

The best support is the combination of three price indicators. This formation consists of the uptrending 1 × 1 angle intersecting the 50% retracement price and the swing-chart target. This is strong support because three independent analysis techniques are identifying the same price level.

It is therefore very important to learn to work with combinations of price indicators, so that you will then have more control over the placement of the stop-loss orders. If you trade using the Gann angles and place your stop accordingly, there will be a time when your stop-loss may have to be placed at a level equal to the 50% price. This may cause your stop to get hit at the same time support is being reached. Also your stop may have to be placed on a Gann angle if you are buying at a 50% price level. Finally, your swing chart may be signaling a corrective break right to the spot you have placed your stop for a percentage retracement buy or a Gann angle buy. By combining two or sometimes three price indicators, you can place a more powerful stop that is less likely to be reached, but when reached is more likely to indicate a change in trend (Figures 9.50 and 9.51).

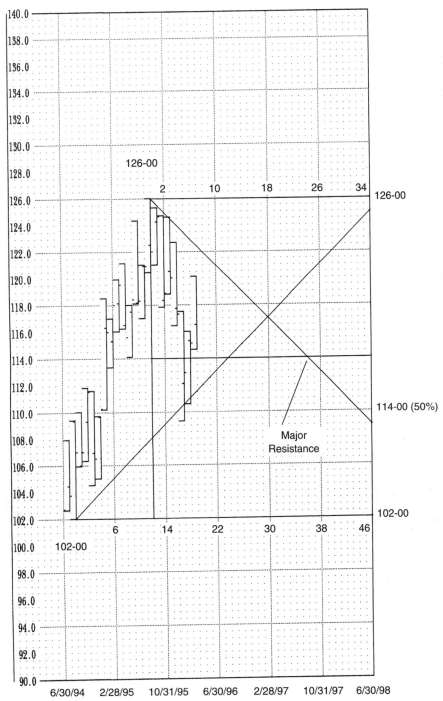

Figure 9.47   Squaring a range with 1×1 angles and 50% level.

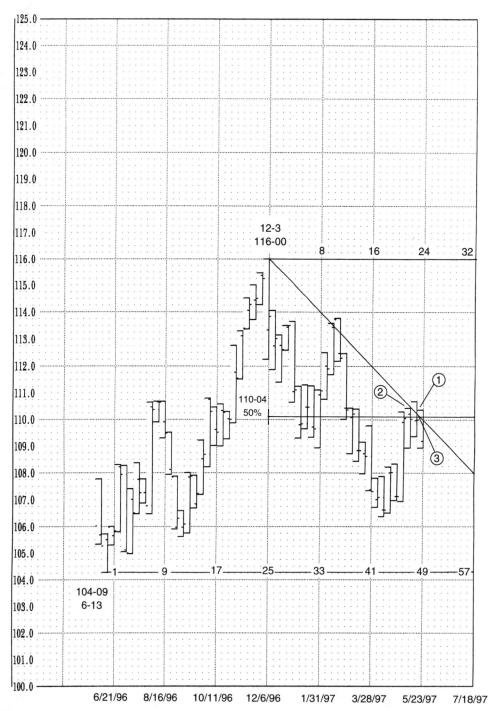

Figure 9.48 Combining the horizontal and diagonal price indicators. Key: ① = Gann angle of 110-08; ② = 50% price of 110-04; ③ = resistance zone of 110-04 to 110-08.

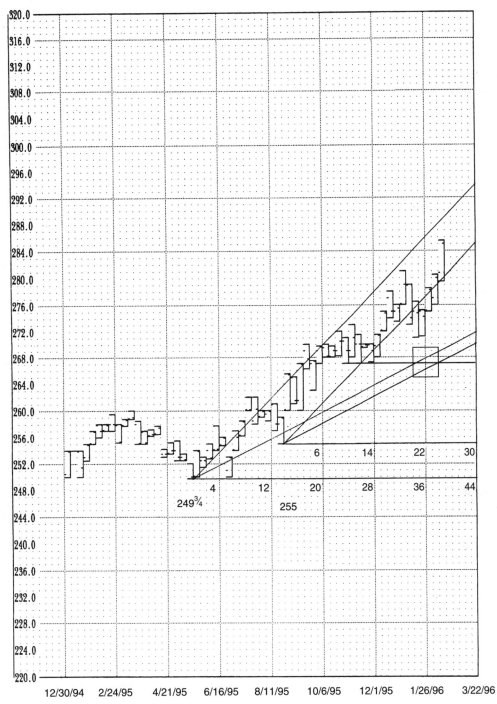

Figure 9.49   An uptrending angle and an old bottom.

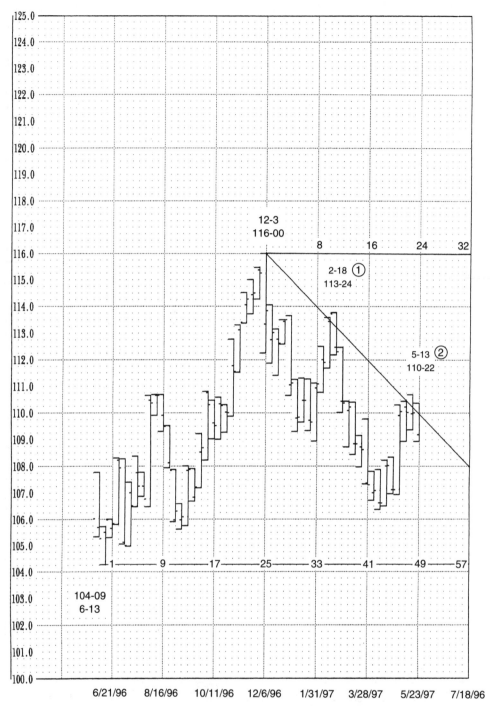

Figure 9.50   Combining price indicators. Key: ① = Gann angle of 113-08, with a high before the break of 113-24 and lost motion of $^{16}/_{32}$nds; ② = Gann angle of 110-08, with a high before the break of 110-22 and lost motion of $^{14}/_{32}$nds.

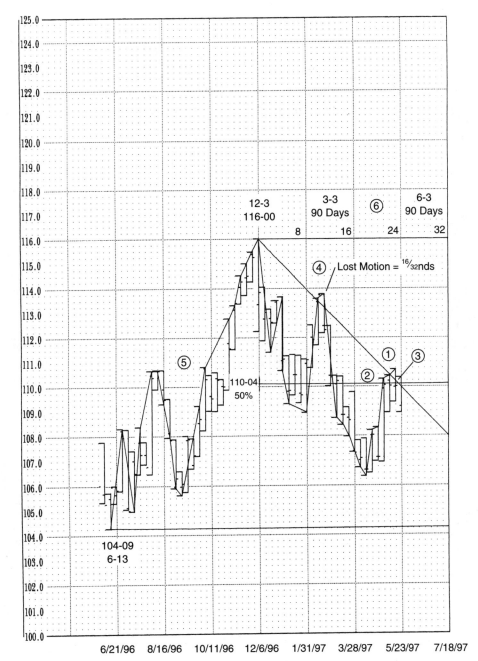

Figure 9.51   Combining the horizontal and diagonal price indicators. With a Gann angle of 110-08 ① and 50% of price at 110-04 ②, the resistance zone is 110-04 to 110-08 ③. Use the previous lost motion to determine a stop ④. Determine the trend ⑤ and the time period ⑥. Conclusion: The trend is down. Time indicates that the market could break until June 3 . Sell at 110-04 to 110-08 with a stop greater than 16 tics.

The same formation is true for sell signals. Instead of taking the sell signal individually, trade the combinations in order to place the stops at more strategic levels.

Following the calculation of valid support and resistance levels, you must determine if time is going to be an important factor. The subject of time is covered in the following chapter. Various forms of time analysis are also explained, along with how to apply it to a trading strategy.

SUMMARY

Gann used a number of methods to determine support and resistance levels. The essence of Gann analysis is that important price levels are determined by diagonal and horizontal support and resistance levels. The diagonal price levels are determined by the Gann angles. The horizontal price levels are determined by the swing tops and bottoms and by the percentage retracement points. While each method can yield strong support and resistance points, the combination of the various methods yields the best results. It should also be noted that calculating Gann angles requires precision. Therefore, proper scaling is important in the construction of this type of chart. Finally, an understanding of the concept of lost motion as it applies to Gann angle and percentage retracement points is equally important in developing a trading system.

This chapter emphasized the importance of price to a trading strategy. The next chapter analyzes time and its applications.

10　Time

Gann considered time the most important factor in determining changes in trend. He measured time in various ways, including natural cycles, anniversary dates, seasonality, swing cycles, and square dates. In this chapter we discuss various ways that time can be used to determine tops, bottoms, and changes. We begin with the most difficult method (natural cycles) and end with the most popular method (the squaring of time). Natural cycles is considered the most difficult concept because it involves the complex topic of financial astrology, which requires hours of outside research before it can be successfully applied. Squaring time is considered the most popular because it involves using charts to forecast tops, bottoms and changes in trend. Many of the techniques learned in Chapter 9 are applied here. Consequently, research acquired from studying the price activity on a chart will be reinforced using this timing technique. Timing analysis involving seasonal charts and swing charts is also discussed. These concepts also utilize information obtained from charts created using techniques in Chapters 4–7.

NATURAL CYCLES

A natural cycle is a time period that can be measured and forecast by natural law and cannot be altered by man.

Celestial Phenomena

The Planets.　The phenomena or the patterns created by the planets are very important, because they move and create patterns such as conjunctions, squares, trines, and oppositions. For example, two or more planets at the same degree are at a conjunction, two or more planets 90 degrees apart are square, two or more planets 120 degrees apart are trine, and two or more planets 180 degrees apart are at an opposition. These patterns have been classified by financial astrologers as bullish or bearish. The bullish phenomena are conjunctions and trines, while the bearish phenomena are squares and oppositions. Gann and other financial astrologers would search the ephemeris (a table of the planets' movements) to find major planetary patterns to predict tops, bottoms, and market direction. Since the future positions of the planets can be predicted using an ephemeris, it was possible for Gann to construct market forecasts years into the future using planetary rulerships as his guide.

Generally speaking, the business planets are Jupiter and Saturn. Jupiter is considered a bullish planet and Saturn a bearish one. Jupiter is usually considered expansive, hence an expanding market is considered a bull market, while Saturn is considered restrictive, and is, therefore, associated with a bear market. Uranus and Mars are associated with volatility and erratic trading. Study and research of these planets and their relationships to market direction is necessary before applying them to trading (Figure 10.1).

Planetary Rulerships. Knowing planetary rulerships is another key to developing a forecast, because the financial astrologer has to associate various markets with the planet or planets that are said to control a specific market's direction. Books are available that identify these relationships, but these books should only be used as guidelines. Although these accepted relationships are a good starting point, study and practice is required to prove the connections and the relationships before a valid forecasting or trading tool can be constructed. Nonetheless, knowing the planetary rulerships plays an important part in constructing a forecast.

Besides using the movement of the larger planets to predict the major moves in the market, Gann also used minor cycles such as the phases of the moon for the 7-day cycle and movement of the sun for the 30-day cycle. The major moves were primarily predicted by the cycles of the major planets and the phenomena of the major planets. For example, the two-year cycle may have been associated with the orbit of Mars, which takes two years to circle the sun, or the 84-year cycle of Uranus, which takes 84 years to orbit the sun. Finally, Gann also used the cycles of the planetary phenomena to forecast future movement. For instance, the conjunction of Jupiter and Saturn is most often associated with a 20-year cycle.

The 30-Day or Sun Cycle. The sun cycle is a natural cycle because it cannot be changed by man. The actual sun cycle is approximately 365 days, which is very close to a circle or 360 degrees. A complete yearly cycle is measured as 360 degrees or 365 days. In other words, one degree is basically the equivalent of one day. This is the basis for Gann's explanation of cycles.

In addition to the complete sun cycle of 365 days, divisions of the yearly cycle are also important. These divisions include ¼, ⅓, ½, ⅔, and ¾ of the year and are important points for tops, bottoms, or changes in trend. Translated into degrees, they represent 90 degrees, 120 degrees, 180 degrees,

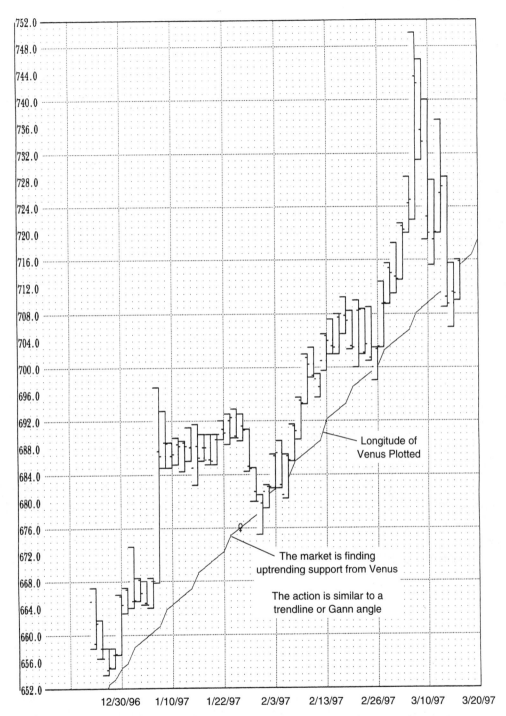

Figure 10.1   Natural cycles of the planets and the 1997 daily November soybeans market. (Heliocentric 90-degree Mercury aspects with the planet angle = 0.5.)

240 degrees, and 270 degrees. Converted into days, they equal 90 days, 120 days, 180 days, 240 days, and 270 days.

Some examples of natural cycles include the Spring Equinox (March 21), Summer Solstice (June 21), Autumnal Equinox (September 21), and Winter Solstice (December 21). These "seasonal dates" are measured by the movement of the sun cycle and are approximately 90 calendar days apart. Although these dates are "quarterly," the man-made quarterly is measured by March 31, June 30, September 30, and December 31, which are not natural quarters or natural dates. These time periods represent the strongest points from a top or bottom from which the next forecasted top or bottom is to occur.

In keeping with the natural cycle of the sun, Gann also assigned importance to the 30-day cycle (Figures 10.2 and 10.3). This is the equivalent of the natural cycle of the sun moving through each sign of the zodiac.

The 7-Day or Moon Cycle.   Another natural cycle Gann recommended to follow is the moon cycle. The moon cycle is a 28-day cycle from new moon to new moon. Key 7-day minor cycles inside of this 28-day main cycle are the different phases of the moon. For example, the 14-day cycle is the new moon to full moon cycle or full moon to new moon cycle.

Financial Astrology.   The study of these cycles falls under the heading of financial astrology, which is beyond the scope of this book. Further research and study is needed to understand how to use and apply this method to forecasting tops, bottoms, and changes in trend. It is also very important to know that Gann wrote in a hidden, veiled language at times. This means that those with a thorough understanding of astrology may be able to find the hidden references to astrological cycles throughout original Gann text and course books.

Gann's Approach

Gann extensively researched the cycles of planets and phenomena. He looked for correlations between the up and down cycles of the market and the up and down movements of the planets. His conclusion after many years of study was that the latitude and longitude of the planets create forces that cause price changes, and that their squares and trines raise and lower prices.

It should be noted at this time that Gann was an active trader as well as a researcher. Therefore, although he had access to and created long-term market forecasts, he updated or adjusted these forecasts according to the short-term movement of the market. This was noted in his forecasts when he told subscribers to adjust tops and bottoms on his original forecasts when market

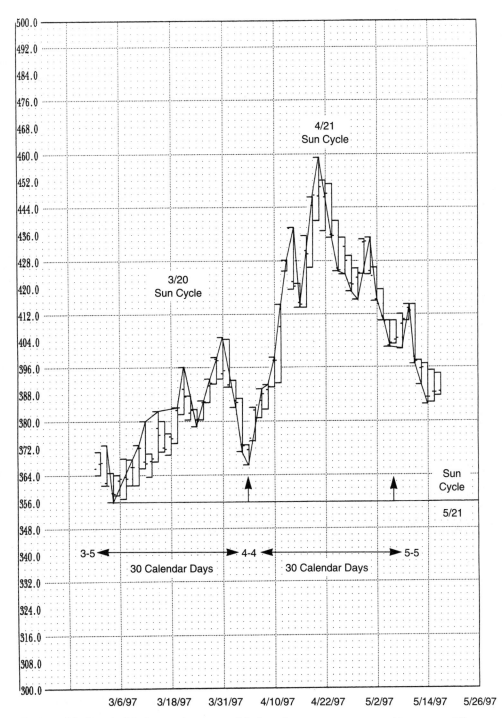

Figure 10.2 A 30-day cycle: count 30 days from major tops and bottoms. (The sun cycle is a natural 30-day cycle.)

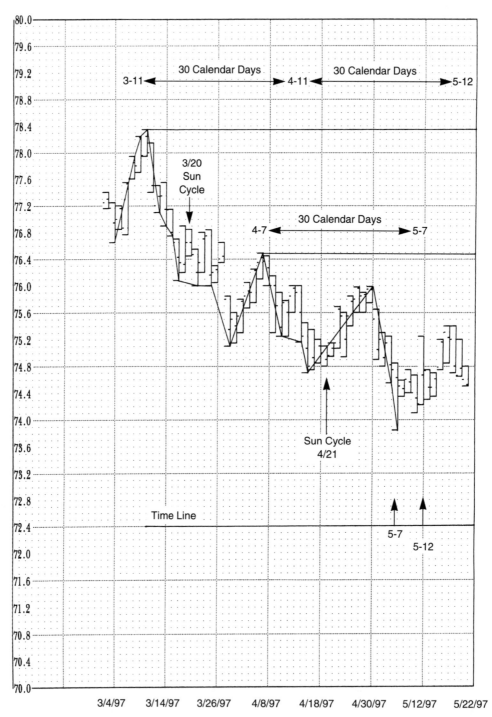

Figure 10.3 Two 30-day cycles set up a zone for the next likely 30-day bottom. (Sun cycle dates remain fixed.)

action dictated such a change. For instance, assume he predicted a January 8 top and a February 10 bottom. If January 8 turned out to be a bottom, then he told traders to look for a top on February 10 instead of a bottom. This tells me that the date of the forecast was more important than the predicted top or bottom. It should be stressed that although he was allegedly very accurate in his forecasts, being able to trade the market correctly was much more important than predicting the direction.

How to Apply Natural Cycles to the Market

First of all, the individual who wants to use natural cycles (Figure 10.4) must be familiar with an ephemeris. The law of motion of the planets can be used to forecast the movement and therefore the positions of the planets well into the future. An ephemeris also identifies various phenomena such as planetary conjunctions, squares, trines, and oppositions. Movement of the planets from zodiac house to zodiac house along with phases of the moon are also identified. Finally, the exact latitude and longitude of the planets are pinpointed (Figure 10.5).

Gann used this information to forecast tops and bottoms as well as the strength of bull and bear markets. Using the ephemeris as his guide, he would predict the strength and direction of the market years in advance.

Gann spent many years studying financial astrology based on the books he had in his library and others, a list of which has been published since his death. Many of these books are available today in reprint. In addition, charting the planets has been made easier through computer programs such as Ganntrader 2. Other financial astrology programs available today contain computerized ephemerides. In short, the data necessary to make a forecast is available today in easy to access form. However, there is still one point that needs to be addressed.

Although the data are readily available, forecasting is more of an art than a science. This is because interpretation of the astrological data requires deep study and practice as opposed to just reading the numbers from a book or computer. This study involves knowing the characteristics of the planets, planetary rulerships of the various markets, and the phenomena created by the planets.

In summary, in order to construct a market forecast using natural cycles, you must have a basic understanding of financial astrology. This basic understanding of astrology should include knowing how to read an ephemeris, learning the planetary rulerships, and knowing how to interpret planetary phenomena. After this basic knowledge is acquired, study and practice is required in order to learn how the information applies to the futures markets. Only after learning how to apply this information should the trader attempt to make a forecast and trade his interpretation of the natural dates.

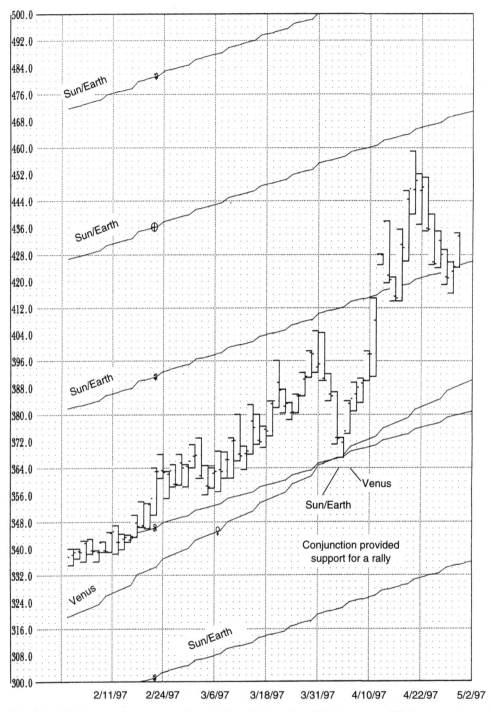

Figure 10.4   Applying natural cycles to the market. (Heliocentric 90-degree sun, earth aspects with the planet angle = 0.5.)

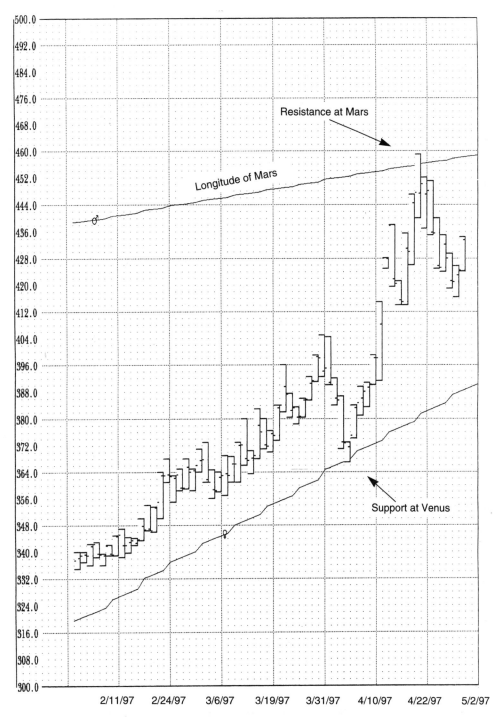

Figure 10.5   Natural cycles and the 1997 daily July wheat market. (Heliocentric 90-degree Jupiter aspects with the planet angle = 0.5.)

Many of Gann's forecasts and trades were triggered by his understanding of natural cycles or financial astrology. The methods that he used included predicting tops and bottoms, changes in trend, and support and resistance. His understanding of natural cycles came from deep research and study of various methods of financial astrology. He was also a trader. While he used the forecasts as a guideline for his trading activity, he did adjust the forecasts to the current market conditions.

ANNIVERSARY DATES

Natural cycles are applied to fixed dates that occur throughout the year (Figure 10.6) in the case of sun and moon cycles, and at predictable intervals in regard to planetary conjunctions, squares, trines, and oppositions. When using these cycles to forecast tops, bottoms, or changes in trend, the trader relied on exact dates that were known in advance.

Anniversary date cycles (Table 10.1) use the same concept as the natural cycle, but are not known until a top or bottom is formed. The basic definition of the anniversary date is a one-year cycle from a major top or major bottom. For example, a major top on June 1, 1996 has an anniversary date cycle due on June 1, 1997, June 1, 1998, etc. Each year on June 1 into the future, the anniversary of that major top will be due. The same holds for a major top anniversary date (Figure 10.7).

Minor Divisions of Time

Variations of the anniversary cycle occur when this cycle is divided into $\frac{1}{4}$, $\frac{1}{3}$, $\frac{1}{2}$, $\frac{2}{3}$, and $\frac{3}{4}$ time periods (Figure 10.8). Since an anniversary cycle is approximately 365 days, a $\frac{1}{4}$ division is 90–91 calendar days, a $\frac{1}{3}$ division is 120–122 calendar days, a $\frac{1}{2}$ division is 180–182 calendar days, a $\frac{2}{3}$ division is 240–244 calendar days, and a $\frac{3}{4}$ division is 270–274 calendar days. These divisions represent the most important anniversary date cycles.

Combining the Yearly Anniversary Date with the Minor Divisions

Another variation of the anniversary date is the combination of the one-year anniversary date and the division of time periods (Figure 10.9). For example,

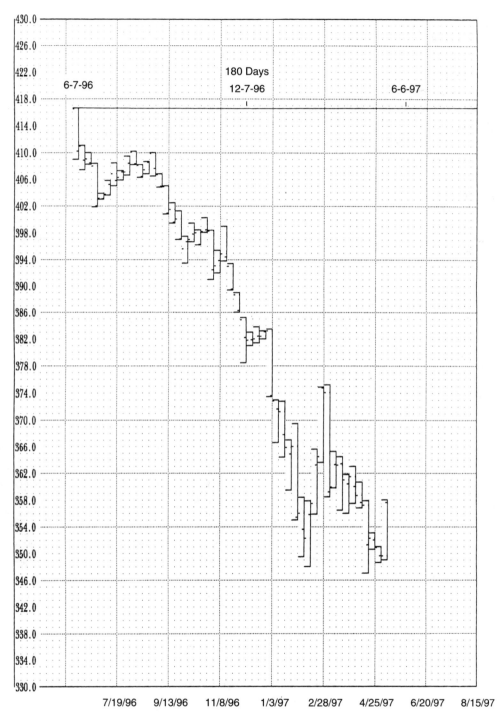

Figure 10.6   Anniversary date cycles.

Table 10.1   September Corn Anniversary-Date Monthly Chart for May

| Number | Month | Monthly High and Low by Date | | | |
		Date	Price	Date	Price
1	5	600520	120.87	600502	117.25
2	5	610515	121.00	610523	116.25
3	5	620504	119.62	620529	114.50
4	5	630531	121.00	630501	117.25
5	5	640506	123.87	640515	120.37
6	5	650505	129.75	650525	124.75
7	5	660531	125.75	660504	122.62
8	5	670526	138.62	670518	132.50
9	5	680508	120.62	680522	117.37
10	5	690521	132.12	690526	124.50
11	5	700501	129.13	700518	126.13
12	5	710528	148.38	710519	139.75
13	5	720524	129.50	720531	126.75
14	5	730530	213.62	730502	165.00
15	5	740501	269.00	740507	238.00
16	5	750520	272.25	750528	251.00
17	5	760527	284.75	760503	269.00
18	5	770503	256.00	770520	242.00
19	5	780530	271.50	780502	241.50
20	5	790502	280.00	790517	263.75
21	5	800505	298.00	800529	284.50
22	5	810501	377.00	810526	349.00
23	5	820503	289.75	820528	276.00
24	5	830503	312.75	830527	290.50
25	5	840525	330.00	840514	314.00
26	5	850501	269.50	850529	256.50
27	5	860509	220.00	860530	199.75
28	5	870512	205.50	870501	183.75
29	5	880531	234.50	880513	211.25
30	5	890505	268.25	890530	239.00
31	5	900511	286.00	900522	268.50
32	5	910506	254.25	910530	241.00
33	5	920515	267.25	920501	247.50
34	5	930503	238.75	930526	228.50

the current time period may be $1\frac{1}{4}$ anniversary cycles from a main top or main bottom. Another example is $2\frac{1}{2}$ anniversary cycles from a main top or bottom. It is important to maintain accurate records of these cycle dates as they extend out into the future. The purpose of studying these cycles is to find clusters of anniversary cycles in the future that can be used to forecast a top, bottom, or change in trend.

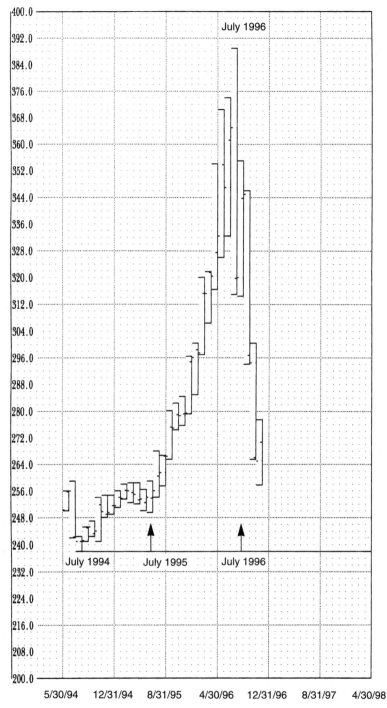

Figure 10.7   Anniversary date monthly chart.

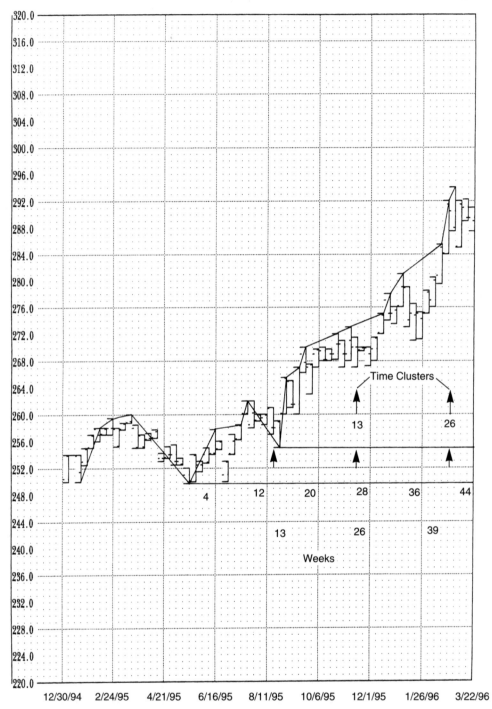

Figure 10.8   A 13-week or 90-day cycle.

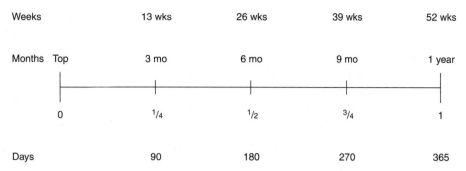

Figure 10.9   Anniversary dates and division of time.

How to Apply Anniversary Dates to Trading

Following the construction of a properly drawn main trend indicator chart, the trader will have before her a chart filled with main tops and bottoms, plus the prices and dates at which these tops and bottoms occurred. These data should be recorded on a spreadsheet in order to have a permanent record of the date of each main top and main bottom.

Monthly Main Trend Chart. The more data the better in the case of analyzing anniversary dates. This is because the trader is looking for important future cycles so that he can accurately forecast future tops, bottoms, and changes in trend. As mentioned earlier, the easiest way to maintain these records is to start with the main trend indicator chart and record all main trend tops and bottoms in a spreadsheet format. The best time period to follow initially is the monthly chart. The monthly main trend indicator chart usually provides the trader with a minimum of two major tops and bottoms during the life of an individual contract. Using the data from 10–20 years worth of monthly charts, he may be able to construct a valid forecast of future tops and bottoms, as indicated by clusters of main tops and main bottoms at or near the same calendar dates.

Weekly Main Trend Chart. The second important trend indicator to construct and analyze for important cycle dates is the weekly main trend indicator chart. This chart offers the trader more anniversary cycle dates for future forecasts. It also contains the contract highs and lows and any other main tops or bottoms that appear on the monthly main indicator chart. The dates that overlap are the most important to use for future forecasts. Once again the key is to note the clusters of main tops and main bottoms at or near the same calendar dates. Five to 10 years of weekly chart main tops and main bottoms will yield a large sample of these anniversary dates.

Daily Main Trend Chart. The third important trend indicator to construct and analyze for important cycle dates is the daily main trend indicator chart. This chart offers the trader even more cycle dates than the weekly main trend indicator chart and the intermediate trend indicator chart for future forecasts. It also contains the contract highs and lows and any other main tops or bottoms that appear on both the monthly and weekly charts. In addition, some of the main tops or bottoms that occur on the weekly chart but not on the monthly chart occur on the daily trend indicator chart.

Short-term traders should focus their attention on the cycles on the daily chart. If the trader charts this contract from the first trading day, then by the time the market reaches the active stage, a series of 90-day cycle dates should have been established. These dates are important in forecasting future tops and bottoms.

Prolonged Moves in Time

When learning how to construct the swing charts, starting the chart after a prolonged move in time is strongly recommended. Studying the short-term cycles of each market shows that a prolonged move from top-to-top, top-to-bottom, bottom-to-bottom, or bottom-to-top is often associated with a 90-day cycle. In other words, if the market is 90-calendar days from a main top and currently in a downtrend, then 90-days from this top the market is most likely to begin showing signs of bottoming. Reverse the signal from bottom-to-top.

In addition to forecasting the up and down swings, the trader may look for topping action when a market is 90 calendar days from a previous main top or 90 calendar days from a previous main bottom. The trader should note that this cycle is used to predict future tops and bottoms and not changes in trend.

Remember that a change in trend occurs *only* when the market crosses a main top or main bottom, not when the market forms a main top or main bottom. This means that although a main top or main bottom has been formed, this action combined with the cycle work will only be a clue that a change in trend may soon take place.

The Importance of the 90-Day Cycle

The basic function of the anniversary date is to identify the dates on which the market is likely to top or bottom in the future. The most common anniversary date cycle is the 90-day cycle. As the market approaches a 90-day top, the trader should watch for a signal top formation, as this will combine the best of time and pattern when forecasting the top. Conversely, as the market approaches a 90-day bottom, the trader should watch for a signal bottom formation, as this will combine the best of time and pattern when forecasting the bottom.

Combining the Three Main Trend Charts to Forecast Tops and Bottoms

The combination of the three main trend charts makes this technique a valuable tool for forecasting future tops and bottoms. The ability to isolate the future month, week, or day of a major top or bottom is very important. For example, by studying 10 years of monthly data, the trader can determine with a high degree of accuracy in which month of the year a contract is likely to top or bottom. She will also be able to determine which week of the month the market is likely to top or bottom, as well as which day of the month and week the market is likely to top or bottom.

Depending on how aggressive the trader is, instead of using the monthly main trend indicator chart to forecast, he may use a monthly intermediate or monthly minor trend indicator chart. These charts will give him more cycle top and bottom dates to choose from and are more likely to post clusters of dates because of the many dates that can be matched up. This technique can also be applied to the weekly and daily charts.

Anniversary Dates Forecast Future Tops and Bottoms

Identifying anniversary dates helps in forecasting future tops and bottoms, not changes in trend. A change in trend only occurs when a swing top or swing bottom is crossed. Such a change may occur several days or weeks after a cycle top or cycle bottom has been formed. Intense study of how far in time after a cycle top or cycle bottom a change in trend occurs may help the trader determine more precisely when to expect a valid change in trend in the future. The way to do this is to gather data on change in trend dates and forecast them into the future in the same way used to forecast future swing tops and swing bottoms. After doing this, look for clusters of anniversary dates showing when these changes in trend have occurred based on the past history. By doing this the trader will be able to accurately predict future changes in trend.

Besides using combinations of swing charts to link time with pattern, another way to predict future trend changes is to combine anniversary dates, especially the 90-day cycle, with the signal top or signal bottom. As stated in

Chapters 3–7, following a prolonged move in time, watch for a signal top or signal bottom to indicate an impending change in trend.

Recall that the definition of the signal top and signal bottom includes the phrase "following a prolonged move in price and time." The 90-day cycle can help the trader pinpoint the signal top and signal bottom. Since many cycle tops and bottoms occur in conjunction with the 90-day cycle, it can be called a *prolonged move in time*. Look for signal tops and signal bottoms when a 90-day cycle is due.

Although the 90-day cycle has been discussed most frequently, the 180 day, 270 day, and 1-year cycles can also be used.

In summary, the goal of using anniversary dates for forecasting is to identify with a high degree of accuracy which month, week, and day the cycle top or bottom will occur. It is therefore important to obtain as much information as possible regarding past tops and bottoms, as this information is useful in predicting future tops and bottoms. Thus, the trader should look at the main trend chart with the largest period of time. Combinations of monthly, weekly, and daily main swing charts should help identify more precisely a future top or bottom.

SEASONALITY

The one-year anniversary date chart can also be called a *seasonal chart* (Figure 10.10). This chart differs from the popular seasonal technique used by many analysts that identifies the time periods in which the market is likely to rally or break based on the historically largest dollar moves throughout the year.

Constructing a Simple Yearly Forecast of Tops and Bottoms Using the Monthly Chart

A simple forecast of tops and bottoms involves the placing of previous main tops and bottoms on blank chart paper at the time of their occurrence (Table 10.2). The data can come from a monthly, weekly, or daily main trend chart. This is another reason why strict records of this information should be kept.

In order to construct a simple yearly forecast of tops and bottoms, the analyst needs a sheet of blank chart paper, a green pen, a red pen, a ruler, and a database of main tops and bottoms, complete with price and time identified. The piece of chart paper should be long enough so that the trader can forecast an entire year on it.

The first step is to place the time periods forecast along the bottom of the chart. List the months along the bottom of the monthly chart, the week-

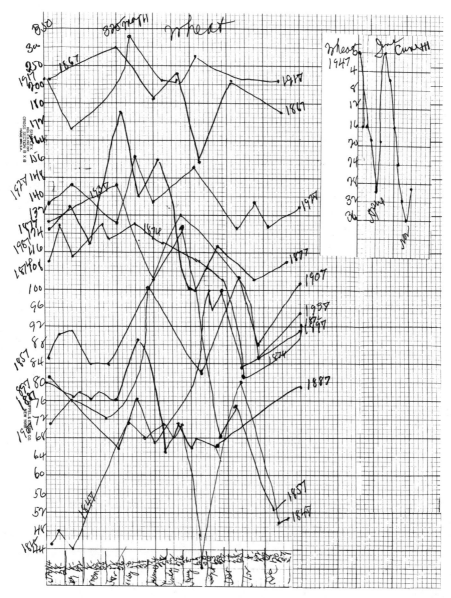

Figure 10.10 Original Gann chart, wheat seasonality, 1847–1937.

ending date along the bottom of the weekly chart, and calendar days along the bottom of the daily chart (Figure 10.11).

Price is irrelevant on this simple forecast chart, but setting prices along the left side of the chart inside the all-time price range or at least the 10-year range could be helpful. Price will be necessary when building a more complex forecast chart.

Table 10.2   November Soybeans Calendar Year Highs and Lows

Number	Year	Price	Date	Price	Date
1	1960	220.00	600811	206.12	600121
2	1961	263.50	610425	215.75	610103
3	1962	250.00	621024	229.25	620806
4	1963	291.50	631108	240.12	630109
5	1964	282.50	641002	237.62	640721
6	1965	259.75	651214	242.25	650526
7	1966	334.50	660719	258.00	660103
8	1967	291.37	670605	261.25	671002
9	1968	273.25	680315	239.25	681202
10	1969	248.00	691024	233.12	690729
11	1970	310.25	701028	242.37	700106
12	1971	342.25	710716	278.00	710104
13	1972	386.75	721115	295.75	720113
14	1973	929.00	730814	345.25	730112
15	1974	956.00	741004	506.00	740408
16	1975	699.00	750102	464.00	751118
17	1976	777.25	760707	483.00	760127
18	1977	797.50	770607	497.00	770816
19	1978	731.00	781030	554.00	780117
20	1979	833.00	790622	625.00	791029
21	1980	930.50	801105	631.00	800402
22	1981	871.00	810409	625.00	811116
23	1982	708.00	820201	518.00	821004
24	1983	968.50	830913	585.25	830104
25	1984	771.00	840620	568.50	840921
26	1985	624.00	850121	488.00	851118
27	1986	552.25	860430	465.25	860825
28	1987	624.50	870616	460.25	870217
29	1988	1046.00	880623	608.50	880104
30	1989	760.50	890320	540.00	891016
31	1990	682.00	900501	552.00	901114
32	1991	650.00	910802	517.00	910710
33	1992	651.00	920601	524.50	921005
34	1993	757.50	930719	576.00	930616

After placing the time periods on the chart, the analyst can use the database to find the main swing tops and bottoms for that particular market.

The second step is to place arrows at the top of the monthly portion of the chart to identify the main tops. Use the red pen to draw the arrows and mark the time period on the chart during the month a main top took place. For example, if a main top occurred during January, place a red arrow at the

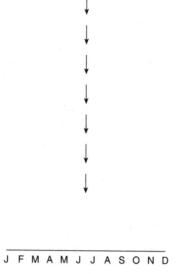

J F M A M J J A S O N D

Figure 10.11   Yearly forecast format for November soybeans, calendar highs. Seven calendar-year highs have occurred during June from 1960–1993.

top of the chart on the time period representing January. If the next main top occurred during March, place the arrow at the top of the chart during the time period representing March. Repeat this procedure for each year in the database (Figure 10.12).

Next, place arrows at the bottom of the monthly portion of the chart to identify main bottoms. Use the green pen to draw arrows and mark the time

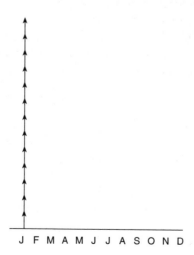

J F M A M J J A S O N D

Figure 10.12   Yearly forecast format for November soybeans, calendar lows. Thirteen calendar-year lows have occurred during January from 1960–1993.

period on the chart during the month a main bottom took place. For example, if a main bottom occurred during February, place a green arrow at the bottom of the chart on the time period representing February. If the next main bottom occurred during July, then place the arrow at the bottom of the chart during the time period representing July. Repeat this procedure for each year in the database.

The fourth step is to identify the months that contain clusters of tops and bottoms. This chart is designed to give the trader a general look at the market, because it contains the main tops and bottoms on the monthly chart. The objective of the chart is to identify which months the market has tended to make tops or bottoms.

Constructing a Simple Yearly Forecast of Tops and Bottoms Using the Weekly Chart

The first step in constructing this chart is to place the identified week-ending dates along the bottom of the chart.

Price is irrelevant on this simple forecast chart, but setting prices along the left side of the chart inside the all-time price range or at least the 10-year range could be helpful. Price will be necessary when building a more complex forecast chart.

After placing the time periods on the chart, the analyst can use the database to find the main swing tops and bottoms for that particular market.

The second step is to place arrows at the top of the weekly portion of the chart to identify the main tops. Use the red pen to draw the arrows and mark the time period on the chart during the week a main top took place. For example, if a main top occurred during the week ending January 4, place a red arrow at the top of the chart on the time period representing the week ending January 4. If the next main top occurred during the week ending March 10, place the arrow at the top of the chart during the time period representing the week ending March 10. Repeat this procedure for each year in the database.

Next, place arrows at the bottom of the weekly portion of the chart to identify main bottoms. Use the green pen to draw arrows and mark the time period on the chart during the week a main bottom took place. For example, if a main bottom occurred during the week ending February 10, place a green arrow at the bottom of the chart on the time period representing the week ending February 10. If the next main bottom occurred during the week ending July 16, place the arrow at the bottom of the chart during the time period representing the week ending July 16. Repeat this procedure for each year in the database.

The fourth step is to identify the weeks that contain clusters of tops and bottoms. This chart is designed to give the trader a more specific look at the market than the monthly chart, but not as detailed as the daily chart, because it only contains the main tops and bottoms on the weekly chart. The objective of the chart is to identify which weeks the market has tended to make tops or bottoms.

Constructing a Simple Yearly Forecast of Tops and Bottoms Using the Daily Chart

The first step is to construct a chart of the entire calendar year.

Price is irrelevant on this simple forecast chart, but setting prices along the left side of the chart inside the all-time price range or at least the 10-year range could be helpful. Price will be necessary when building a more complex forecast chart.

After placing the time periods on the chart, the analyst can use the database to find the main swing tops and bottoms for that particular market.

The second step is to place arrows at the top of the daily portion of the chart to identify the main tops. Use the red pen to draw the arrows and mark the time periods on the chart on the day a main top took place. For example, if a main top occurred on March 5, place a red arrow at the top of the chart on the time period representing March 5. If the next main top occurred on April 10, place the arrow at the top of the chart during the time period representing April 10. Repeat this procedure for each year in the database.

Next, place arrows at the bottom of the daily portion of the chart to identify main bottoms. Use the green pen to draw arrows and mark the time period on the chart on the day a main bottom took place. For example, if a main bottom occurred on February 10, place a green arrow at the bottom of the chart on the time period representing February 10. If the next main bottom occurred on July 16, place the arrow at the bottom of the chart during the time period representing July 16. Repeat this procedure for each year in the database.

The fourth step is to identify the days that contain clusters of tops and bottoms. This chart is designed to give the trader a more specific look at the market than the monthly and weekly charts. The objective of the chart is to identify which day of the year the market has tended to make tops or bottoms.

Top and Bottom Forecasts and Price Levels

The previous section dealt with the tendency of the market to form main tops and bottoms at various time periods throughout the calendar year. This section discusses a technique that identifies price levels at which the market has tended to make tops and bottoms. As stated several times throughout this book, price and time analysis has to be emphasized. The trader must learn to use price and time together and not stress one over the other.

Monthly Main Tops and Bottoms with Price Levels

This technique is basically the same as the previous one, only instead of placing red arrows at the top of the chart to identify main tops, the analyst places an "X" on the chart during the month and at the price the main top occurred.

For example, the November soybeans made a main top in June 1988 at $10.46. On the price and time seasonal monthly chart, the analyst would place a red "X" on the time line representing June and on the price line representing $10.46 (Figure 10.13).

The technique is basically the same as the previous method for bottoms also, but instead of placing green arrows at the bottom of the chart to identify main bottoms, the analyst places an "X" on the chart during the month and at the price the main bottom occurred.

For example, the December corn made a main bottom in July 1988 at $2.72½. On the price and time seasonal monthly chart, the analyst would place a green "X" on the time line representing July and on the price line representing $2.72½.

This procedure is repeated for the weekly chart. Here, the November soybean main top occurred the week ending June 24, 1988, at $10.46. On the price and time seasonal weekly chart, the analyst would place a red "X" on the time line representing the week ending June 24, 1988, and on the price line representing $10.46.

The December corn made a main bottom the week ending July 29, 1988, at $2.72½. On the price and time seasonal weekly chart, the analyst would place a green "X" on the time line presenting the week ending July 29, 1988, and on the price line representing $2.72½.

Repeat this procedure for the daily chart. Here, a November soybean main top occurred on June 23, 1988, at $10.46. On the price and time seasonal daily chart, the analyst would place a red "X" on the time line representing June 23, 1988, and on the price line representing $10.46.

A December corn main bottom occurred on July 28, 1988, at $2.72½. On the price and time seasonal daily chart, the analyst would place a green "X" on the time line representing July 28, 1988, and on the price line representing $2.72½.

Value of the Price and Time Seasonal Chart

The value of the price and time seasonal chart is that the analyst will be able to see at which price level the market is likely to make tops and bottoms. This is important because sometimes a seasonal tendency fails. This usually happens when a market with a seasonal uptrend is trading at a historically high

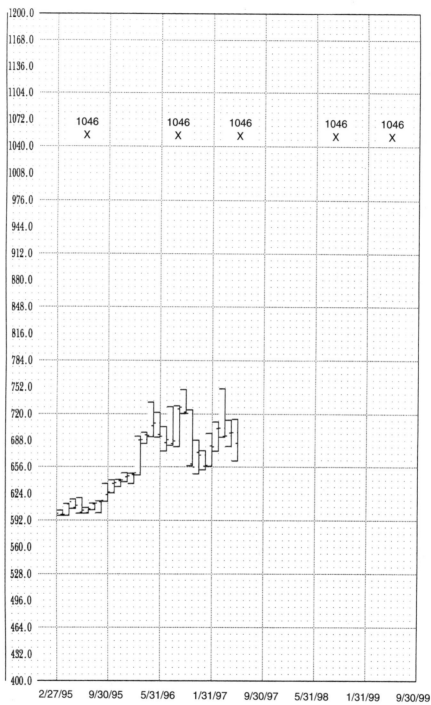

Figure 10.13   Monthly forecast chart. Place the all-time high on the monthly chart during the month it took place; for example, November soybeans all-time high for June 1998 was 1046. This technique gives you price and time.

price level or when a market with a seasonal downtrend is trading at a historically low price level.

For example, the November soybeans have a seasonal tendency to trade lower starting June 23. This is usually a valid analysis if the market is trading at a high price level, but a poor one if trading at a low price level. Using seasonal price and time analysis, the trader will be able to see at which price levels or zones the market is likely to top and break in confirmation of the seasonal trend, and at which price levels or zones the market is likely to fail by trading in the opposite direction.

Variations of the Seasonal Chart

The previous sections used main tops and main bottoms to identify possible future main tops and main bottoms. A variation of this technique is to use monthly tops and bottoms instead of main tops and bottoms.

Using this technique the analyst takes a specific calendar month and identifies the calendar days on which the market has made a monthly high or low. This is different from the monthly chart that identifies main tops and main bottoms, because a monthly high or low is not necessarily a monthly main top

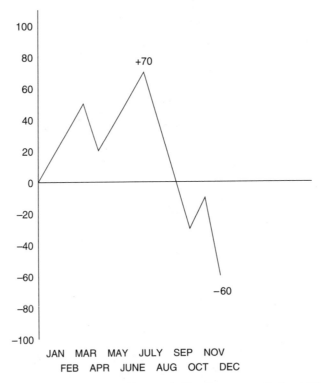

Figure 10.14   A 10-year seasonal forecast. This forecast calls for a 70-cent rally from the beginning of the year to July, then breaks sharply lower to –60 by December.

or bottom; for example, a main top or bottom that occurs prior to the start of the new month and continues in one direction throughout the month.

This technique helps to identify the tendency of a market to top at the beginning, in the middle, or at the end of a month.

Monthly Seasonal Chart. The chart sets the previous month to zero, and up and down moves are tracked (Figure 10.14). It shows the trader how far above the previous month's close the market is likely to rally, and how far below the previous month's close the market is likely to break.

Ten-year Seasonal Chart. One of Gann's favorite charts was the 10-year seasonal chart. It shows the trader the seasonal tendency of a market based on a 10-year cycle. On this chart the analyst starts the new year at zero, then tracks the swings of the previous 10-year increments. For example, for a 1997 forecast, the analyst would draw the swings of the market for 1987, 1977, 1967, 1957, 1947, and each year that ends in 7. The outcome gives the trader an opportunity to see how the market trades during 10-year cycles (Figure 10.15). This chart can be used to forecast the direction of the market and time bottoms and tops.

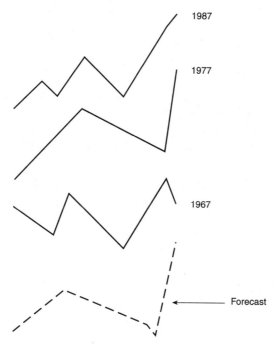

Figure 10.15 A Gann 10-year seasonal chart to forecast 1997. Gann would create a seasonal forecast by making a curve of the market based on 10-year patterns. To forecast 1997, use the charts from the years ending in 7: 1987, 1977, 1967, 1957, 1947.

SWING CHARTS

Basic Use

The swing or trend indicator charts were covered extensively earlier in the book (Chapters 3–7). A properly constructed swing chart can provide the trader with valuable timing information. This information can aid the trader in forecasting the duration of both rallies and corrections during an uptrend and breaks and corrections during a downtrend.

By definition the rallies in an uptrending market in terms of time should increase over the life of the uptrend. One of the first signs of an impending top is a rally that falls short of a previous upswing in terms of time. In addition, the rallies in terms of time should be greater than the corrections. Other signs of an impending top are a correction that lasts longer than the previous upswing, and a correction in terms of time that is greater than a previous correction in terms of time. Finally, the combination of a shorter-than-expected upswing in terms of time and a longer-than-expected correction in terms of time should be seen as a strong indication that the trend is getting ready to change.

The opposite is valid in a downtrending market. By definition the breaks in a downtrending market in terms of time should increase over the life of the downtrend. One of the first signs of an impending bottom is a break that falls short of a previous downswing in terms of time. In addition, the breaks in terms of time should be greater than the corrections. Other signs of an impending bottom are a correction that lasts longer than the previous downswing, and a correction in terms of time that is greater than a previous correction in terms of time. Finally, the combination of a shorter-than-expected downswing in terms of time and a longer-than-expected correction in terms of time should be seen as a strong indication that the trend is getting ready to change.

In Figure 10.16, the market is in a downtrend. A break from March 13, 1997 to March 21 was six market days. The correction was three market days. The next break was six market days and the correction was three market days. The next swing down was seven market days, followed by a three-market-day rally.

The forecast is for another break of six market days or more from the last top. A break that fails to equal or exceed the previous break is a sign of a bottom. In addition, if the market doesn't have a minimum six-market-day break and the next correction is greater than three market days, then the trend is getting ready to turn up.

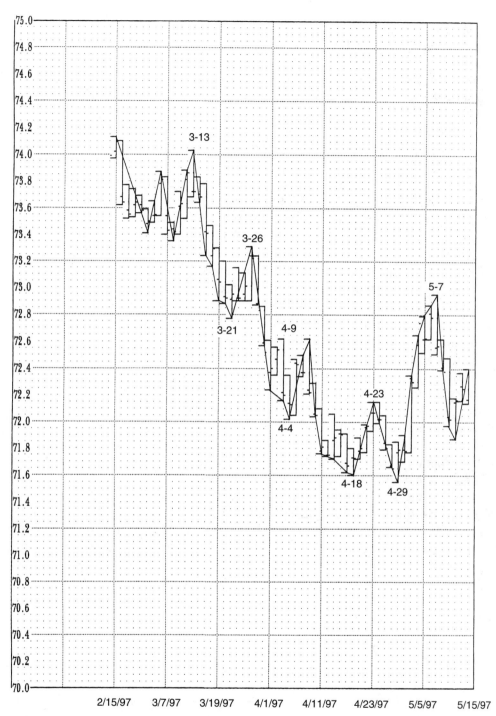

Figure 10.16   Time swings, 1997 daily June Canadian dollars. During the major decline, the rallies often balanced on the third day.

Setting Time Objectives and Stops
with the Swing Chart

The swing chart can also be used to set time objectives and stops. This chart offers the trader an opportunity to go with the market rather than trying to beat it.

For example, during an uptrend, a trader could use the swing chart to forecast the duration of the next upswing. After establishing a long position in the direction of the trend, she should strongly consider liquidating the position when either a time objective or a time stop is reached.

A time objective is reached if the trader has a profit on a trade and the market has reached the date on which the market is expected to make a correction based on the swing chart (Figure 10.17). On this date, the trader should take the profit on the opening, on the close, or at a price predetermined by either a percentage retracement or Gann angle. The key is to liquidate the position on the day that the swing chart forecast the next top or bottom is due. This form of profit taking allows the trader to trade with the market according to time. Holding on to the position will indicate the trader wants to beat the market. In that case, the trader can accomplish his objective by staying in longer while looking for a strong move that exceeds the previous move in time. At the same time he assumes more risk, because if the swing reaches its objective exactly, he may give back some or all of his profits.

A time stop is reached if the trader has a loss on a trade and the market has reached the date on which the market is expected to make a correction based on the swing chart. On this date, the trader should take the loss on the opening, on the close, or at a price predetermined by either a percentage retracement or Gann angle. The key is to liquidate the position on the day that the swing chart forecast the next top or bottom is due. This form of stopping out of a losing trade allows the trader to trade with the market according to time. Holding the position will indicate the trader wants to beat the market. In that case, the trader can accomplish her objective by staying in longer than the swing suggests while looking for a strong move that exceeds the previous move in time. At the same time she assumes more risk, because if the swing comes to an end exactly, she may increase her loss by holding on to the position.

Chapters 3–7 should be carefully studied, as a properly constructed swing chart can yield valuable information on market timing. The duration of the up- and downswings should be recorded and analyzed to help determine market strength and rhythm. Clues about when a market is going to form a top or bottom or change trend can be found in the swing chart. The keys to remember are that during an uptrend, the rallies in terms of time should equal or exceed the previous upswings, and that during a downtrend, the breaks in

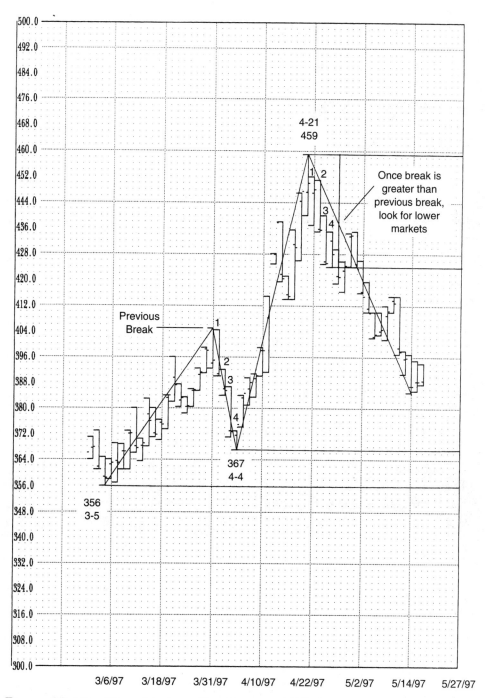

Figure 10.17   Time objectives. From a top at 4.59, the market had four consecutive lower tops. This break equals the previous break of four days. Once the market exceeds the previous break in terms of time, consider this a sign of weakness and look for lower markets.

terms of time should equal or exceed the previous downswings. Finally, the duration of the swings can be used to take profits or stop out a loss.

SQUARE CHARTS

Squaring a Range

The chapter on Gann angles showed the analyst how important the range of a market is in determining support and resistance. This chapter also covered the price zones created by the Gann square. Another important aspect of the Gann square is timing, a feature we now address. The Gann square chart uses a range and important divisions of time inside the range to identify further tops and bottoms.

Constructing the Square Chart and Divisions in Time. The steps for constructing the Gann square for timing are the same as for the Gann square for pricing support and resistance.

> Step 1: Find a main range. (A main range is created by a main top and a main bottom.)
> Step 2: Divide the range vertically into time periods.

The major time periods are 25, 50, and 75% of the range (Figure 10.18). These points represent ¼, ½, and ¾ retracements of time, respectively. For example, if the range is 50, then 25% of the square in time is the range times 0.25. In this example,

$$50 \times 0.25 = 12.5$$

The time period will be represented by the type of chart used, either monthly, weekly, or daily. In this case, 25% of time represents 12.5 months, weeks, or days.

Fifty percent of the square in time is the range times 0.50. In this example,

$$50 \times 0.50 = 25$$

The time period will be represented by the type of chart used either monthly, weekly, or daily. In this case, the 50% of time represents 25 months, weeks, or days (Figure 10.19).

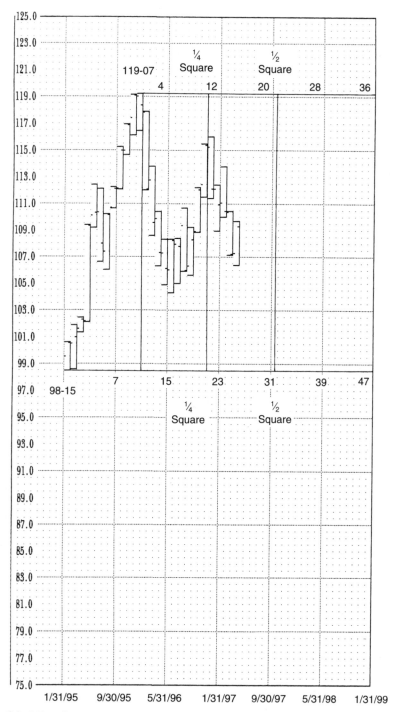

Figure 10.18   Squaring a range. Main top = 119-07; main bottom = 98-15; range = 20-24. Scale = 0.50, ½ square of time = 20.75 months. Scale = 0.50, ¼ square of time = 10.38 months.

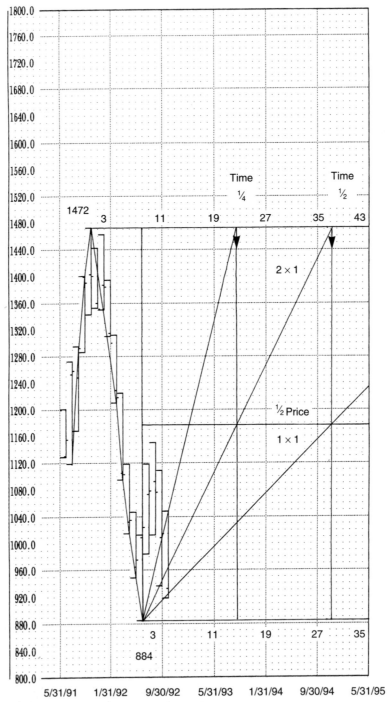

Figure 10.19 Squaring a range, time divisions. Top = 1472, bottom = 884, range = 588; ½ square = 29.4 months, ¼ square = 14.7 months. Tops, bottoms, or changes in trend are expected on ¼ and ½ time divisions.

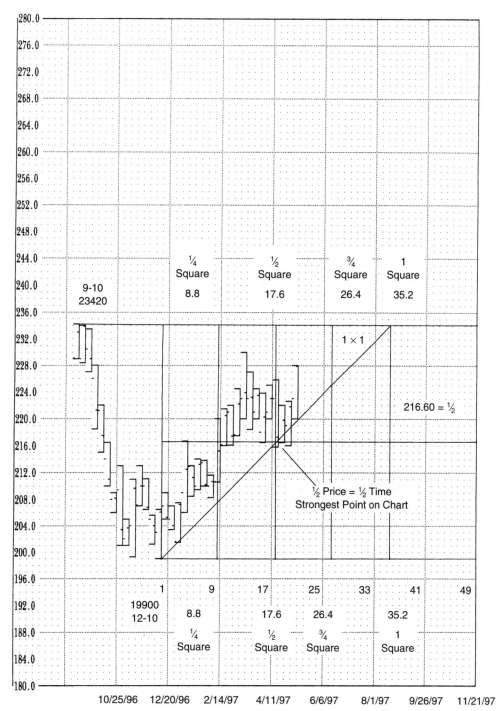

Figure 10.20 Squaring a range, important time periods. Top = 234.20, bottom = 199.00, range = 3520, scale = 100, 1 square = 35.2 weeks; ¼ = 8.8 weeks, ½ = 17.6 weeks, ¾ = 26.4 weeks.

Seventy-five percent of the square in time is the range times 0.75. In this example,

$$50 \times 0.75 = 37.5$$

The time period is represented by the type of chart used either monthly, weekly, or daily (Figure 10.20).

Step 3: Identify these time periods on the chart.

It is important to mark these time periods on the chart, as they represent dates on which the market may have a top or bottom. Often the market exhibits high volatility on these dates.

These time periods remain intact as long as the market remains inside the range used to identify them. When the range is violated, the dates are no longer valid for tops and bottoms. Because these ranges are more likely to remain intact over a longer period of time, it is suggested that major ranges, such as the all-time range or the second- or third-largest range be used. In addition, they are more likely to signal major top or bottom formations. The contract range may also be used, as can the large ranges on the daily chart, but remember that these ranges are likely to be exceeded often throughout the life of the contract.

Other divisions of time that could be used to identify future tops or bottoms are the 33% and 67% time periods. These represent $\frac{1}{3}$ and $\frac{2}{3}$ retracements of time. A 33% retracement of time is found by taking the range times 0.33, and a 67% retracement of time is found by taking the range times 0.67. In our example, if the range is 50, then a 33% retracement of time is 16.5 months, weeks, or days. A 67% retracement of time in a range of 50 is 33.5 months, weeks, or days.

Time Clusters. As stated earlier in the chapter, the best time to anticipate tops or bottoms is when two or more timing dates land on the same time periods. The market is made up of several main ranges that combine to form the contract range or the all-time range. Because of this overlap, conditions exist at times when several "square dates" are due at the same time.

For example, there may be a time when $\frac{1}{4}$ of one square is due the same weeks as $\frac{1}{2}$ square of another range (Figure 10.21). These are important setups to watch for, as they are often associated with the formation of major tops or bottoms. This is especially true if the market is trading at or near a historical top or bottom (Figure 10.22).

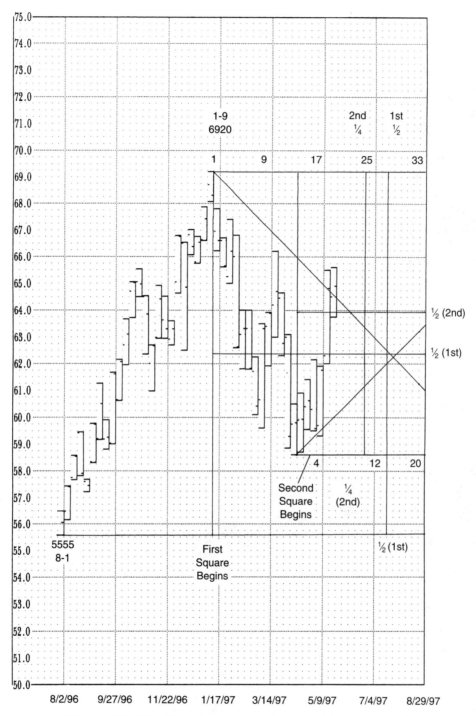

Figure 10.21   Squaring a range, "square within a square."

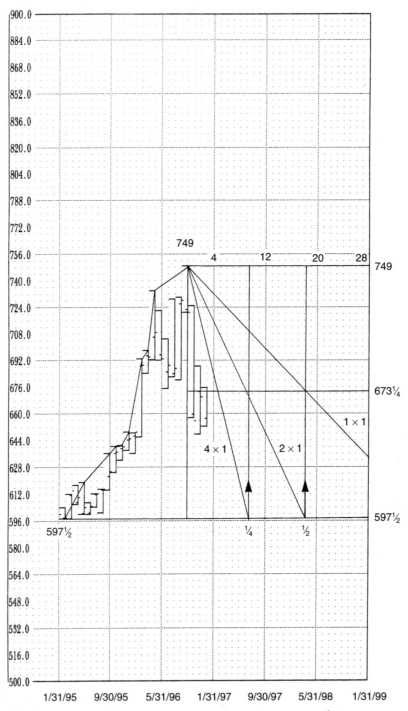

Figure 10.22   Square of a range. Top = 749, bottom = 597½, range = 151½; ½ = 18.94 months, ¼ = 9.47 months.

Squaring a High Price

One technique utilized by Gann was squaring a high price. Squaring a market by a high price yields additional time periods to watch for tops and bottoms. This is especially important on the weekly chart. In order to square a high, the analyst must know the main top and the scale used by a particular market. Once again, the all-time high, or the second- or third-highest high, is important to use to project future tops and bottoms. Unlike squaring a range, squaring a high price extends into infinity, as each high from the past is related mathematically to each high or low in the future.

For example, the November soybeans have an all-time high of $10.46\frac{1}{2}$. Based on a scale of 4 cents per week for soybeans, a top or bottom has been projected every 262 weeks since the major top formed in the week ending June 24, 1988. The squaring of the high was determined by dividing the all-time high of $10.46\frac{1}{2}$ by 4 cents per week. The result was a cycle of 262 weeks. Every 262 weeks, or approximately 5 years from the week ending June 24, 1988, traders should watch for future tops and bottoms.

Although squaring a high is used primarily in conjunction with the weekly chart, other charts can be used, especially the monthly chart. For example, using November soybeans once again, the all-time high of $10.46\frac{1}{2}$ occurred in June 1988. Based on a scale of 8 cents per month, the November soybean monthly chart would square every 131 months. This means that from this high a major top or bottom could be forecast every 131 months, or close to 11 years. In that case, June 1999 is an important time period for a major top or bottom.

Squaring a Low Price

Another technique utilized by Gann was squaring a low price. Squaring a market by a low price yields additional time periods to watch for tops and bottoms. This is especially important on the weekly chart. In order to square a low, the analyst must know the main bottom and the scale use by a particular market. Once again, the all-time low, or the second- or third-lowest low, is important to use to project future tops and bottoms. Unlike squaring a range, squaring a low price extends into infinity as each low from the past is related mathematically to each high or low in the future (Figure 10.23).

For example, July corn has a major low of 1.54 from February 17, 1987. Based on a scale of 2 cents per week for corn, a top or bottom has been projected every 77 weeks since the main bottom formed the week ending February 21, 1987. This squaring of the low was determined by dividing the major low of 1.54 by 2 cents per week. The result is a cycle of 77 weeks. Every 77 weeks, or approximately $1\frac{1}{2}$ years from the week ending February 21, 1987, traders should watch for future tops and bottoms.

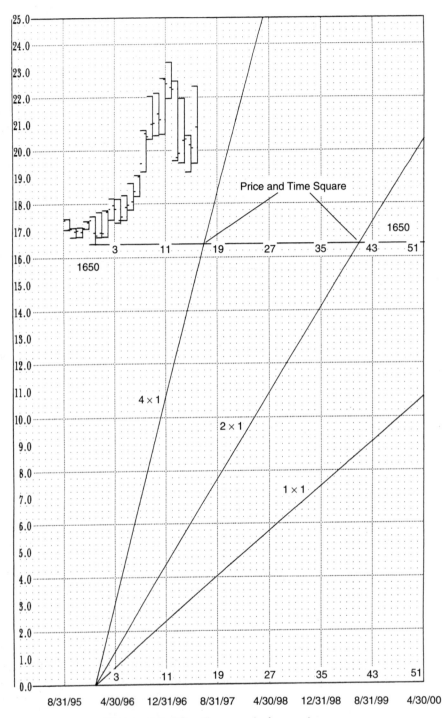

Figure 10.23   Zero angle from a low.

Although squaring a low is used primarily in conjunction with the weekly chart, other charts can be used, especially the monthly chart. For example, using the July corn once again, the major low of 1.54 occurred in February 1987. Based on a scale of 8 cents per month, the July corn monthly chart would square every 19 months. This means that from this major low a major top or bottom could be forecast every 19 months. In that case, March 1998 is an important time period for a major top or bottom.

This concludes our discussion of square charts. Possibly the three most important timing tools Gann used to forecast tops and bottoms were the square of the range, the square of the high, and the square of the low. These tools use prices to determine when tops and bottoms may be due. Study and practice are necessary in order to use this technique. Careful analysis should be done to determine the accuracy of this method. While exactness is aimed for, using a square can give a good indication of where the top or bottom is going to occur. Learn the characteristics of this timing device and of the market to which it is being applied in order to determine its usefulness in predicting tops and bottoms.

SUMMARY

It is important to note that markets are made of both price and time. The idea behind successful trading is to balance the two. Of the two, however, time is the most powerful. In order to time a top or a bottom, the trader should be aware of the various methods used to determine these tops and bottoms. Timing can come in the form of cycles that can be natural and adaptive. These cycles can be represented by natural phenomena, such as planetary movement, or they can be applied directly from past market action, such as the anniversary dates and time divisions. Timing can also be achieved by using an adaptive method that uses the actual price movement of the market to determine and forecast future tops and bottoms, such as the square of the price range, the square of the high, and the square of the low. In addition, the duration of the up and down swings can be used to forecast future tops and bottoms. Finally, it should be noted that a combination of the timing methods is strongly suggested. Experience shows that market tops and bottoms will most likely occur when "clusters" of time indicators come together simultaneously.

You have now been introduced to the basics of Gann analysis. The next chapter gives examples of how to apply these techniques to real markets.

11 Using Gann Techniques

1997 DAILY JUNE CANADIAN DOLLARS

The Intermediate Trend Indicator

We begin the analysis of the 1997 daily June Canadian dollar contract (Figure 11.1) at an extreme level just slightly below the contract high of 76.35. An intermediate trend top was formed at 7568 on January 22, 1997 following two consecutive days of lower-lows. The first two-day bottom was formed at 7475 on January 24. The next lower two-day top was formed at 7545 on January 28. The intermediate trend turned down on February 6, 1997 when the market crossed the swing bottom at 7475. A short signal was given and a protective stop was placed over the last swing top at 7523. As the market continued to post lower tops and lower bottoms, the trend indicator moved down and stops were also moved to just above each new swing top. The downtrend continued until March 13, 1997 when the swing top at 7387 from March 6, 1997 was crossed and the position was stopped out.

In addition to crossing the swing top, the rally exceeded the previous rally in terms of price and time. A buy signal was triggered on the breakout, but failed when the market crossed the swing bottom at 73.35. One clue that the rally might fail was the minor signal top formed on March 13, 1997. Although this did not occur after a prolonged move up, the market failed to hold the uptrend and triggered another sell following the break under the March 10 bottom at 7335.

The next swing down was 7403 (March 13) to 7277 (March 21), or 126 points in six days. The subsequent correction was 7277 (March 21), to 7331 (March 26), or 54 points in three market days. The forecast was for a 126 point break over the next six market days. The market broke from 7331 (March 26) to 7202 (April 4). This break was 129 points in six market days. Time balanced the previous move exactly, but price was off by three ticks. With the market balanced, a correction of 54 points in three market days was

285

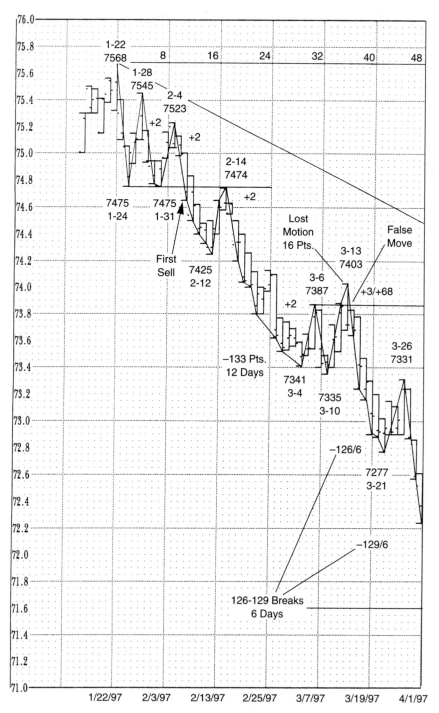

Figure 11.1   Chart for 1997 daily June Canadian dollar.

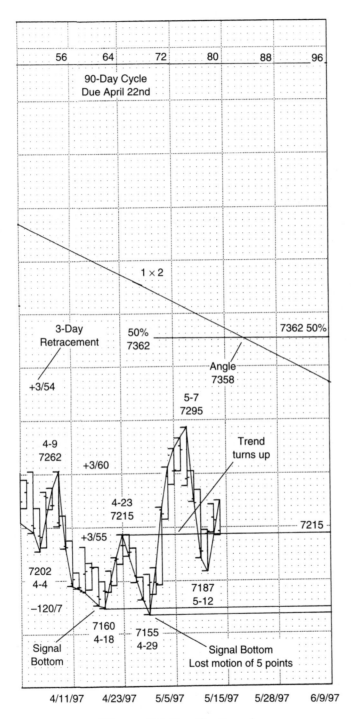

Figure 11.1 Continued.

expected. The next correction was 7202 (April 4) to 7262 (April 9) or 60 points in three market days. Time once again balanced exactly and price was off by six ticks. The next forecast was for 126–129 points in six market days. The break from 7262 took the market to 7160, or 102 points in seven market days. The break was one day too long, but price finished well short of the target of 7139–7136. This was the first sign the market was getting ready to change the trend.

With the market at an extreme level by virtue of a new contract low, it was time to start watching for bottoming action. The bottom at 7160 on April 18 was formed by a signal bottom. This was another sign the market was getting ready to bottom or change trend. The subsequent correction from 7160 to 7215 was 55 points in three days. This correction balanced with the previous corrections, which was an indication that the market may fail and that the 7160 bottom would not hold. The next break traded down to 7155 on April 29 and posted another signal bottom. Generally speaking, two signal bottoms within seven days is usually a strong sign that a final bottom is near. The market rallied from 7155, and the intermediate trend indicator turned up when the market crossed the last swing top at 7215.

The break through 7160 to 7155 was only five points before the trend changed to up. This break could be attributed to lost motion. With the main trend now up, the market began to take on the characteristics of a bull market, as rallies began to exceed previous corrections in terms of both price and time. With the main trend up and the position long, a forecast was necessary. The first leg up was 7155 to 7295, or 140 points in six market days. The first break following the trend change was 108 points in three days. This action forecast a 140-point rally in six market days from the 7187 bottom. The forecast called for a trade to 7327 by May 20, 1997. Although the market rallied to 7350 on May 16, price was ahead of time and the market corrected back to 7327 on May 20. The actual close was 7329. This action proved that price and time balance.

Combination of Gann Angle and Percentage Retracement Level

The rally from 7155 came to an end when the market traded into 7362 on May 21, 1997. The market sold off following a trade into a major resistance zone. The main range from the January 22 top to the April 29 bottom was 7568 to 7155. This range created a 50% level at 7362. A 1×2 Gann angle moving down at a rate of $2\frac{1}{2}$ points per day was at 7358 on May 21. This created a resistance zone at 7358–7362, which is why the market broke following a test of this resistance zone.

Time Analysis. The first intermediate top was made on January 22, 1997. Looking ahead with the 90-day cycle, the next major bottom or change in trend was forecast by April 22, 1997. The first bottom was reached at 7160 on April 18, two market days ahead of the cycle date. The final bottom at 7155 was posted on April 29. This bottom came in five market days late.

Pattern Analysis. The two bottoms at 7160 and 7155 were formed by signal bottom days following a prolonged move down in price and time and with the market at a new contract low (an extreme price level). Following a confirmation of these bottoms with a follow-through rally, the first countertrend buy signals were issued following 50% corrections of the first leg up following the reversal bottoms.

1997 DAILY JULY PLATINUM

Intermediate Trend Indicator and Gann Angle Combination

Following a top on February 28, 1997 at 403.50, the market broke down to 364.00 (Figure 11.2). The first rally from this bottom stopped at 377.50 on April 11, 1997. The subsequent two-day break took the market down to 364.50 on April 15, 1997. On April 17 the main trend turned up when the market crossed the swing top at 377.50.

The market did not follow through after the change in trend to the upside. The subsequent break formed a minor range of 364.50 to 384.50 with a 50% price at 374.50. Uptrending Gann angle support from the 364.50 bottom crossed 374.50 on April 29, 1997. With the main trend up, a buy was triggered at 374.50 with stops under the last swing bottom at 364.50. This was also the strongest support zone. The market did not react swiftly and decisively off of 374.50 when tested and broke to 369.00. This price was on an uptrending support angle from the 353.00 contract low. In addition, a signal bottom was formed.

After spending five consecutive market days under the 50% level at 374.50, the market finally broke out to the upside on May 8. On May 9, the uptrend was reaffirmed when the last top at 384.50 was crossed. The market rallied sharply higher into 397.50, where it posted a top. The next break stopped short of the old top at 384.50, finishing at 385.50. This came close to confirming our "old top/new bottom" rule. The next rally took the market slightly above the old top at 397.50, but failed to follow through to the upside. This action created a new bottom at 385.50.

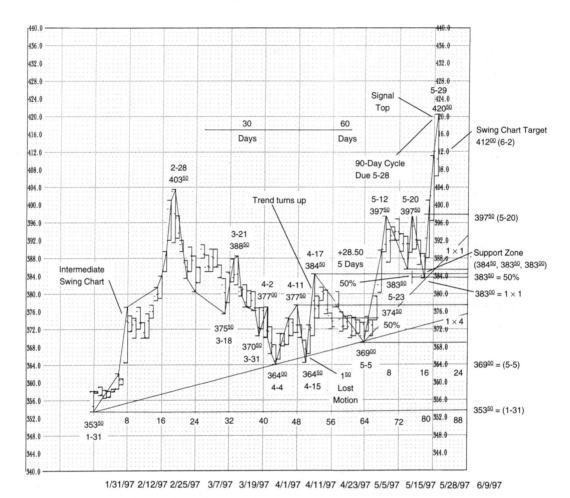

Figure 11.2   Chart for 1997 daily July platinum.

Following a break from 397.90, a main range was formed by 369.00 to 397.90 with a 50% price at 383.50. On May 23, a Gann angle from 369.00 moving up $1.00 per day was at 383.00. The percentage retracement point and uptrending Gann angle formed a range of 383.50–383.00 on May 23. With the trend up, a buy signal was issued following a test of this level.

On May 23, the market crossed the trend indicator bottom by only $2.00 and stopped at 383.50. Although technically the trend turned down at this point, it may not have been enough to trigger a sell signal, since it fell within the lost-motion point associated with platinum. The combination of an old top/new bottom (384.50), a 50% price (383.50), and an uptrending Gann angle (383.00) provided strong support and the market rallied.

The first rally from 369.00 to 397.50 was $28.50 in five market days. From the 383.50 bottom, a $28.50 rally in five market days was forecast. This pegged the upside target at 412.00 by June 2. On May 28, the market reached 411.00 on the close. On May 29, the market reached 420.50 and posted a signal top. At this point price was ahead of time. This indicated that the market was due for a correction back to 412.00 on June 2.

In addition to the swing chart forecasting a price and time target of 412.00 on June 2, the market reached the 90-day cycle date on May 28. With price and time clustered at May 28–June 2 and the market at a new contract high, a top was forecast. The signal top on May 29 and the subsequent confirmation break on May 30 were strong signs a major top was being formed. At this time, look for a return rally to 412.00 to balance price and time with the swing chart, and for a break to begin. Based on the first leg down from the 420.50 top to the 399.20 low, look for a 50% retracement of this range to 409.90. This makes 409.90 to 412.00 the next resistance zone and countertrend selling level.

1997 DAILY JUNE LIVE HOGS

Following a prolonged move up in price and time from the 7565 bottom on March 11, 1997, the June live hogs made a two-day top at 8660 on April 24, 1997 (Figure 11.3). This top was close to the 90-day cycle from the January 27, 1997 top. The subsequent break from 8660 took out a swing bottom at 8435 and turned the intermediate trend to down. Since this top was the contract high and an extreme price level, a short was triggered at this point with a stop above the top.

Following a break to 8270 on May 5, the market rallied. The first upside objective was 50% of the first range. With the range 8660 to 8270, the 50% price level came in at 8465. Since the main trend was down, selling into the 50% price level on the day the 1 × 1 downtrending angle crossed triggered another short at 8465–8480 on May 7. The market did not break immediately and rallied into the 1 × 2 angle from the top at 8540 on May 12 before making a final top. This final top was an outside move down and a signal top. With the trend already down, this was a strong sign of a major top.

The first break was 8660 to 8270 from April 24 to May 5 or 390 points in seven days. This created a forecast of a break from 8577 to 8187 by May 21. The actual break was to 8050 on May 21. This was a balance of time. On this day the market posted a signal bottom and rallied for one day.

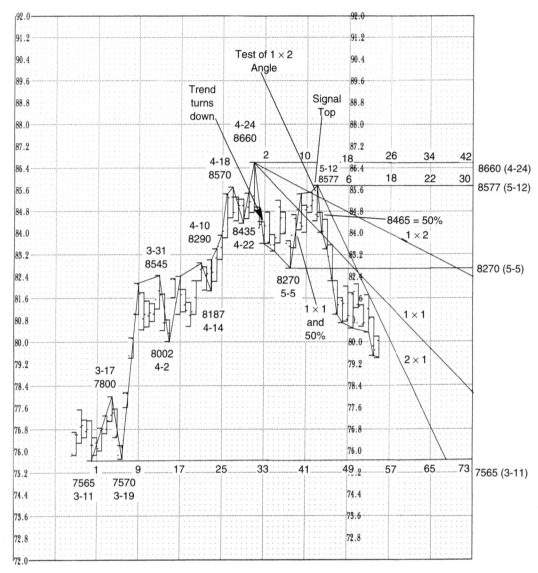

Figure 11.3   Chart for 1997 daily June live hogs.

1997 WEEKLY JUNE TREASURY BONDS

The main range is 104-09 to 116-00, with a 50% price at 110-04 (Figure 11.4). During the week ending May 16, 1997, the downtrending angle from the 116-00 top is at 110-08. This creates a strong resistance zone at 110-04 to 110-04.

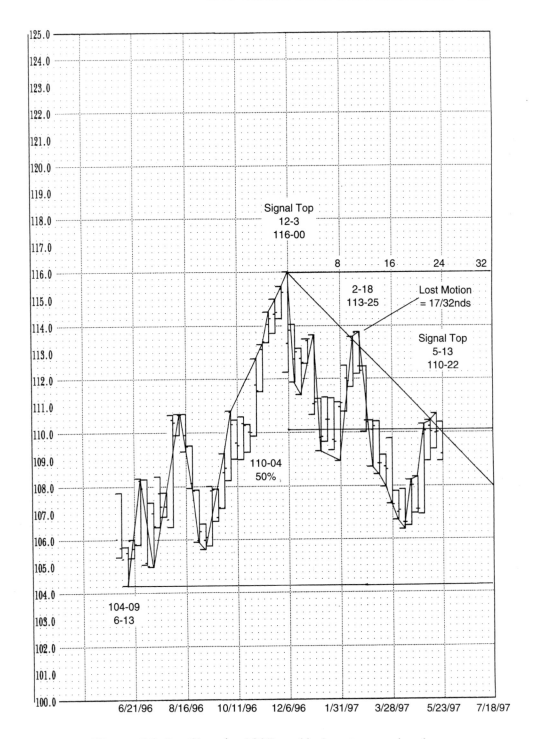

Figure 11.4 Chart for 1997 weekly June treasury bonds.

The main trend is down according to the two-day trend indicator. This creates a selling opportunity at 110-04 to 110-08. The first rally was through the 1 × 1 angle to 113-25 on February 18, 1997. The angle was at 113-08 and the top was 113-25. This created lost motion of $^{17}/_{32}$nds. This means the next sell into this angle must accompany a stop of greater than $^{17}/_{32}$nds.

On May 13, the market traded 110-22. This price exceeded the 50% price by $^{18}/_{32}$nds and the 1 × 1 angle by $^{14}/_{32}$nds. Selling into this angle required a stop placed at the lost motion point of $^{17}/_{32}$nds plus two or more ticks.

Following a test of this resistance zone, the market posted a daily and weekly signal top and began a correction that eventually broke the market down to 108-17.

This is a good example of how to use a combination of the 50% price and a downtrending resistance angle.

Index